Monitoring the Worker
for Exposure and Disease

The Johns Hopkins Series in Environmental Toxicology
Zoltan Annau, Series Editor

Monitoring the Worker for Exposure and Disease

Scientific, Legal, and Ethical
Considerations in the Use of
Biomarkers

Nicholas A. Ashford

Christine J. Spadafor

Dale B. Hattis

Charles C. Caldart

The Johns Hopkins University Press
Baltimore and London

The Johns Hopkins University Press, 701 West 40th Street
Baltimore, Maryland 21211
The Johns Hopkins Press Ltd., London

The paper used in this book meets the minimum requirements of American
National Standard for Information Sciences—Permanence of Paper for Printed
Library Materials, ANSI Z39.48-1984.

Library of Congress Cataloging-in-Publication Data

Monitoring the worker for exposure and disease : scientific, legal, and ethical
   considerations in the use of biomarkers /
   Nicholas A. Ashford . . . [et al.].
        p.   cm.—(The Johns Hopkins series in environmental toxicology)
     Includes bibliographical references (p.
     ISBN 0-8018-3982-3 (alk. paper).—
     ISBN 0-8018-3989-0 (pbk. : alk. paper)
     1. Industrial toxicology.   2. Biological monitoring.   3. Patient monitoring.
   I. Ashford, Nicholas Askounes.   II. Series
   RA1229.4.M67   1990
   363.11′63—dc20   89-43479
                                                              CIP

To my father, Theodore Askounes Ashford, who by his example set for me a high standard of scholarship and whom I miss terribly.

—N.A.A.

To my parents, for their values, support, and personal sacrifices.

—C.J.S.

To Kathy and David.—D.B.H.

To my parents.—C.C.C.

Contents

About the Authors

Nicholas A. Ashford, Ph.D., J.D., is an associate professor of technology and policy at the Center for Technology, Policy and Industrial Development, Massachusetts Institute of Technology; member and chair of the Committee on Technology Innovation and Economics, Environmental Protection Agency National Advisory Council on Environmental Technology Transfer; former public member and chair of the National Advisory Committee on Occupational Safety and Health; and former member of the Science Advisory Board to the Environmental Protection Agency. He received his B.A. from Washington University, and his Ph.D. and J.D. from the University of Chicago.

Christine J. Spadafor, J.D., Sc.M., R.N., is an attorney at Hill and Barlow, Boston. She was formerly a health scientist at the Occupational Safety and Health Administration Office of Health Standards and a special assistant to the director of chemical control at the Environmental Protection Agency Office of Toxic Substances. She received her R.N. from Montefiore Hospital School of Nursing, her B.S. from LaRoche College, her Sc.M. from the Harvard School of Public Health, and her J.D. from Harvard Law School.

Dale B. Hattis, Ph.D., is a research associate professor at the Center for Environment, Technology, and Development, Clark University, and a principal research associate at the Center for Technology, Policy and Industrial Development, Massachusetts Institute of Technology. He received his B.A. from the University of California, Berkeley, and his Ph.D. from Stanford University.

Charles C. Caldart, J.D., M.P.H., is a lecturer in the department of civil engineering and a research associate at the Center for Technology, Policy and Industrial Development, Massachusetts Institute of Technology. He is the director of the Public Interest Litigation Project, Massachusetts Public Interest Research Group Education Fund, Boston. He received his B.A. and J.D. from the University of Washington and his M.P.H. from the Harvard School of Public Health.

Introduction

Human monitoring to supplement or replace environmental (ambient) monitoring of toxic substances in the workplace has become a major issue within the last decade and has led to increased activity and discussion among those concerned with occupational health and safety. Congressional hearings and a study by the Office of Technology Assessment (OTA) have addressed problems associated with the genetic testing of workers.[1] The Occupational Safety and Health Administration's (OSHA's) standard for occupational exposure to lead focuses on the biological monitoring of workers for lead uptake.[2] A conference held in December 1980 in Luxembourg, in which the United States, the European Community, and other countries participated, addressed the problems arising from a variety of methods for monitoring and screening workers.[3] The American Conference of Governmental Industrial Hygienists sponsored a symposium in 1981 on the protection of sensitive workers,[4] and human monitoring has been a topic of major concern at the annual meetings of the American Industrial Hygiene Association.

These activities prompted an extensive review in 1984 of the scientific, legal, and ethical issues related to human monitoring by three of the authors of this book.[5] Since that time, there has been an explosion of activity and interest in the subject. The papers presented at the Luxembourg conference have been published.[6] In 1986, the National Institute for Occupational Safety and Health, the National Cancer Institute, and the Environmental Protection Agency published papers presented at a conference on medical screening and biological monitoring in Cincinnati in July 1984.[7] In 1987, the papers presented at a conference in Milan in May 1986 on cellular and biochemical indices for monitoring toxicity were published.[8] The OTA expects to release its second study on genetic testing in 1990. With the exception of the Milan conference,[9] this book significantly updates our 1984 review and takes note of the papers presented at the conferences cited above, as well as other new literature. However, the subject has become a rapidly moving target.

Most of the literature, until recently, has lent itself to a characterization based on the *type of monitoring* conducted, for example, medical surveillance, biological monitoring, genetic monitoring and screening, and sensitivity screening (see Chap. 1 for definitions). However, a new focus has emerged on *biological markers,* that is, the actual substance or biochemical marker being monitored.[10] The National Academy of Sciences offered the following definitions.

> Biological markers are indicators signaling events in biological systems or samples. It is useful to classify biological markers into three types, those of *exposure, effect, and susceptibility,* and to describe the events particular to each type. A biological marker of *effect* may be an indicator of an endogenous component of the biological system, a measure of the functional capacity of the system, or an altered state of the system that is recognized as impairment or disease. A biological marker of *susceptibility* is defined as an indicator that the health of the system is especially sensitive to the challenge of exposure to a xenobiotic compound (a compound originating outside the organism). A biological marker of *exposure* may be the identification of an exogenous substance within the system, the interactive product between a xenobiotic compound and endogenous components, or other event in the biological system related to the exposure. Of utmost importance is the correlation of biological markers of exposure with health impairment or potential health impairment.
>
> It must be emphasized that there is a continuum between markers of exposure and markers of health status, with certain events being relatable to both types of markers. The terms biological monitoring and health monitoring are also in common use, and their distinguishing features are subject to debate. In essence, biological markers can be used for both biological monitoring and health monitoring.
>
> Once exposure has occurred, a continuum of biological events may be detected. These events may serve as markers of the initial exposure, internal dose, biologically effective dose (dose at the site of toxic action, dose at the receptor site, or dose to target macromolecules), altered structure/function with no subsequent pathology, or potential or actual health impairment [Figure 1]. Even before exposure occurs, there may be biological differences between humans that cause some individuals to be more susceptible to environmentally induced disease. Biological markers, therefore, are tools that can be used to clarify the relationship, if any, between exposure to a xenobiotic compound and health impairment.[11]

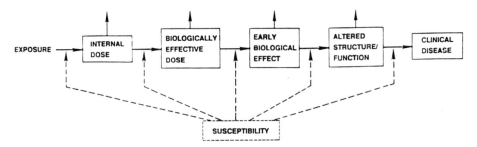

Figure I. *A simplified flow chart of classes of biological markers (in boxes). Solid arrows indicate progression, if it occurs, to the next class of marker. Dashed arrows indicate that individual susceptibility influences the rates of progression, as do other variables described in the text. Biological markers represent a continuum of change, and the classification of change may not always be distinct. Reprinted from NRC Committee on Biological Markers,* "Biological Markers in Health Research," Environmental Health Perspectives *(1987) 74:3–9, 4.*

The National Academy of Sciences formed four subcommittees to study biological markers for specific biological systems.[12] They have published their first study of markers for reproductive and developmental effects, and reports on markers for other specific biological systems are expected (see "Application of Biological Monitoring" in Chap. 5.).

As compelling as a focus on biological markers is from a scientific perspective, for our purposes in this book a discussion of the application of monitoring for these biomarkers lends itself better to an organization by type of monitoring than by type of biomarker. Some of the recent literature, by lumping together biomarkers for exposure, effect, and susceptibility, describes all biomarker monitoring as "biological monitoring," thus obscuring important technical and legal differences among medical surveillance, biological monitoring, and genetic monitoring or screening (see discussion in Chap. 1).

A look through the literature reveals the diverse and sometimes conflicting purposes for undertaking human monitoring. One purpose is to reduce occupational disease or injury to the working population as a whole by providing indicators of *average* harm or risk of harm from exposure to toxic substances. The monitoring need not involve all workers, only a statistically informative sample, to ensure an adequate average level of toxic material control. Another purpose is to protect especially sensitive workers,[13] workers exposed to a toxic material by means other than inhalation, and workers for whom nonoccupational sources may add to occupational exposure. An employer (or employer–manufacturer) may institute human monitoring to remove workers from potentially harmful exposures, thereby avoiding liability for increased workers' compensation premiums and tort or products liability suits. Employers may also use human monitoring results to avoid increased worker demands for preventive technology or other health and safety measures.

Previous writers have focused their attention on the problems of screening workers in general, rather than on the significant distinctions among the several kinds of monitoring.[14] This book discusses additional scientific distinctions and their legal implications; for example, the differences between monitoring hypersensitive workers and monitoring workers at high risk (see Chap. 8). It places a broad proscriptive emphasis on protecting workers by integrating the self-initiated right to refuse hazardous work with remedies available under the Occupational Safety and Health Act (OSHAct), the Toxic Substances Control Act (TSCA), the National Labor Relations Act (NLRA), and common law, with an eye toward encouraging the employer to use monitoring as a basis for positive change in the workplace, rather than as a basis for discharging affected workers.

In this book we discuss

1. The legal basis for OSHA monitoring requirements and for access to monitoring records provided under the OSHAct, TSCA, and NLRA (Chap. 2);
2. The scientific basis, appropriateness, usefulness, and timing of various human monitoring activities (Chaps. 3–7);
3. Human variability and consequences to the worker of medical removal (Chaps. 8 and 9);
4. The legal and ethical problems of conducting monitoring tests on workers and possible misuse of the results (Chaps. 10–12); and
5. Policy recommendations for the proper use of human monitoring in reducing occupational disease and injury (Chap. 12).

Although worker monitoring for drugs and acquired immune deficiency syndrome markers are related and ethically challenging practices under intense discussion, they are beyond the scope of this book.

PART I
Definitions and Legal Authority

I. Overview and Definitions: Monitoring, Surveillance, and Screening

The scientific and legal literatures commonly use the terms *monitoring, surveillance,* and *screening* interchangeably, but the terms are not identical. Monitoring and surveillance programs involve the repeated performance of an observation or measurement used to detect an unfavorable trend that may be altered by appropriate intervention.[1] These programs include medical surveillance, biological monitoring, genetic monitoring, and environmental monitoring (see "Monitoring and Surveillance" in this chapter). In contrast, screening is an observation or measurement performed only once and generally conducted on a large population to identify a subpopulation with a high likelihood of having a treatable disease or an avoidable risk of developing or aggravating disease.[2] Screening programs that seek to exclude those with a greater likelihood of developing disease are termed *sensitivity screening.* We prefer to use this term rather than "genetic" screening because it is broader, includes human characteristics that have not been identified with specific genes, and more accurately describes what is being investigated in the screening process. Sensitivity screening is discussed later in this chapter and in Chapter 6.

GOALS OF THE PROGRAM

Before implementing monitoring or screening programs, it is necessary for the intervenor to formulate specific goals of the program and to provide for the collection of data that will be needed to decide whether the goals are being met.[3] Goals of such programs may vary according to employer, industry, or costs of implementation, but generally the primary goal should include the prevention of disease.[4] The utility of monitoring and screening methods is believed ultimately to depend on whether they contribute to the prevention of occupational disease and injury.[5] They are the important means of prevention, not ends in themselves. Once the testing results are properly interpreted, only appropriate intervention can give the prevention sought.[6]

The ability of monitoring and screening programs to serve as preventive tools depends on a continuum of measures:[7]

1. Primary preventive measures that interrupt the initiation of the disease process and entail certain precautions such as the testing and prohibition of certain dangerous industrial chemicals before they enter into commerce, the substitution of less hazardous agents, the control of exposure through engineering measures, and the monitoring of the workplace environment to ensure compliance with established standards.

2. Secondary prevention measures that detect a disease process at an early stage before a worker would normally seek clinical care. Preventive action at this point may cause a disease process to be reversed (or at least arrested) upon discontinuation of exposure.

3. Epidemiologic surveillance, which is late in the continuum of prevention of occupational disease because cases of the disease must have already occurred for the affected workers to be counted. The data collected are interpreted and disseminated.

4. Tertiary prevention measures including the appropriate medical care of symptomatic clinical disease.

The National Institute for Occupational Safety and Health (NIOSH) agrees that monitoring and screening programs can serve as tools in the prevention of occupational injuries and diseases. NIOSH compiled its list of the leading 10 work-related diseases and injuries and believes that these programs can serve as preventive measures in decreasing the number and severity of the following occupational diseases and injuries:[8]

1. Occupational lung disease,
2. Musculoskeletal injuries,
3. Occupational cancers,
4. Severe occupational traumatic injuries,
5. Cardiovascular disease,

6. Disorders of reproduction,
7. Neurotoxic disorders,
8. Noise-induced loss of hearing,
9. Dermatologic conditions, and
10. Psychologic disorders.

Although prevention of disease and injury may be viewed as the primary objective in implementing monitoring and screening programs, other rationales for instituting such programs exist. For example, the programs may be undertaken for diagnostic and treatment purposes. They may also be undertaken in an attempt to decrease the morbidity and mortality among persons tested, as a feature of a benefit package, or as a method of early detection to decrease hospitalization and medical care costs.[9] The goals may be even more specific. For example, the goals of a cancer screening program may include a shift toward earlier stages of detection, a reduction in case fatality rates, and a reduction in site-specific cancer mortality among the screened population.[10]

Regardless of whether programs are designed only for prevention or are designed to achieve multiple goals, the data from the programs should be uniformly reported, compiled, and summarized for epidemiologic use.[11] Currently, neither the Occupational Safety and Health Administration (OSHA) regulations nor the NIOSH recommendations suggest epidemiologic assessment of the programs' data. One researcher concluded, "A collection of screening information on unremitting disease is pointless if the data will not be analyzed epidemiologically and used to protect other workers similarly exposed."[12]

MONITORING AND SURVEILLANCE

There are multiple components to a comprehensive monitoring and surveillance program. Various commentators suggest that the program should

1. Be relatively inexpensive;[13]
2. Be simple to administer;[14]
3. Be acceptable to both participants and providers;[15]
4. Be free from serious complications and reasonably painless for the participant;[16]
5. Take minimal work time;[17]

6. Use methods that are highly sensitive and specific;[18]
7. Be targeted for diseases that produce serious morbidity and high mortality among those affected;[19]
8. Be targeted for diseases with a preclinical phase that is reasonably common among the population to be screened;[20]
9. Have a recognizable latent, asymptomatic/preclinical stage or early asymptomatic stage that precedes the usual time the worker would seek care for symptomatic disease[21] (treatment is more effective during the preclinical phase than treatment applied after the onset of clinical symptoms);[22]
10. Be targeted to the specific risks consistent with the exposure or occupation and be reassessed periodically to ensure consistency with evolving knowledge;[23]
11. Be conducted in situations in which an accepted treatment exists for the recognized disease and the data will be useful in improving the prevention for others similarly situated;[24]
12. Be carried out by a professional skilled in conducting and interpreting screening tests for occupational disease;[25]
13. Be linked with a plan for care;[26] and
14. Be ongoing, with the frequency of screening depending on the incidence of disease, the length of the preclinical detection period, the level and frequency of exposure, and the worker turnover rate.[27]

The discussion of terms and definitions that follows—medical surveillance, genetic monitoring, biological monitoring, and environmental monitoring—is consistent with the meaning and usage of the same in regulations promulgated by OSHA.[28]

Medical Surveillance

The *Assessment of Toxic Agents at the Workplace: Roles of Ambient and Biological Monitoring* defines *health surveillance* as "the periodic medico-physiological examinations of exposed workers with the objective of protecting health and preventing occupationally related disease."[29] We prefer to use the term *medical surveillance* because we believe it more accurately describes the nature of the tests performed and because it is used in OSHA regulations. Medical surveillance is designed in an occupational setting to detect adverse health *effects* (or health status) resulting from hazardous exposures in the workplace. Medical surveillance tests are generally diagnostic tools used in routine medical practice. They most commonly include tests such as chest X-rays, pulmonary function tests, routine blood analyses, serum liver function tests, serum kidney function tests, and routine urinalyses.

Medical surveillance testing serves to obtain certain types of information, such as the identification of workers who are suffering from an occupational injury or illness, the epidemiological data on occupational disease, and the general or specific data on categories or types of workers. These data are intended to aid in testing workers by monitoring specific organ systems that may be affected by exposure to workplace hazards. Testing may be instituted by an employer on its own initiative, in response to OSHA requirements, or at the request of employees or their unions.

Medical surveillance is most useful in three situations: (1) if compliance with the permissible exposure limits established by OSHA will not adequately ensure worker health, (2) if air measurement cannot sufficiently monitor worker exposure (e.g., if a significant route of entry is not inhalation), and (3) if high-risk groups are exposed.[30] Medical removal may also be appropriate in these three situations.[31]

The *Assessment of Toxic Agents* implies that in some circumstances medical surveillance can prevent occupationally related disease.[32] If a disease is reversible or arrestible, medical surveillance may be preventive insofar as it serves as a warning signal prompting timely action to avoid future exposures and continuing or progressive adverse health effects.

Pursuant to statute, OSHA can require employee medical surveillance (see "Occupational Safety and Health Administration" in Chap. 2). Medical surveillance provisions in OSHA standards traditionally include both the general diagnostic tools as well as some laboratory tests that could be classified under "biological monitoring" (see Chap. 5 and "Biological Monitoring" in this chapter). For this reason, it has been suggested that the OSHA provisions should be recharacterized as "Medical Surveillance and Monitoring."[33] The required medical surveillance provisions vary for the 24 OSHA health standards promulgated since 1972 (see Table 1), but generally they are routine diagnostic tests used in medical practice. All OSHA health standards contain required medical surveillance provisions that articulate the tests that physicians are required to perform. However, the ethylene oxide standard relaxes such requirements. In that standard, OSHA departed from giving specific medical guidance as it had in previous standards, opening up the possibility of unchecked discretion in testing.[34] This new approach of providing only very general guidelines for testing gives further cause for concern

Table I. Chemical Substances for Which the Occupational Safety and Health Administration (OSHA) Has Promulgated Health Standards 1972–1989[a]

2-Acetylaminofluorine	4-Dimethylaminoazobenzene
Acrylonitrile	Ethylene oxide
4-Aminodiphenyl	Etyleneimine
Arsenic (inorganic)	Formaldehyde
Asbestos, tremolite, anthophyllite,	Lead (inorganic)
and actinolite	Methyl chloromethyl ether
Benzene	α-Naphthylamine
Benzidine	β-Naphthylamine
bis-Chloromethyl ether	4-Nitrobiphenyl
Coke oven emissions	N-Nitrosodimethylamine
Cotton dust	β-Propiolactone
1,2-Dibromo-3-chloropropane	Vinyl chloride
3,3'-Dichlorobenzidine (and its salts)	

[a]Adapted from 29 C.F.R. 1910, Subpart Z (1989). OSHA has initiated rule making for nine other substances, including 1,3-butadiene, cadmium dust and fume, 2-ethoxyethanol (Cellosolve), 2-ethoxyethyl acetate, ethylene dibromide, methyl Cellosolve, methyl Cellosolve acetate, methylene chloride and 4,4'-methylenedianiline [53 *Fed. Reg.* 21,246 (June 7, 1988)].

because many examining physicians are not specially trained and certified in occupational health.[35] Realizing this lack of specialized medical expertise, OSHA should propose and promulgate standards that provide detailed medical guidelines, sufficient for all examining physicians, which are essential to promoting good health in the workplace.

In January 1981, OSHA and NIOSH published the *Occupational Health Guidelines for Chemical Hazards.*[36] This volume includes a variety of information on approximately 450 substances for which OSHA adopted consensus standards under section 6(a) of the OSHAct.[37] The information for each substance usually includes chemical, toxicological, and health hazard data, as well as recommendations for industrial hygiene and medical surveillance practices.

On June 7, 1988, OSHA issued a notice of proposed rule making updating the section 6(a) health standards by lowering the permissible exposure limit (PEL) for 100 substances, raising the PEL for one, establishing PELs for 205 new substances, and adding or changing the short-term exposure limit for 70 substances.[38] Following intense criticism that no worker monitoring requirements were included, OSHA published two advance notices of proposed rulemaking on September 27, 1988, on exposure monitoring and on medical surveillance programs.[39]

Genetic Monitoring

One particular type of medical surveillance that has received much attention is genetic monitoring.[40] This monitoring includes the periodic testing of employees working with or possibly exposed to certain substances (such as known or potential carcinogens) that cause changes in chromosomes or deoxyribonucleic acid (DNA) and is classified in two categories. The first, *cytogenetic monitoring*, involves monitoring for changes in chromosomes. A sample of blood is usually collected, and the chromosomes are visualized after inducing cell division in specific types of white cells. The second, *noncytogenetic monitoring*, includes monitoring for DNA reaction products (adducts), small changes at specific places in DNA, or the presence of mutagens in body fluids. Generally, both types of genetic monitoring are conducted in an attempt to determine if environmental exposures of a specific population (e.g., workers in the same job category) to particular substances cause changes in genetic material in statistically significant numbers above background levels.[41]

Biological Monitoring

The third type of monitoring practice is biological monitoring. Biological monitoring is defined in the *Assessment of Toxic Agents* as "the measurement and assessment of workplace agents or their metabolites either in tissues, secreta, excreta, expired air or any combination of these to evaluate *exposure and health risk* compared to an appropriate reference."[42] More broadly defined, biological monitoring is a collection of activities designed to determine whether a person has been exposed to and whether his or her body fluids or organs contain unusual amounts of a particular substance or its metabolites. Using this broader definition, biological monitoring would include what we and others call "genetic monitoring," discussed in the previous subsection. Indeed, Perera categorized genetic monitoring as a subset of biological monitoring. Table 2 makes a distinction between monitoring for "internal dose" and monitoring for "biologically effective dose."[43] In this book, we treat the former as biological monitoring; the latter we term genetic monitoring.

Ideally, the best indicator of biologically relevant exposure or risk would be a direct measure of the chemical or its metabolite at the target site (see "General Considerations" in Chap. 5), not the broad concept of toxin "uptake." According to one researcher,

Table 2. Examples of Human Biological Monitoring Methods[a]

End point	Method	Sites and fluids
Internal dose		
Carcinogen or metabolite	Physical and chemical techniques: immunoassay	Body fluids and tissue
Thioethers	Physical and chemical techniques	Urine
Mutagenicity	Bacterial mutation assay	Body fluids
Thymine or thymidine glycol	HPLC[b] with ultraviolet detection	Urine
Biologically effective dose		
Adducts (DNA)	Immunoassay, postlabeling, fluorescence spectrometry	WBC[c]
Adducts (protein)	Mass spectrometry, ion-exchange amino acid analysis, HPLC, gas chromatography	RBC[d]
Excised adducts	HPLC, fluorescence	Urine
Unscheduled DNA synthesis	Cell culture, thymidine incorporation	WBC
Sister chromatid exchange	Cytogenetics	WBC
Micronuclei	Cytogenetics	Bone marrow, WBC
Chomosomal aberrations	Cytogenetics	WBC
Somatic cell mutation	Autoradiography, light microscopy	WBC
Somatic cell mutation (glycophorin A)	Immunoassay	RBC
Sperm quality	Analysis of count, morphology, motility	Sperm

[a]Reprinted from L. Tomatis, ed., *Monitoring of Humans with Exposures to Carcinogens: Mutagens and Epidemiological Applications* (Lyon, IARC Scientific Publications, 1987) as modified by F. P. Perera, "Molecular Cancer Epidemiology: A New Tool in Cancer Prevention," *Journal of the National Cancer Institute* (1987) 78(5):887–898.

[b]High-pressure liquid chromatography.

[c]White blood cells.

[d]Red blood cells.

direct measure [at the site of action] is not usually feasible because the sites of action are frequently located in tissues not accessible for sampling (e.g., brain acetylcholinesterase activity). The concentration of the pollutant or its metabolites in another body compartment (blood, urine) or the amount bound to another molecule may be used for this purpose if one has demonstrated that the latter parameter is in equilibrium with the amount at the site of action.[44]

In practice, biological monitoring is used to measure the actual total "uptake" (intake × fractional absorption) through several pathways simultaneously (inhalation, ingestion, and dermal absorption).[45] Biological monitoring differs from medical surveillance in that the former measures uptake (and sometimes also the persistence of the measured substance in the body) and the latter is used to determine the effects of exposure. For example, medical surveillance (e.g., chest X-ray) would be an appropriate part of a pulmonary evaluation for a worker exposed to silica dust, because the X-ray would most likely show any major effects due to such exposure. An X-ray, however, would not yield useful biological monitoring information in this situation because the X-ray would not assess the worker's level of uptake of silica dust.

Biological monitoring measures primarily the levels of an agent and/or its metabolites in biological specimens.[46] For some chemicals, it may also measure agent-specific reversible nonadverse effects (e.g., blood zinc protoporphyrin levels for exposure to lead) but the definition of biological monitoring does not include the measurement of nonspecific effect parameters (e.g., decreased nerve conduction velocity or decreased forced expiratory volume).[47] The analysis most commonly uses urine, breath, and blood specimens, but sometimes uses hair, nails, tears, breast milk, or perspiration as well.

Some observers believe that the information obtained from biological monitoring can be used in conjunction with environmental monitoring results to determine whether ambient data predict the true exposure of workers and thereby evaluate occupational hygiene control methods.[48] Others, however, believe that ambient environmental measurements cannot accurately be correlated with biological measurements because of individual pharmacokinetic and metabolic variability. One researcher stated, "Biological measurements reflect *uptake* and not *exposure*. . . . there are numerous instances in which significant uptake of toxic materials have [sic] occurred in spite of low air-levels of the contaminant in question."[49] Obviously the use of particular biological monitoring tests for evaluating specific exposures needs to be evaluated on a case-by-case basis in the light of both (1) the degree of interindividual variability and (2) the dynamics of the marker that is being measured in the workers in relation to the dynamics of their exposures.

Biological monitoring should not substitute for environmental monitoring. Rather, "environmental and biological monitoring are ways of investigating different problems and should be seen as complementary and not mutually exclusive procedures."[50] The general substitution of biological monitoring in favor of environmental monitoring to determine compliance and control consistent with the OSHA standards is not appropriate for the following reasons:[51]

1. It is not clear whether OSHA has the authority to require workers to submit to biological monitoring procedures for determining compliance.

2. A biological standard may provide an incentive for employers to intervene in altering specific parameters in their workers. For example, chelation therapy may be used in industrial settings to decrease worker blood lead levels.

3. Biological standards may reinforce a "blame the worker" attitude among employers with regard to specific employees, rather than focusing attention on the workplace.

4. In some cases, biological standards may involve greater risk of health damage due to possible delays between dangerous air exposure and the monitored biological response.

Biochemical tests cannot always be defined as either medical surveillance or biological monitoring. Certain tests not only are indicators of metabolic effects (medical surveillance) but also can be quantitatively linked to effects of exposure. Examples of these effect tests include zinc protoporphyrin and delta aminolaevulinic acid dehydrase, both of which are quantitatively related to lead exposure.[52]

Environmental Monitoring

Environmental monitoring measures the concentration of harmful agents *in the workplace,* whereas the other types of monitoring involve tests performed *on the workers.* It is used primarily to assess whether there is actual or impending overexposure in the workplace and whether there is a related increased health risk from that exposure.[53] The multiple components of a comprehensive environmental monitoring program are listed below. The program should

1. Signal an unhealthy environment;
2. Effectively monitor the atmosphere;

3. Detect unexpected noxious contaminants;
4. Maintain surveillance on the efficacy of their containment;
5. Help determine the effectiveness of alteration of the environment (e.g., workplace renovation, removal from exposure);
6. Test for compliance with workplace standards; and
7. Help evaluate the effectiveness of corrective or possibly therapeutic measures.[54]

Environmental monitoring includes both ambient monitoring and personal monitoring. Personal monitoring is "a term designating the determination of the inhaled dose of an airborne toxic material or of an air-mediated hazardous physical force by the continuous collection of samples in the breathing or auditory zone, or other appropriate exposed body area, over a finite period of exposure time."[55] Personal monitors placed in the breathing zone (e.g., on shirt collars) are considered to provide a representative dose of inhaled air that transports any airborne hazardous agents.[56] Ambient monitoring is defined as "the measurement and assessment of agents at the workplace and [the evaluation of] ambient exposure and health risk compared to an appropriate reference."[57] Ambient (work area) monitoring is useful if the hazard is a specific one for which a permissible exposure limit is known (e.g., a consensus guideline or legal standard). An advantage is that it does not use the worker as a sampling device. In this book, we do not discuss environmental monitoring in detail, but mention it only in reference to the other monitoring practices.

SENSITIVITY SCREENING

A fourth kind of human monitoring, sensitivity screening (see Chap. 6), is practiced on an employee only once, usually as part of a preemployment or preplacement exam (see "Preemployment Examination" and "Preplacement Examination" in Chap. 7). Such examinations are very common. In the National Occupational Exposure Survey conducted in 1981–83, medical screening of potential new workers was mandatory in 22% of "small" manufacturing plants (less than 100 workers), 57% of medium-sized plants (100–499 workers), and 78% of larger plants.[58]

Sensitivity screening seeks to determine whether an individual possesses certain inherited or acquired traits that may predispose him or her to an increased risk of disease if exposed to particular substances. If that trait is inherited, the term *genetic screening* applies. (One example of this is an inherited deficiency in alpha-1 anti-trypsin, which is associated with increased susceptibility for emphysema, particularly among smokers.[59]) Laboratory tests on body fluids (usually blood) identify these traits. However, a number of other common components of medical examinations can also be thought of as more general forms of sensitivity screening, such as back X-rays (intended to detect susceptibility to back injuries) or inquiries about past histories of allergic responses or cardiovascular symptoms.

2. Legal Authority for Human Monitoring

AGENCY AUTHORITY

The Occupational Safety and Health Act (OSHAct) covers most private (i.e., nongovernmental) workplaces. The OSHAct grants both the Occupational Safety and Health Administration (OSHA) and the National Institute for Occupational Safety and Health (NIOSH) the authority to promulgate regulations that require employers to conduct human monitoring. The authority granted to NIOSH for monitoring is broader in scope than that vested in OSHA, but financial limitations on NIOSH in exercising that authority give OSHA the greater practical grant of authority. Each agency's authority is discussed in this section, after first considering employee participation.

Although employers are mandated to make medical testing programs available (generally consisting of medical surveillance alone or coupled with biological monitoring in some circumstances), participation by employees in all OSHA health standards testing programs is not required as a matter of law.

The implication that participation by employees in medical testing is voluntary for health standards provisions is found in section 6(b)(7) of the OSHAct, which states that medical examinations "shall be made available" to certain employees.[1] There is no mention that employees must participate, only that employers must make such tests available.

Certain standards such as the asbestos,[2] vinyl chloride,[3] and carcinogen[4] standards imply the voluntary nature of the employees' participation as well as articulate the mandatory nature of the employer's duties. The OSHA standard for coke oven emissions furthers the notion of voluntary employee participation by providing guidelines for an employer on what to do when an employee refuses to be tested.[5] The regulation states that the employer is to inform the employee who refuses to be examined of any possible health consequences of such refusal and to obtain a statement signed by the employee that the employee understands the risk taken by refusing to be examined.[6] The OSHA lead standard specifically states that participation in the medical surveillance program is not mandatory for the employee.[7] The agency did, however, initially consider mandating that all employees participate in the medical surveillance program. It finally decided not to institute a mandatory program because the program could interfere with the voluntariness and meaningfulness of worker participation. This participation was believed to be essential to the success of the medical surveillance provisions and consistent with employees' personal privacy and religious concerns.[8]

The policy decision to permit voluntary participation in medical surveillance programs has not been significantly opposed by either employee or employer representatives.[9] Employees' rights and privacy interests are believed to be protected if the examinations are made available.[10] Further, there are concerns that the results of mandatory examinations could be used as a basis for adverse personnel action against them.[11] Employers find acceptable the voluntariness of participation because mandatory provisions could prove difficult to enforce.[12]

Authority of the Occupational Safety and Health Administration

Some types of medical surveillance provisions are contained in all OSHA health standards promulgated under section 6(b) of the OSHAct. The agency's authority to promulgate such provisions is found in section 6(b)(7) of the OSHAct, which specifies that, where appropriate, section 6(b) standards (standards issued, modified, or revoked through rule-making procedures) "*shall* prescribe the type and frequency of medical examinations or other tests which *shall* be made available, by the employer or at his cost, to employees exposed to [the regulated hazard] in order to most effectively determine whether the health of such employees is adversely affected by such exposure." Further, if such examinations are "in the nature of research," NIOSH may provide the funding.[13] These provisions give clear authorization for OSHA to require medical surveillance to determine the health effects of hazards regulated under section 6(b), even if such surveillance is considered "research."

In addition, OSHA may order *biological monitoring* under each of three sections of the OSHAct: sections 8(c)(1), 8(c)(3), and 6. Section 8(c)(1) provides general authority:

> Each employer shall make, keep and preserve . . . such records regarding his activities relating to this chapter as the Secretary, in cooperation with the Secretary of Health, Education, and Welfare, may prescribe by regulation as necessary or appropriate . . . *for developing information* regarding the causes and prevention of occupational accidents and illnesses. In order to carry out the provisions of this paragraph such regulations may include provisions requiring *employers to conduct periodic inspections.*[14]

Section 8(c)(3) contains a more specific mandate. It provides that OSHA "*shall* issue regulations requiring *employers to maintain accurate records of employee exposures* . . . which are required to be monitored or measured under Section 6." This section also requires employers to "promptly notify" employees if they have been or are being exposed to any hazard in violation of "an applicable occupational safety and health standard promulgated under section 6."[15] The Senate deliberated over this provision while considering the OSHAct. Senator Peter H. Dominick (R–Colo.), who led an unsuccessful effort to pass a substitute Nixon administration bill,[16] proposed an amendment that would have eliminated the provision. In objecting to the language of section 8(c)(3), Senator Dominick noted that it "indirectly requires excessive employer monitoring of his entire operation," and thus requires the employer "to be his own policeman, judge and jury."[17] The language of this section is broad as enacted. The fact that Congress chose to include it in the OSHAct, rather than accept the substitute bill deleting this language,[18] supports the proposition that the OSHAct requires employers to conduct biological or environmental monitoring or both for any exposure regulated under section 6.

Section 6 itself, however, casts some doubt on this interpretation. On the one hand, section 6(a) makes no mention of human monitoring, but merely requires OSHA to adopt previously existing health standards.[19] Section 6(b), on the other hand, specifically discusses both biological monitoring and medical surveillance. Section 6(b)(7) mandates that, where "appropriate," a section 6(b) standard "*shall* provide for monitoring or measuring employee exposure . . . in such manner as may be necessary for the protection of employees."[20]

This last provision raises an interesting issue. Unquestionably, section 8(c)(3) applies to both section 6(a) standards (national consensus standards and established federal standards adopted without rule making) and section 6(b) standards, because both are occupational health standards that require "employee exposures to be measured" within the meaning of section 8(c)(3). If section 8(c) grants broad power to order biological monitoring, the question is raised as to why section 6(b) also grants such power. The solution may lie in the "accuracy" limitation of section 8(c).

Section 8(c)(3) requires only that employers maintain "accurate" records of employee exposures. For many exposures, accurate measurements may be possible without biological monitoring, that is, by using environmental monitoring. Arguably, section 8 would not require biological monitoring in those situations. Under section 6(b), however, OSHA could go further and order biological monitoring if it were "necessary for the protection of the employees." This interpretation finds an implicit Congressional attempt to balance the need for reliable information against the cost and inconvenience of a physically invasive monitoring procedure. Accordingly, potentially invasive monitoring would be subject to the specificity and increased scrutiny of the section 6(b) standard-setting procedure.

Currently, only the OSHA lead standard requires routine biological monitoring.[21] The recently promulgated benzene standard requires biological monitoring for urinary phenol in emergency situations (see "Urine Analysis" in Chap. 5). Concerning the consensus health standards adopted under section 6(a) of the OSHAct, OSHA recommends biological monitoring for certain substances such as carbon monoxide, fluoride (inorganic), and pesticides, including endrin and parathion.[22]

Under the *NIOSH/OSHA Occupational Health Guidelines*, OSHA issued biological monitoring guidelines for some consensus health standards adopted under section 6(a). These guidelines "provide a basis for promulgation of *new* occupational health regulations."[23] Because these guidelines are not regulations, they are not subject to judicial review. On September 27, 1988, OSHA issued an advance notice of proposed rule making on a generic standard for exposure monitoring.[24] No specific mention of biological monitoring is made, but OSHA might well include it as well as environmental monitoring. (See "Application of Biological Monitoring" in Chap. 5 for a discussion of biological exposure indices.)

Biological monitoring results must be preserved as a part of an employee's *exposure* record under the OSHA rule governing access to employee exposure and medical records.[25] The OSHA rule defines this record as including any information concerning "biological monitoring results which directly assess the absorption of a substance or agent by body systems (e.g., the level of a chemical in the blood, urine, breath, hair, fingernails, etc.) but not including results which assess the biological *effect* of a substance or agent."[26] This OSHA definition of biological monitoring clearly distinguishes the results of these tests from the results of medical surveillance tests. OSHA further distinguished between exposure records and medical records by providing that an employee medical record must contain any information concerning the health status of the employee including "the results of medical examinations (preemployment, preassignment, periodic, or episodic) and laboratory tests (including X-ray examinations)."[27]

The "OSHA Log": Record Keeping and Reporting Occupational Injuries and Illnesses

Results from medical surveillance and biological monitoring testing must also be included in the OSHA Log, which is maintained to develop information related to the causes and prevention of occupational illnesses and to collect, compile, and analyze occupational health standards.[28] The specific regulation, entitled "Recording and Reporting Occupational Injuries and Illnesses," requires employers with more than 10 employees to (1) maintain a log and summary of all recordable occupational *injuries and illnesses* in each establishment and (2) enter each recordable injury and illness in the log and summary as soon as practicable, but no later than 6 working days after receiving the information that the incident occurred.[29] The logs are to be retained by the employer for 5 years after the end of the year of recording and are to be made available by the employer upon request, to any employee, former employee, or representative.[30]

The regulation requires that "recordable occupational injuries or illnesses" be entered in the log. There are three categories under this classification:[31]

1. Fatalities, regardless of the amount of time between the injury and death or of the length of the illness;

2. Lost workday cases, other than fatalities, that result in lost workdays; and

3. Nonfatal cases without lost workdays that result in transfer to another job or termination of employment, require medical treatment (other than first aid), or involve loss of consciousness or

restriction of work or motion. This category also includes any diagnosed occupational illnesses that are reported to the employer but are not classified as fatalities or lost workday cases.

Medical surveillance and biological monitoring test results apply most logically to the third category, or "nonfatal cases." Yet, the implementation of this reporting requirement may be difficult and produce inconsistent recordings because it is not clear what constitutes a reportable item under this catagory when applied to the testing results.

Because medical and biological testing results are not specifically mentioned in the regulation, it is necessary to parse its language to better understand how the regulation might apply. First, it must be determined that an illness or injury occurred in the work environment before an entry is made in the log.

INJURY

An occupational injury is defined as "any injury such as a cut, fracture, sprain, amputation, etc., which results from a work accident or from an explosion involving a single incident in the work environment."[32] One time-exposure to chemicals is also included in this definition,[33] but the *Brief Guide to Recordkeeping Requirements* does not articulate what level of exposure or what types of effects are required to constitute an "injury." Injuries are recordable only when they require medical treatment other than first aid[34] or involve loss of consciousness, restriction of work or motion, or transfer to another job.[35]

Regarding medical and biological testing results, it seems that any results not within normal limits would be entered in the log only if shown to be caused by a chemical spill or other event causing acute or emergency overexposure. This approach may lead to erroneous or inconsistent reporting. For example, in some instances, the precision of a test may not be developed enough to determine with certainty if an acute exposure caused an injury such as a chromosomal aberration in a worker who was also exposed to chronic low levels of the same chemical. In addition, if there are no baseline testing results (i.e., preexposure) for the same parameter, the postexposure results may not be helpful.

ILLNESS

An occupational illness is defined as "any abnormal condition or disorder, other than one resulting from an occupational injury, caused by exposure to environmental factors associated with employment. It includes acute and chronic illnesses or diseases which may be caused by inhalation, absorption, ingestion, or direct contact."[36]

Examples of occupational illnesses include but are not limited to the following:[37]

1. Occupational skin diseases and disorders;
2. Dust diseases of the lungs (pneumoconioses);
3. Respiratory conditions due to toxic agents (e.g., pneumonitis, acute congestion due to chemicals, dusts, gases, or fumes);
4. Poisoning (systemic effect of toxic materials, such as poisoning by lead or other metals, carbon monoxide or other gases, carbon tetrachloride or other organic solvents, insecticide sprays, other chemicals such as formaldehyde, etc.);
5. Disorders due to physical agents (other than toxic materials, such as heat exhaustion and other effects of environmental heat, frostbite and other effects of exposure to low temperatures, effects of ionizing and nonionizing radiation, etc.);
6. Disorders associated with repeated traumas (such as noise-induced hearing loss, Raynaud's phenomenon, and other conditions due to repeated motion, vibration, or pressure); and
7. All other occupational illnesses (such as malignant and benign tumors, histoplasmosis, infectious hepatitis, etc.).

In general, exposures related to illness ultimately result in conditions of a chemical, physical, biological, or psychological nature.[38]

To be recorded, the occupational illness must be diagnosed. The physician can use the results of "past biological or medical monitoring (blood, urine, other sample analyses)" and previous physical examinations in arriving at a diagnosis.[39]

TWO ADDITIONAL CONCERNS

Two additional concerns relate to the accuracy and consistency of reporting medical and biological results in an OSHA Log. First, many of the types of illnesses and disorders of an occupational nature can also occur from nonoccupational sources (e.g., lung cancer from smoking), so it may be difficult to determine if an illness or disorder is linked to the workplace. Second, how the problem is defined—as an illness or as an injury—has a significant impact on record keeping. Care must be taken in determining the categorization, because whereas *all* work-related illnesses must be recorded, the only injuries to be recorded are those that require medical treatment (other than first aid) or involve loss of consciousness, restriction of work or motion, or transfer to another job.[40]

The Authority to Require Medical Surveillance on Consensus Standards

Section 6(a) of the OSHAct does not mention human monitoring. The *NIOSH/OSHA Occupational Health Guidelines,* however, contains extensive medical surveillance guidelines for approximately 450 substances.[41] Because the *Guidelines* provides a basis for new regulations and does not constitute required practices, the legality of adding medical surveillance requirements to existing section 6(a) standards was not an issue at the time the guidelines were established. With a proposed rule on medical surveillance programs for section 6(a) standards under consideration (as mentioned in "Medical Surveillance" in Chap. 1), the issue may be raised.

Genetic Screening Not Authorized for Any Promulgated Health Standards

The particular kind of medical surveillance involving genetic testing of workers has caused some concern.[42] Some standards that OSHA promulgated under section 6(b) and for the 13 carcinogens standards require medical examinations to include a personal history of an employee, his or her family, or both, including "genetic and environmental factors."[43] OSHA issued a clarification of these standards, emphatically denying that the standards require genetic testing of any employee.[44] (Genetic testing includes both cytogenetic and noncytogenetic monitoring, as well as genetic screening; see Chaps. 4 and 6.)

The Authority to Require Medical Removal Protection

The OSHAct of 1970 does not contain specific language that expressly authorizes medical removal protection (MRP) in occupational health standards.[45] Various sections of the act, however, indicate congressional intent to include MRP as part of the agency's rulemaking authority.[46] The mechanism of MRP is consistent with section 2(b) of the OSHAct, which requires that "so far as possible every working man and woman in the Nation [has] safe and healthful working conditions." Section 2(b)(4) of the OSHAct asks that employers protect worker health "by building upon advances already made through employer and employee initiative for providing safe and healthful working conditions," and section 2(b)(5) requires employers to provide healthful working conditions "by developing innovative methods, techniques, and approaches for dealing with occupational safety and health problems."[47]

Sections 3(8), 6(b)(5), 6(b)(7), and 8(g)(2) of the OSHAct grant the statutory authority for including MRP in occupational health standards. Section 3(8) states that a standard can require "the adoption or use of one or more practices, means, methods, operations or processes, reasonably necessary or appropriate to provide safe or healthful employment and places of employment." Accordingly, MRP meets the definitional criteria of section 3(8). Section 6(b)(5) requires OSHA to base occupational health standards on "experience gained under this and other health and safety laws." Section 6(b)(7) of the act specifies that an OSHA standard shall prescribe such control procedures "as may be necessary for the protection of employees." The general rule-making authority of section 8(g)(2) provides additional authority for the agency to include MRP in a health standard. It states, "The Secretary . . . shall . . . prescribe such rules and regulations as he may deem necessary to carry out [his] responsibilities under this chapter."[48]

After promulgating the final lead standard in 1976, OSHA considered the merits of developing a generic standard for medical removal protection.[49] To date the agency has not taken any further action on issuing a generic MRP rule.

Authority of the National Institute for Occupational Safety and Health

In its capacity as a research agency, NIOSH has broad power to order human monitoring. Inherent authority to do so is granted in sections 20(a)(1), 20(a)(4), and 20(a)(7) of the OSHAct, all of which include mandates to NIOSH to conduct various studies pertaining to occupational health. Section 20(a)(5) gives specific authority to order both biological monitoring and medical surveillance. It states that NIOSH may

> prescribe regulations requiring employers to measure, record, and make reports on the *exposure* of employees to substances or physical agents which [NIOSH] reasonably believes may endanger the health or safety of employees . . . [and] establish such programs of *medical examinations* and tests as may be necessary for determining the incidence of occupational illnesses and the *susceptibility* of employees to such illnesses.[50]

This section envisions collecting information for extensive epidemiological studies and is not limited to hazards already regulated under section 6. Therefore, its potential scope is much broader than that pertaining to OSHA. Section 20(a)(5), however, also directs NIOSH to "furnish full financial or other assistance" to "any employer who is required to measure and record *exposure* of employees . . . under this subsection," to defray "any additional expense" the employer incurs in fulfilling those requirements.[51] Budgetary limitations thus place a decided constraint on NIOSH's ability to impose biological monitoring requirements. The reimbursement provision does not appear to apply to medical surveillance for the measuring and recording of *effects*.

Authority of the Environmental Protection Agency under the Toxic Substances Control Act

The Toxic Substances Control Act (TSCA) imposes substantial requirements on chemical manufacturers and processors to develop health effects data.[52] Section 4 of TSCA requires chemical testing, section 5 requires premarket manufacturing notification, and section 8 requires the reporting and retention of certain information.[53] TSCA imposes no specific medical surveillance or biological monitoring requirements. However, human monitoring may be used to meet the more general TSCA reporting and record-keeping requirements discussed below, and the data resulting from such monitoring presumably are subject to an employer's recording and retention obligations under the OSHAct (see "OSHA Access Rule" in Chap. 11). Further, the Environmental Protection Agency (EPA) has proposed agencywide generic guidelines for exposure assessment used in risk assessment under TSCA and other statutes, and these guidelines cover the gathering of exposure data through biological monitoring.[54]

Beginning in 1982, EPA promulgated a series of "chemical information rules" under section 8(a) of TSCA. Presently, these rules require the submission of certain data, including information on occupational health effects and exposure, on some 350 chemicals.[55] Section 8(a)(2) allows the agency to require the reporting and maintenance of such data "insofar as known . . . or . . . reasonably ascertainable."[56] EPA would thus appear to be authorized to require human monitoring under section 8(a)(2), as a way of securing information that is "reasonably ascertainable." However, the chemical information rules require only the reporting of "information that is readily obtainable by management and supervisory personnel."[57] Nonetheless, if monitoring is undertaken, the results must be reported.

To supplement this general reporting requirement, the EPA issued "specific chemical reporting requirements" under section 8(a) in 1988. The focus of these requirements is a Comprehensive Assessment Information Rule (CAIR), which sets forth 10 categories of information that, depending on the circumstances, may be required to be reported. One of these categories—"worker exposure"—encompasses data gathered through human monitoring. Although initially applicable to only 19 chemicals, the CAIR is intended by EPA to "standardize certain section 8(a) rules" by establishing uniform questions, reporting forms, and reporting and record-keeping requirements for a detailed list of TSCA-related data.[58]

Beyond the section 8(a) regulations, EPA has promulgated a rule under section 8(d) of TSCA requiring submission of health and safety studies for more than 400 chemical substances and mixtures.[59] As defined in the regulation, a health and safety study includes "any data that bear on the effects of a chemical substance on health." Examples are "monitoring data, when they have been aggregated and analyzed to measure the exposure of humans . . . to a chemical substance or mixture."[60] Although section 8(d) requires that all such data as are "known" or "reasonably ascertainable" be reported,[61] the regulation itself is somewhat less inclusive.[62]

Section 8(c) of TSCA mandates that records of any "significant adverse reactions to [employee] health" alleged to have been caused by a chemical be maintained for 30 years.[63] The rule implementing this section defines significant adverse reactions as those "that may indicate a substantial impairment of normal activities, or long-lasting or irreversible damage to health."[64] Under the rule, human monitoring data, especially if derived from a succession of tests, clearly appears reportable.[65] Genetic monitoring of employees, if some basis links the results with increased risk of cancer, also seems to fall within the rule.

Finally, section 8(e) imposes a statutory duty to report "immediately . . . information which supports the conclusion that [a] substance or mixture presents a substantial risk of injury to health."[66] In a policy statement issued in 1978, EPA interpreted "immediately" in this context to require receipt by the agency within 15 working days after the reporter obtains the information and "substantial risk" to be defined exclusive of economic considerations. Evidence can be provided by either designed, controlled studies or undesigned, uncontrolled studies, including "medical and health surveys" or evidence of effects in workers.[67] EPA has distinguished this reporting requirement from the "significant adverse reactions" requirement of section 8(c) by noting that a "report of substantial risk of injury, unlike an allegation of a significant adverse reaction, is accompanied by information which reasonably supports the seriousness of the effect or the probability of its occurrence."[68] Human monitoring results indicating a substantial risk of injury would thus seem reportable to EPA. Either medical surveillance or biological monitoring data would seem to qualify.[69]

EMPLOYER AUTHORITY IN THE ABSENCE OF AGENCY DIRECTIVE

Even without statutory authority, employers have the authority at common law to gather information regarding the health, fitness, and physical and mental capabilities of their employees. This authority grows out of the employer's right to set reasonable conditions of employment that will protect his or her interest in having work performed in an efficient and socially acceptable fashion. The Kansas Court of Appeals stated the rationale for this right:

> As a matter of public policy, employers must have the right to establish reasonable standards of physical fitness for their employees to insure insofar as possible that work is performed by employees who will not endanger themselves, their fellow employees, or the public at large.[70]

Because human monitoring is one method by which an employer can obtain the information necessary to determine whether an employee meets "reasonable standards of physical fitness," employers have the general authority to implement human monitoring programs even without state or federal regulation directing them to do so.

PART II
Scientific and Technical Concerns

Introduction

Conducting any of the human monitoring or screening tests is certain to be a complex activity. Before deciding how to interpret the results of the tests and what possible action to take, one must assess the goodness of the tests. To determine whether a test is an appropriate tool for monitoring a certain worker population and if it reliably detects a certain disease or abnormality, one must consider the test's sensitivity, specificity, and predictive value; the frequency of the condition within a population; and the reproducibility of the results (see Table 3).

The *sensitivity* of a test is a measure of how accurately the test identifies those people with the disease or abnormality who will correctly test positive. Those who have the disease or abnormality and are correctly identified by a positive test are classified as "true positives." *Specificity*, in contrast, is a measure of how accurately the test identifies people who do not have the disease or abnormality. Those persons correctly identified by a negative test are classified as "true negatives." The *predictive value* of a test is the test's accuracy in avoiding either false positive (people without the disease who test positive) or false negative (people with the disease who test negative) results. For example, among all people who test positive for having the disease or abnormality, the "predictive value positive" is the proportion of those who truly have the condition. Merely because someone tests positive does not necessarily mean that person actually has the condition for which he or she has been screened.

The frequency or prevalence of the disease or abnormality within the test population is an important but commonly overlooked factor that can dramatically influence a test's predictive value. When applying diagnostic test results to unselected populations, false positive errors may be magnified as a result of the relatively low prevalence of disease in the general population. *Prevalence* is the number of subjects with the disease per 100,000 population,[1] and *point prevalence* is the frequency of the disease at a designated time.[2] The *incidence* of a disease is the number of new cases of the disease that come into being during a specified period of time,[3] such as the number of new cases per year per 100,000 population.[4] Both of these terms relate to the frequency of disease in a population.[5] *Unless one knows the frequency of the condition in the population to be screened, one cannot estimate the test's predictive value.* Unfortunately, few frequencies are in fact known for conditions related to work environments. The following example illustrates the importance of the frequency factor:

Table 3. Sensitivity, Specificity, and Predictive Value of a Test[a]

		Disease		
		Present	Absent	Total
Test outcome	Positive	a (true positives)	b (false positives)	$a + b$
	Negative	c (false negatives)	d (true negatives)	$c + d$
	Total	$a + c$	$b + d$	

Sensitivity $= \dfrac{a}{a + c} = \dfrac{\text{true positives}}{\text{true positives + false negatives}}$

Specificity $= \dfrac{d}{b + d} = \dfrac{\text{true negatives}}{\text{false positives + true negatives}}$

Predictive value positive $= \dfrac{a}{a + b} = \dfrac{\text{true positives}}{\text{true positives + false positives}}$

Predictive value negative $= \dfrac{d}{c + d} = \dfrac{\text{true negatives}}{\text{false negatives + true negatives}}$

[a]Adapted from R. M. Thorner and Q. R. Remein, "Principles and Procedures in the Evaluation of Screening for Disease," *Public Health Monograph* (1967) 67:1–24; T. J. Vecchio, "Predictive Value of a Single Diagnostic Test in Unselected Populations," *New England Journal of Medicine* (1966) 274(21):1171, 1173; P. Cole and A. S. Morrison, "Basic Issues in Population Screening for Cancer," *Journal of the National Cancer Institute* (1980) 64:1263–1272.

An electrocardiogram (EKG) taken during exercise.. . . is about 95 percent sensitive and 95 percent specific for coronary artery disease. If this test is given to 1000 patients with angina pectoris (chest pain), . . . and the frequency of coronary artery disease (in the group) is 80 percent, then of the 800 persons with disease, 95 percent or 760 persons will have positive exercise tests. Of the 200 persons without the disease, 95 percent or 190 persons will have negative exercise tests, but 10 will have positive tests.

Therefore, . . . the positive predictive value of the test is

$$\frac{760}{(760 + 10)} = 98.7\%.$$

This percentage indicates that of all those who tested positive for coronary artery disease (total of 770), 98.7 percent or 760 persons actually have the disease. Conversely, if the same EKG test were given to healthy job applicants (e.g., 18 to 30 years old), a group in which the frequency of coronary artery disease is 2 percent, one would see very different results in the predictive value. If 1000 applicants were tested, then of the 20 persons with the disease, $(20 \times .95)$ or 19 persons would have positive tests and one would have a false negative test. Of the 980 applicants without the disease, (980 × .95) or 931 persons would have negative tests, but 49 would have false positive results. Therefore, the predictive value positive of the test is

$$\frac{19}{(19 + 49)} = 28\%.$$

The predictive value positive of 28 percent means that of those who tested positive (total of 68), only 28 percent or 19 persons actually have coronary artery disease. The other 72 percent or 49 persons in fact have no coronary disease.[6]

This example demonstrates a major problem with the use of certain diagnostic tests, particularly in an occupational setting for pre-employment exams. Individuals free of disease may falsely test positive, and if such a test were to be conducted on a similar population as a condition of employment, 72% might wrongly be denied work on the basis of the misclassified test results. False positive results not only may cause denial of employment but also may cause persons without the disease to undergo further testing. This second level of testing may subject the person to more risky diagnostic procedures and cause unnecessary social costs associated with testing persons who are in fact free of disease.

Reproducibility of results is an important component in any testing program. One or more laboratories should repeat a test often enough to ensure the reliability of the results. Comparability of test results also depends on the standardization of techniques and methods.[7] Currently, however, little data exist to compare the testing methods used in various occupational health studies.[8] Along with the standardization of techniques, laboratory quality assurance and quality control are essential.[9]

Chapters 3–6 address the specific types of tests used to conduct medical surveillance, genetic monitoring, biological monitoring, and sensitivity screening, discussing certain limitations that affect test interpretation and use of the results.

3. Medical Surveillance

A medical surveillance program typically consists of a medical history, physical examination(s), and special tests, some of which may come under the classification of biological monitoring. Each component of the program must be analyzed and limits recognized before commencing with the program.[1] A medical history and physical examination can be as important as special laboratory tests, but neither have received much attention for standardization or for evaluation of their predictive value.[2] The history and examination determine what special tests, if any, will be ordered by the physician. A complete medical history that includes an occupational history is particularly important because evidence of exposure must be ascertained before a diagnosis of occupational disease can confidently be made.[3] The results of a physical examination are limited by the large variability in the physician's measuring and recording. Also, the examinations are generally conducted in a group atmosphere that is not conducive to the worker's giving confidential information to a physician.[4]

Special laboratory tests routinely performed as part of a medical surveillance program may also have limitations. These tests are regularly given emphasis in Occupational Safety and Health Administration (OSHA) health standards (e.g., serum liver function tests and certain parameters of a complete blood count) but because there may be a low prevalence of the disease in the population being tested, the predictive value of a test may be poor.[5] It is, therefore, important for an employer (i.e., the employer's physician) to determine the predictive values positive and negative before selecting certain tests to be included in the program. Further, the finding of both low prevalence and low predictive value in populations studied under OSHA regulations indicates an even greater need for comprehensive medical examinations that include an occupational history and a complete physical examination.

Other limitations of medical surveillance tests in an occupational setting include nonspecificity, nonselectivity, and the fact that the tests may detect a disease or abnormality *after* possibly serious and irreversible adverse health effects have already occurred. For example, serum blood tests will detect an elevated serum blood urea nitrogen (BUN) level in workers who have nephrotoxicity as a result of lead exposure only after 66% of kidney function is lost or when symptoms of renal failure are present.[6] If the health condition is not detected before a worker would seek help anyway (e.g., when the worker becomes symptomatic), then medical surveillance has no additional preventive benefit.[7]

The frequency of false positive and false negative results in routine tests is another limitation of medical surveillance testing methods. The frequency depends on where the "normal" limits of the test are set.[8] A test that measures a biological distribution of variables is normal when the result falls within a predetermined range of values.[9] The question is how far above normal must the result be to indicate that a disease state exists or that additional testing or some other action (e.g., medical removal) must be undertaken.[10] Normal limits are also related to the frequency of the condition tested for in the population under scrutiny. For variables on a continuum such as serum blood measurements, it is often difficult to distinguish between health and disease[11] and to define the "normal" range because of individual variability due to metabolism, age, and gender (see "'Stochastic,' Genetic, Age, and Sex Variability" in Chap. 8). Time of day and method of performing the test also can make it difficult to determine a referent value. In fact, what may be "normal" for one person may be a disease state for another; it is not uncommon for the results in healthy and diseased groups to overlap (see the shaded area in Figure 2).[12]

It is also difficult to determine if a result is normal for the tested individual when the "normal" designation for a population spans a wide range. For example, the accepted range for BUN results is considered to be 10–20 mg/100 ml of whole blood.[13] A person who is initially monitored as having a BUN of 10 mg/100 ml and then increases to 19 mg/100 ml still falls within accepted limits, even though that individual's kidney function may have been appreciably impaired. In this situation, the diseased individual has a serum level that may also be exhibited by "normal" nondiseased individuals. Therefore, a false negative result occurs because the serum measurement is not a perfect predictor of disease. Similarly, problems deter-

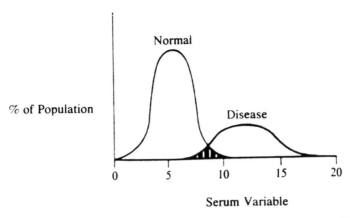

Figure 2. *False positives and false negatives relative to "normal" limits. Reprinted from P. Cutler,* Problem Solving in Clinical Medicine: From Data to Diagnosis *(Baltimore: Williams & Wilkins, 1979), 16. © 1979 by the Williams & Wilkins Co., Baltimore.*

mining a "normal" result have also occurred in serum cholinesterase testing for exposure to pesticides. One researcher noted that the upper range limit may be 225% of the lower range limit, so workers suffering substantial declines from their initial baseline results may still have levels within the accepted normal range.[14]

Exposure to noise and resultant hearing loss is an example of a different difficulty in determining "normal" levels. Figure 3 demonstrates how the definition of "normal" can obscure the full impact of exposure to an occupational hazard. Curve I represents the hearing loss in a population that has not been exposed to noise. Curve II represents the hearing loss in an exposed population. The vertical line, called a "fence," separates the population with "normal" hearing acuity from the population with impaired hearing. The "fence" is placed somewhat arbitrarily. Persons with impaired hearing lie to the right of the fence on both curves. When the entire population is exposed to noise, the population's hearing shifts. The handicaps of those with impaired hearing before noise exposure increase after the population shift. They are not counted, however, as an increase in the number of impaired persons because they were impaired from the beginning. Other persons who had no hearing impairment initially crossed the fence after exposure to noise. They are considered newly impaired. Finally, a sizable number of persons who do not cross the fence, and who therefore are not considered impaired, nonetheless suffer a significant loss in hearing acuity.

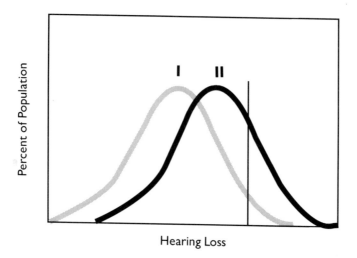

Figure 3. *Shifts in the population distribution of hearing acuity in response to noise. Curve I represents the hearing loss in a population that has not been exposed to noise. Curve II represents the hearing loss in an exposed population.*

Another limitation of the results of routine medical surveillance tests is that they may be nonselective and nonspecific in that they do not identify a particular pollutant or agent as the cause of disease. The health effects observed may be due to any one of several factors (both occupational and nonoccupational) other than the one for which the worker is being considered for treatment or removal. One researcher pointed out that "when new tests are first discovered many are thought to be specific for certain diseases. . . . Subsequent studies showed these tests [e.g., rheumatoid factor for rheumatoid arthritis, serum glutamic-oxaloacetic transaminase and serum glutamic pyruvic transaminase for acute myocardial infarction or liver cell necrosis] to be nonspecific and positive in other diseases which were either closely related or not related at all."[15]

Colorectal cancer testing is one illustration of nonselectivity and nonsensitivity in medical surveillance. Hemoccult testing is a common method used to test for colorectal cancer. A problem using the nonselective and nonspecific guiac testing method is the number of false results obtained. For example, red meat, peroxidase-containing vegetables (e.g., beets, tomatoes, and cherries), and aspirin may cause false positive Hemoccult results.[16] Conversely, vitamin C, a delay in developing specimen slides, or a low-bulk diet can cause a false negative Hemoccult result.[17] The test is limited further when it is used as a preventive or early detection method for colorectal disease.

The sensitivity of the hemoccult test has been reported to be low, and this is true especially when the sensitivity of the guiac stool test is compared to a procedure using flexible sigmoidoscopy.[18] For example, in a study of nearly 1,500 pattern makers conducted to evaluate the sensitivity and feasibility of both the guiac stool test and flexible sigmoidoscopy in the detection of asymptomatic colorectal cancer among workers at high risk, the sensitivity of the guiac test was 25%, compared with the 91.7% sensitivity of the flexible sigmoidoscopy.[19]

Another illustration of the inability of a routine medical surveillance test to identify the cause of a disease can be made by again using serum BUN as an example. The OSHA lead standard requires that BUN analysis be conducted on all employees who are or may be exposed to lead concentrations above 30 $\mu g/m^3$ of air, averaged over an 8-hour period, for more than 30 days/year.[20] This measurement is required because BUN levels serve as an indicator of renal function, and exposure to lead causes known adverse effects to the renal system. Although exposure to lead may cause an increase in the BUN measurement, an increase in BUN levels may also be seen from other causes of impaired kidney function or decreased renal blood flow, such as salt and water depletion or decreased fluid intake.[21] Therefore, if testing for elevated BUN levels was conducted in a foundry where workers were exposed to lead, a number of workers might test positive for BUN elevation, not necessarily because lead exposure affected their kidneys, but because of physical stress and sweating, causing salt and water depletion.

One physician cites pulmonary function tests, which medical surveillance programs frequently use, as another example of nonselectivity. He observes, "pulmonary function tests tell only the physiologic derangement, not the cause of disease."[22] A further limitation is the ability of the tests to meet the frequently stated goals of prevention or early detection of pulmonary disease. Some pulmonary tests used in medical surveillance are discussed below in detail, because they are the subject of many occupational studies and because occupational lung disease ranks first on the National Institute for Occupational Safety and Health list of the leading 10 work-related diseases and injuries.

Pulmonary medical surveillance testing for lung cancer most commonly includes a chest X-ray and sometimes also sputum cytology. Neither method may be useful for the purposes of detection if the cancer is of the small cell type.[23] A chest X-ray is considered to be the best method of detecting adenocarcinomas, large cell cancers, and small cell cancers in the more peripheral regions of the lung.[24] If a chest X-ray is used as a surveillance method, the tumor must increase from the unicellular stage, which is not detectable by X-ray, to a mass of 0.8–1.0 cm in diameter before it can be detected by X-ray.[25]

Sputum cytology is considered to be a good method for detecting atypical squamous cells in the mucosa of a major or segmental bronchus of the central region of the lung.[26] Absent a lesion of at least 0.8 cm, the detection of atypical cells is possible only by using cytological methods. These atypical cells, however, may be only an inflammatory response or a chronic irritation—both conditions that are able to heal and reverse to a normal state.[27] Current technology is not helpful in designating with certainty between those conditions indicating potentially dangerous environmental situations and those that are simply nonharmful changes.[28] Nonetheless, some believe that automated cytology systems hold great potential for future use in determining with increasing accuracy and reproducibility whether an atypia is the result of a harmless, reversible response or the result of neoplastic development.[29]

Sputum cytology may be useful in detecting changes on the cellular level that may indicate a precancerous condition, but because these changes are too small to be detected by chest X-ray it may be difficult to determine the location of the atypical cells. It is believed that treatment is not feasible until the lesions progress to a size that is visible by chest X-ray.[30] A proposed solution for this problem of locating the atypia is to inject a hematoporphyrin derivative, followed in 48–72 hours by bronchoscopy using an argon laser beam to locate the lesion.[31]

It therefore appears that the usefulness of either a chest X-ray or sputum cytology as a predictor or early detector of pulmonary pathology depends on the type of cell and location of the lesion. The use of computerized axial tomography (CAT scan) has been suggested as an alternative to chest X-rays for detecting peripheral tumors. It is unlikely this would be a satisfactory substitute, however, because the chest X-ray is faster, simpler, less expensive, and less time intensive.[32]

The question, then, is whether using either a chest X-ray or sputum cytology, alone or in combination, achieves the goals of prevention and early detection of pulmonary pathology, thereby detecting cancers earlier for treatment and subsequently decreasing the mortality in a tested population.

The effect of chest X-rays and sputum cytology on reducing lung cancer mortality was evaluated in three randomized clinical trials.[33]

These studies evaluated whether sputum cytology in conjunction with a chest X-ray was more beneficial in detecting pulmonary lesions than using the chest X-ray alone. In two studies, there was no statistically significant difference in the rate of detection between the groups who received both a chest X-ray and sputum cytology test and the group who received only the chest X-ray.[34] The third study noted that the low prevalence of lung cancer (20%) detected by cytology alone was "disappointing and unexpected."[35] All three studies noted an extended survival period as a result of earlier detection that lengthened the interval between diagnosis and death, but they noted that earlier detection did not necessarily produce a later date of death. Such results led one researcher to draw the following two conclusions:[36]

1. Preclinical lung cancer is not a condition suitable for surveillance because either the condition is too advanced by the time it is able to be detected using current methodologies or because current therapies provide no better outcome even if applied at an earlier stage of the disease.
2. Chest X-rays and sputum cytology are not adequately sensitive to detect biological precursors of clinical cancer; the rate of biological progression of most lung cancers seems to be too rapid to be amenable to screening by current methodologies.

Although chest X-rays and sputum cytology are considered to be "complementary procedures that remain the most effective techniques for detecting asymptomatic lung cancer,"[37] the American Cancer Society does not recommend either procedure for asymptomatic persons at high risk for lung cancer.[38] Two of the studies note that longer follow-up observations must be conducted in order to better evaluate the role of these procedures in the detection of lung cancer and the possible reduction in mortality.[39]

Another study was conducted to evaluate the efficacy of sputum cytology in decreasing the mortality of a population also screened by chest X-ray,[40] and the results are similar to those noted above. The researchers determined that testing by sputum cytology and chest X-ray compared with surveillance using chest X-ray alone did not demonstrate a decrease in mortality from all types of primary lung cancer.[41] However, a preliminary analysis of the data indicated a statistically significant decrease in mortality among those with squamous cell carcinoma who received both a chest X-ray and sputum cytology testing.[42] The researchers hypothesized that such testing may benefit certain groups of workers, but they cautioned that the hypothesis needed rigorous testing before sputum cytology testing was conducted on a routine basis to reduce mortality.[43]

Pulmonary surveillance programs for nonmalignant respiratory diseases frequently include pulmonary function testing, most commonly forced vital capacity (FVC), forced expiratory volume in 1 second (FEV_1), and their ratio. These tests have the advantages of easy measurement, acceptability to employees, and reproducibility.[44] They are limited, however, by their lack of sensitivity and specificity and may not be useful in detecting the early stages of coal miners' pneumoconiosis or occupational asthma.[45] In order to overcome these limitations, the use of newer methods has been proposed, designed to achieve the same goal as traditional measures of detecting occupational lung diseases at asymptomatic stages when intervention may be more helpful. The proposed new methods include bronchial hyper-reaction and either methacholine challenge or cold air challenge, barriers to diffusion and diffusing capacity, and abnormalities in gas distribution.[46] None of these methods, however, has been evaluated for its effectiveness in identifying asymptomatic cases.[47] As a result, no data are available at this time to assess these methods' effectiveness as testing tools with a high predictive value at a point when intervention would reduce mortality or morbidity in the tested population.[48]

In sum, it is believed that not many methods used in testing for occupational lung disease, even the traditional methods of chest X-ray and sputum cytology, have been substantiated to yield an improved health outcome.[49] This is because the traditional methods are limited in their ability to identify subclinical or asymptomatic disease at a time when removing the worker or instituting engineering controls would prevent the development of disease.[50] In the case of some newer tests, sufficient randomized clinical testing with long-term follow-up to evaluate success may simply not have been carried out yet.

The interpretation of medical surveillance results provides an opportunity for two kinds of abuse. We have already discussed the practice of removing workers on the basis of positive test results when occupational factors might not, in fact, have been relevant to the positive indications. Another questionable practice may occur when employers attribute elevated BUN levels in workers exposed to lead to other causes such as physical stress and water depletion. Thinking that those two factors rather than lead exposure are the cause for elevated BUN levels, an employer may incorrectly believe that he or she need not impose further controls for lead in the workplace.

4. Genetic Monitoring

We are indebted to Professor Karl Kelsey and Dr. Diane Brenner for assistance with this chapter.

One controversial type of medical surveillance is *genetic monitoring*, the periodic testing of blood and body fluids of employees working with or possibly exposed to substances that may cause alterations in chromosomes or DNA.[1] As discussed earlier, genetic monitoring attempts to determine whether environmental exposures to particular substances are associated with a statistically significant increase in observable changes in genetic material.[2] Genetic monitoring is usually used to determine whether the exposures are *clastogenic* (capable of causing the breakage and/or large-scale rearrangement of chromosomes)[3] or *mutagenic* (capable of causing heritable changes in the information coded in DNA—either in the "germ line" cells involved in reproduction [sperm or egg progenitors] or in normal body cells [somatic cells]).[4] Mutagenic and/or clastogenic changes in normal body cells are of interest because a small minority of these types of changes are key events in the sequence of events that leads to cancers.[5]

There are two types of genetic monitoring—cytogenetic and noncytogenetic. *Cytogenetic* techniques, which have been more extensively studied and used, detect major changes in the gross structure of chromosomes. Structural chromosome aberrations (CAs), sister-chromatid exchanges (SCEs), and micronuclei are the most common markers or end points employed (see below for definitions of these terms). Tests to detect the gain or loss in chromosome number, a phenomenon linked to adverse reproductive outcome and some cancers, are being developed but have not yet been applied to occupational groups.[6] Tissues commonly examined include blood (lymphocytes), exfoliated epithelial tissue, and, more recently, sperm.[7] At the present time, however, the chromosomal analysis of human sperm is

39

Table 4. Examples of Biomonitoring Studies[a]

End point	Method	Sample	Study population	Exposure
Mutagenicity of fluids	Bacterial cell systems	Urine	Rubber workers	Mixture
Protein adducts	Ion-exchange amino acid analysis	RBC[b]	Sterilization plant workers and controls	Ethylene oxide
DNA adducts	Immunoassays	WBC[c]	Roofers, coke oven workers, foundry workers	Benzo(a)pyrene (BP) in mixture
DNA adducts	Synchronous fluorescence spectrophotometry	WBC	Coke oven workers	BP in mixture
Antibodies to DNA adducts	Immunoassays	WBC	Coke oven workers	BP in mixture
Unscheduled DNA synthesis	Cell culture and thymidine incorporation	WBC	Workers and controls	Propylene oxide
Chromosomal aberrations	Cytogenetics	WBC	Workers and controls	Vinyl chloride
Sister chromatid exchange	Cytogenetics	WBC	Workers and controls	Ethylene oxide
Micronuclei	Cytogenetics	Lymphocytes	Tank cleaners and controls	Organic solvents, heavy metals
Sperm abnormalities	Abnormal count	Sperm	Workers and controls	DBCP[d]

[a]F. P. Perera and S. A. Hearne, "Identification and Regulation of Occupational Carcinogens: The Role of Biologic Monitoring," *Seminars in Occupational Medicine* (1987) 2(4):325–329, 328.

[b]Red blood cells.

[c]White blood cells.

[d]Dibromochloropropane.

in its very earliest stages of development. It is technologically complex, prohibitively expensive, and time consuming. Thus it is not a likely biomarker for large-scale occupational monitoring studies.

Noncytogenetic techniques detect actual damage to DNA or the presence of mutagens in body fluids, using any of multiple tissues and a variety of methodologies.[8] Both types of genetic monitoring are discussed in more detail in subsections that follow.

Some researchers believe that genetic monitoring tests may provide advanced warnings for *populations* at risk. For example, the dangers from ethylene oxide exposure were suggested by cytogenetic examination of workers accidentally exposed 10 years before epidemiological evidence confirmed the chemical as a leukemogen.[9] Early cytogenetic studies of nurses and other hospital workers exposed to anticancer agents also provided an early warning of the potential for these occupational exposures to induce adverse reproductive outcomes.[10]

It has also been proposed that such monitoring techniques might also identify *individuals* who are particularly susceptible to certain agents and serve as an "early warning system" before clinical signs become apparent.[11] However, there is a general consensus among most experts in the field that interpretation of results on an individual basis is as yet unjustified. Most existing assays are still at a rudimentary stage of development and testing, because environmental factors and temporal variations in tested parameters within individuals may bias and/or confound the results.[12]

Biological markers for biologically effective dose (i.e., the concentration of the toxin or its metabolite acting at the target organ of interest) of carcinogens have been reviewed.[13] Table 4 shows typical markers used for both cytogenetic and noncytogenetic monitoring.

CYTOGENETIC MONITORING

Structural CAs are common markers or end points in cytogenetic monitoring. Such aberrations are stable and unstable changes that result from breakage and rearrangement of chromosomes. The most important lesions leading to the production of chromosome breaks are double-strand breaks in DNA.[14] Such lesions are efficiently induced by radiation, chemicals that react with DNA (e.g., alkylating agents), or chemicals that distort the DNA helix (e.g., intercalating agents that insert between the helix strands and interfere with the transcription and replication of DNA).

Significantly elevated levels of CAs have been found in lymphocytes of workers exposed to arsenic, asbestos, benzene, chloroprene, hexavalent chromium, DDT, diesel fumes, epichlorohydrin, ethylene oxide, lead, pentachlorophenol, styrene, toluene, and vinyl chloride.[15] Other mixed exposures have also been reported to elevate CAs.[16] CAs have also been validated as a dosimeter in workers exposed to ionizing radiation;[17] however, the sensitivity of the assay for measuring low-dose exposures to chemicals has not been demonstrated. Clear, consistent dose–response relationships have not been measured, perhaps in part because of limitations in available data on worker exposures to the chemicals involved over the time period during which the CAs could have been produced.

There is some evidence linking increases in CAs with increased risk of subsequent disease, especially among groups of workers exposed to ionizing radiation, although this has not been shown on an individual level.[18] In addition, several genetic diseases that are associated with an inherited predisposition to chromosomal instability are also associated with elevated cancer risk.[19] Hence, whereas CAs are generally thought to be important in terms of assessing population cancer risk, they cannot be used to predict individual risk with any confidence.

The assay for chromosomal aberrations has several drawbacks. It must be performed on dividing cells, where the chromosomes can be examined microscopically. The technique is also time consuming, expensive, and subject to variability from observer to observer from time to time. Standardized or automated classification systems do not yet exist, and therefore identification of aberrations depends on the subjective judgment of highly trained technicians.[20] For this reason concurrent studies of unexposed controls are essential for credible demonstration of excess CAs in exposed populations.

Sister-chromatid exchanges are symmetrical exhanges between sister chromatids (chromatids from the same parent chromosome) that do not result in changes in chromosome morphology. The mechanism of their formation and the extent to which they reflect risk of disease are unclear. It is clear, however, that SCEs reflect DNA damage and/or repair.[21]

Despite a large body of research, the mechanism of SCE formation remains obscure. It is known that SCEs are produced only in the S phase of the cell cycle, when DNA is being synthesized,[22] and that SCEs and CAs can be caused by different mechanisms.[23] Hence, although CAs and SCEs are both manifestations of cytogenetic damage, they arise and are measured in very different ways.

Studies of human populations have shown that alkylating agents (such as ethylene oxide and many anticancer agents) are efficient inducers of SCEs.[24] Elevated SCEs have also been measured in workers exposed to a number of other agents, including benzene, mixed organic solvents, styrene, vinyl chloride, and mercury and cadmium.[25] Like the CA assay, the SCE assay must be performed on actively dividing cells and depends on the subjective judgment of trained technicians. The technique has not yet been standardized, and variations in technique have been clearly shown to affect outcome. Nonetheless, SCEs are easier to detect than CAs and the assay is relatively inexpensive.[26] SCEs are widely advocated as an early screen for carcinogenic or other genetically active agents.[27] Others believe that the assay is sufficiently sensitive and well developed to be used in biomonitoring studies of worker *exposures* in cases where available experimental data indicate the SCE-inducing capacity and dose–response relationship for the agent in question. A recent large-scale study of workers exposed to ethylene oxide gave strong support to this view.[28] On the other hand, most researchers would caution that it is "currently impossible to quantitate [sic] the *health risk* associated with increased frequency of SCEs for a group of exposed individuals, and even more so, for the individual."[29]

Micronuclei are DNA-containing fragments that are found within the cytoplasm and have no connection to the cell nucleus. These fragments may be pieces of chromatids or chromosomes, or entire chromosomes that have been excluded from the nuclei of the daughter cells or have lagged behind at replication.[30]

Micronuclei are induced both by substances that cause direct damage to the genetic material and by "spindle poisons," which are substances that affect the process by which the long pieces of DNA are "condensed" into chromosomes. Because of the latter mechanism, micronuclei may reflect damage by processes other than those that could be detected by assays for SCEs or CAs. As is the case for the other cytogenetic assays, the link between micronuclei and disease risk has not been demonstrated. The assay is very easy to carry out, however, and is less prone to observer error. Another advantage is that it does not require mitotic cells.[31] Finally, micronuclei may be useful in distinguishing agents that principally cause clastogenic damage from those that act principally to cause other types of genetic changes.[32]

Although promising, the assay for micronuclei has as yet been applied in relatively few studies of exposed workers. Because of this, its sensitivity at relatively low levels of exposure has not been established. Increased levels of micronuclei have, however, been measured in workers exposed to agents such as ethylene oxide and styrene, as well as in workers exposed to ill-defined mixtures of petroleum hydrocarbons.[33]

Several common problems arise in using cytogenetic techniques for monitoring purposes. First, data concerning cytogenetic changes are meaningless unless there are valid baseline data with which to compare them. On the group level this means establishing valid "normal" mean values and/or aberration frequency distributions in concurrently studied unexposed populations. For individuals, levels of markers must be ascertained *before* a worker is exposed to provide a basis for comparison with levels found after exposure. On both the population and individual levels, background frequencies for each cytogenetic end point fluctuate significantly. For example, it is not uncommon to find larger differences between levels of SCEs among control groups in different studies than are found between controls and exposed workers in studies reported as positive.[34] Repeat measures on a single individual may vary as much as 30–50%, giving highly variable baseline data.[35]

Second, although all three assays have been shown to be sensitive to a wide range of chemicals in culture systems and at high dose levels, their sensitivity to exposures at the lower dose levels usually found in occupational studies has not been generally established.[36] These uncertainties led the Congressional Office of Technology Assessment (OTA) to conclude, "The appropriateness of chromosomal endpoints for occupational monitoring needs to be determined on a case-by-case basis for each chemical."[37] This is a time-consuming and costly process.

Third, such testing has not developed to the point that scientists know the meaning of "positive" or "negative" findings, with "positive" implicitly defined as a statistically significant increase in the number of abnormal chromosomes relative to an appropriate control group. As noted above, sufficient numbers of substances have not yet been tested and adequate epidemiological evidence does not yet exist to directly link these markers with risk of developing specific human diseases.[38] Whereas some researchers have provisionally concluded that chromosomal aberrations are at least qualitatively related to the occurrence of cancer,[39] the association of SCEs and micronuclei to disease must be regarded as even more uncertain.[40] Some supposed noncarcinogens, such as lead and mercury, cause elevations in CAs and SCEs,[41] whereas other important carcinogens, such as asbestos, may not induce SCEs in observable numbers in specific test situations.[42]

Fourth, none of these markers is specific. CAs, SCEs, and micronuclei can all be induced by a number of different substances, and the sets of substances inducing each type of change overlap extensively. Because of the nonspecificity, external variables other than the suspected agent may affect the outcome of the assays, and these must be controlled for if the results are to be properly interpreted. For example, an observed excess of CAs may result not necessarily from exposure to the substance in question but from a viral infection, exposure to ionizing radiation, previous or simultaneous exposure to another chemical, or poor nutrition status.[43] Substances other than the one suspected in monitoring may similarly induce SCEs (e.g., cigarette smoking, viral infections, caffeine, steroids, saccharin, or other medications).[44] Micronuclei levels are not elevated in smokers, but are increased by radiation and poor nutritional status.[45] Individual differences in age, disease status, and metabolism or diet may influence not only the amount of carcinogen available but also its effect on genetic material.[46] Further, where multiple exposures are present at relatively high doses, substances may interact to promote or repress production of abnormalities in ways that are not yet known.

Differences in the longevity of aberrations found in lymph cells have important implications for when a worker is monitored and for interpretation of the results. With regard to CAs, one researcher notes that the "persistence of aberrations for years and decades in long-lived lymphocytes makes them an indicator of past damage, but limits the value of the test in monitoring present low-level exposures in subjects with past exposure(s)."[47] Also, workers with intermittent vinyl chloride exposure would need to be tested more frequently than benzene workers because the chromosomal changes seem to disappear more rapidly for vinyl chloride.[48] Without more frequent monitoring, the CAs from vinyl chloride exposure would not be detected.

Finally, flaws in study design, such as the failure to appropriately characterize background or control levels, inconsistent interpretation of results, inadequate validation, and the lack of a standardized assay procedure, classification methods for abnormalities, and methods for statistical analysis, have frequently clouded the results of cytogenetic monitoring studies in well-defined industrial settings.[49]

NONCYTOGENETIC MONITORING

Noncytogenetic monitoring techniques detect directly or indirectly the presence of mutagens or DNA damage resulting from the presence of mutagens.[50] The tests are designed to measure (1) mutagens in body fluids (most commonly urine); (2) reaction products (adducts) between reactive chemicals and DNA, or similar reaction products with hemoglobin, a major blood protein; (3) cells that have undergone specific kinds of mutations, or (4) germ cell (sperm) damage. The possible methods for evaluating populations exposed to mutagenic hazards for each of these three testing schemes are beyond the scope of this discussion. Details and reviews of these methods are available elsewhere in the literature.[51]

Analysis of urine for mutagenic activity (as indicated by any of a number of tests, including the Ames assay using bacteria) is now believed to be readily applicable to human monitoring situations for a number of reasons: (1) preliminary studies have demonstrated that mutagens can be detected in the urine of humans exposed, under typical exposure regimens, to various therapeutic drugs, industrial chemicals, and cigarette smoke; (2) the collection of urine samples is noninvasive and easy to obtain on a repetitive schedule; (3) biological analysis can be coupled with qualitative and quantitative chemical analysis; (4) dose–response studies can be performed on target "indicator" cells of several phylogenetic levels including human cells, if desired; and (5) the costs and performance time of urine analyses are amenable to large-scale sampling.[52] There are limitations, however, to the use of urine analysis in detecting the presence of mutagens. For example, "only recent exposures can be measured" and "the presence of mutagens in urine has not been translated into a known risk to the individual."[53] One must know the metabolic fate(s) of the mutagen(s) to know when to test and how to interpret the results properly.[54] In general, analysis of urine for mutagens cannot measure cumulative exposure and the results cannot be translated directly into quantitative risks for either individuals or populations.[55] Urine analysis can, however, be a useful tool in isolating potential mutagenic agents from exposures to complex mixtures, or, if the mutagen is known and its pharmacokinetics are well characterized, in indicating the level of recent exposures.

The measurement of DNA and hemoglobin adducts as an indicator of exposure to reactive and potentially mutagenic chemicals has been the subject of a considerable amount of research in recent years.[56] This research has even given birth to the new term *molecular epidemiology,* although this term is also sometimes used to include cytogenetic markers.[57] The research has yielded dramatic increases in sensitivity. For example, in different cases DNA adduct frequencies between 1 in 10 million normal bases and 1 in 10 billion have been measured.[58] Prominent examples where these measurements have begun to be applied in *experimental* studies of working populations include hemoglobin adducts for measurement of ethylene oxide exposure and benzo(a)pyrene–DNA adducts for coke oven workers, roofers, and foundry workers.[59]

In contrast to most of the other groups of genetic monitoring assays, adducts are generally highly specific for particular chemical exposures.[60] A finding of a particular chemical linked to DNA can only have been produced by exposure to that chemical or something that is metabolized to that chemical. If there is good characterization of (1) the dose–response relationship between adduct formation and external exposure and (2) the dynamics of production and loss of the adduct in question, then measurements of DNA or hemoglobin adducts can provide valuable information on the internal exposure (or biologically effective dose) of groups of workers to reactive agents. Such characterization is difficult, however. As with cytogenetic assays, interindividual variability will tend to limit the accuracy of dose estimates for individuals, particularly in the case of agents like benzo(a)pyrene, which must be metabolized to more reactive forms before DNA adducts can be formed. In fact, the enzymes that make this particular metabolic transformation are among the most highly variable among individuals.[61] Another limitation, of course, is that as indicators of internal *exposure*, adducts can be used for estimation of risks only to the extent that there is other information on the relationship of exposure to risk.

Another promising type of noncytogenetic assay seeks to determine the frequency of cells of specific types whose ancestors have undergone particular mutations. Perhaps the most developed of these is the Albertini system,[62] which measures the frequency of T lymphocytes that have become resistant to the toxic action of 6-thioguanine. Frequencies of these variant cells tended to increase somewhat with age and, probably, smoking, but were not detectably elevated in a small sample of health care workers with exposure to anticancer agents.[63]

Another assay system for variant cells indicating previous mutation uses red blood cells and a common blood group antigen (the MN blood group system, known as the "glycophorin A" locus).[64] In individuals who contain genes for both red blood cells and the antigen of the blood group, referred to as MN heterozygotes, nearly all the red cells can be stained with fluorescent antibodies to both the M and the N cell surface markers. However, a few can be found that stain only with one marker or the other—M0 or N0 variants, respectively— suggesting that the activity of the gene producing one of the antigens has been lost in the variant cells' ancestors. As indicated in Graph b of Figure 4, such assay measurements in *groups* of atomic bomb sur-

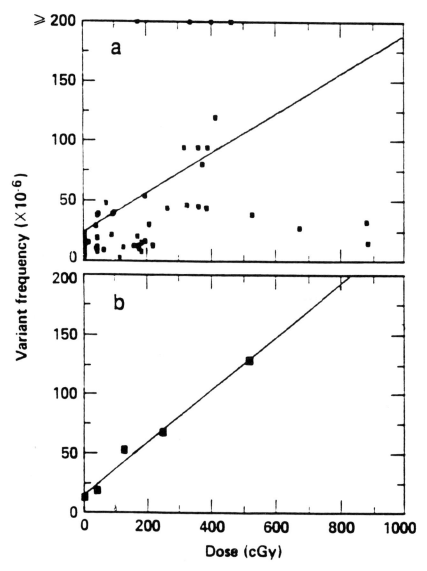

Figure 4. *Plots of hemizygous variant frequency (VF) versus T65DR dose for control and exposed donors. The VF calculated for each donor is the mean value of all NO and M0 measurements performed on that donor. Graph a, individual data; graph b, group data. Reprinted from R. G. Langlois, W. L. Bigbee, S. Kyoizumi, N. Nakamura, M. A. Bean, M. Akiyama, and R. H. Jensen, "Evidence for Increased Somatic Cell Mutations at the Glycophorin A Locus in Atomic Bomb Survivors,"* Science *(1987) 236:445–448, 447. © 1987 by the AAAS.*

vivors show a clean linear relationship between variant frequency and estimated radiation dose, even though the test was conducted decades after the exposure. On the other hand, the individual data points, as indicated in Graph a of Figure 4, show enormous scatter that indicates serious limitations for using the test on an individual basis.

Germ cell tests use sperm for mutation analysis. As with somatic cell testing, studies using germ cell analysis show promise. Germ cell tests, however, need further development. The end points have not been (and because of the difficulty of measuring human mutation rates, may never be) shown to be associated with changes in risks of heritable diseases. At this time, they must be regarded as experimental.[65]

In general, nearly all of the noncytogenetic techniques are considered to be in a developmental phase. At present, there is not enough research experience using humans for most noncytogenetic techniques to determine accurately their usefulness in workplace monitoring situations. The most obvious general deficiencies in these tests are the lack of information on (1) the normal baseline incidence of the abnormalities quantified, (2) the degree of response that can be expected for given exposures to known active agents, and (3) the dynamics of repair/reversal of induced increases in the abnormalities quantified.[66]

Although many of these tests hold promise in the identification of mutations, "extrapolations of these test results to human health is difficult. . . . Given our limited understanding of, and experience with, direct laboratory tests for mutations in man, current use of these tests should be limited largely to studies aimed at evaluating the *tests* rather than evaluating exposed human populations."[67]

The OTA is currently undertaking a second study/survey of genetic monitoring and screening. This assessment will (1) examine the state of the art (e.g., efficacy, accuracy, and cost) of technologies used by employers for genetic screening and monitoring; (2) survey, at a minimum, the 500 largest U.S. industries, 50 largest utilities, and 11 major unions to determine the current and future nature and extent of employer testing; (3) analyze the impacts genetic testing may have had since the 1982 OTA survey; (4) discuss ethical issues pertinent to worker testing, including worker involvement in testing decisions; and (5) examine legal issues, including employment discrimination, and the role of the Occupational Safety and Health Administration and the National Institute for Occupational Safety and Health in matters related to genetic monitoring and screening.

5. Biological Monitoring

GENERAL CONSIDERATIONS

Biological monitoring determines both the occurrence of exposure and the uptake (or presence) of a particular substance or its metabolites in body fluids or organs; it can be used to estimate the dose to effector organs and possibly the concentration at binding sites (receptor compartment) in the critical organs.[1] It may complement both medical surveillance and environmental monitoring.

Biological monitoring may be an important tool when inhalation is not the only significant route of exposure because it detects *total uptake* from all routes (inhalation, ingestion, and skin absorption). In addition, it can estimate individual health risk when an exposure–effect response relationship is known,[2] by measuring or approximating the internal dose or the biologically effective dose.[3] The practice is based on the "impact of man on the agent" and refers to "toxicokinetic" parameters including uptake, distribution, biotransformation, accumulation, and excretion.[4] It can take account of individual differences in uptake, metabolism, and response, and thereby reflect the risk for an individual worker.[5] As discussed earlier, we consider monitoring for the biologically effective dose to be genetic monitoring (see Chap. 4).

Results from biological monitoring procedures may in some instances indicate the presence of a medical disorder much earlier than those of medical surveillance. Biological monitoring serves as an indicator that exposure and uptake have occurred, although harm may not yet have occurred.[6] In contrast, medical surveillance results show possible adverse effects from such exposure, indicating that harm, sometimes irreversible, has already occurred.

In conducting biological monitoring tests, one must assess the *appropriateness of the biological parameter* (the toxin itself, a metabolite, or a biological effect) under consideration. To select an appropriate parameter, the examiner must have sufficient toxicological information about the mechanisms of action and/or the fate (absorption, biotransformation, distribution, and excretion) of the xenobiotic.[7] For example, trichloromethane (chloroform) is partially metabolized to carbon dioxide and the remainder is exhaled unchanged.[8] Conducting biological monitoring for metabolites in blood or urine would not be useful because, to date, there are no metabolites considered helpful in evaluating occupational exposures to chloroform.[9] Ideally, the "value of the biological parameter should be defined on the basis of the relationship between the changes in the biological parameter and the occurrence of health-relevant biological effects in groups of exposed workers."[10] One reviewer believes that most biological monitoring studies conducted in recent years used the presence of the original toxins as the parameter of interest and metabolites were used most frequently after those toxins.[11] The review concluded that little research has been conducted on the relationship between internal dose and adverse health effects.[12] Another researcher believes that there is no justification for undertaking biological monitoring unless the relationship between internal dose and adverse health effects is established; the presence of the toxin or metabolite alone is not sufficient. He believes that biological monitoring can be justified only "if markers can be found which reveal the process of the disease while it is still at reversible stages so that its progress can be arrested. [Biological monitoring] cannot be justified if it is incapable of reducing morbidity and mortality."[13] Thus, one must also question whether a change in the parameter selected is an indicator of actual or potential health damage and not of exposure alone.

If, in fact, the observed change does indicate an actual or potential adverse health effect, one must then determine the *goodness of the test,* or how well the test monitors that change. In selecting a biological test, one must consider the predictive value, specificity, sensitivity, and occurrence of false positives and false negatives (see Table 3 and related discussion in the Introduction to Part II). The factors to consider in selecting a biological monitoring test are as follows:

1. The test should measure or evaluate absorption of an agent;
2. The test should provide reproducible results;

3. The analytical error and biological variability should be small;

4. The test should be quantitatively relatable to the relevant range of occupational exposure;

5. Convenience and risk factors (associated with obtaining a specimen) should be considered;

6. The concentrations of the agent measured in the body media should be quantitatively relatable to a health effect; and

7. The test should provide useful information over and above that obtained by ambient monitoring.[14]

The *frequency* with which biological monitoring should be conducted "does not follow any general rule, [but] depends on the variability and the intensity of exposure, the toxicity of the agent, and the pharmacokinetic properties [such as] short versus long biological half-time[s]" of residence in the body.[15] These factors have an effect on the degree of fluctuation in the measurements over a period of time.[16]

Monitoring should take place at intervals consistent with the goals of the program. For example, if the program is designed to monitor substances suspected of producing irreversible changes in the body, then testing should be frequent. More frequent testing is also recommended if the purpose of the program is to monitor an individual worker rather than to check the workplace and obtain a representative sample.[17] Monitoring conducted too infrequently may fail to reflect changes in both individual exposure and workplace conditions. More frequent testing should also be conducted if the substance is highly volatile, if the level of exposure is high, and at each change in production technology.[18]

Biological monitoring should be promoted only if the positive aspects outweigh the negative.[19] Assurances that the positive aspects outweigh the negative include the following: the procedure measures exposure and leads to progress; the procedure detects disease early and improves prognosis; the data are gathered and devoted to improving conditions in the workplace; the research is applied for a good purpose; and the rights of workers are articulated and respected.[20]

There are also *limitations for the use of biological monitoring.* These include (1) a paucity of reliable tests, (2) weak links between exposure and changes of the biological parameter or "biomarker," (3) interindividual variability, (4) a potential for manipulating the test results, and (5) intraindividual variability.

First, only a *few reliable tests are available,* and of these,

> only a few have well-established predictive validity. . . . Considering biologic tests in general, many score high in sensitivity, but unfortunately, rather low in specificity. The results are then difficult to interpret. . . . So while the search goes on for chemical tests relatively simple to perform, yet of a high degree of specificity, the results of which may be interpreted with reasonable confidence, there are not very many such tests at hand today.[21]

It is not uncommon for studies involving biological monitoring to note that more research and data collection are needed in a particular area before any meaningful biological parameters can be established.[22] Further, the review of articles on biological monitoring published over a 5-year period concluded that little research has been conducted on the relationship between internal dose and adverse effects and that, aside from lead and cadmium, there has been little research on agents that are common in industry or have unusual toxicity.[23] Research efforts are not certain to be focused on the gaps in knowledge or the needs of the work force.[24] In addition, some of the biological monitoring tests available (e.g., for blood analyses) are invasive (see related discussion in the Introduction to Part II), and an invasive technique may deter workers from participating in monitoring activities.

Second, it is difficult to establish *whether exposure to the substance in question causes any observed changes in the biological parameter or biomarker.* This makes it difficult to pinpoint a cause–effect relationship. Cells and tissues generally respond in a limited number of ways to a wide variety of stresses, and the changes observed are often not specific.[25] Frequently, workers are exposed simultaneously to multiple substances, so one must also consider whether a different substance or a combination of substances caused the observed changes in the parameter of interest. A review of recent biological monitoring studies concluded that few of the studies involved combined exposures or exposure to mixtures.[26] Multiple exposure interactions have not yet been extensively studied in humans but they "should be paid particular attention in combined exposure to two or more exogenous substances or in consumption of drugs that can interfere with the metabolism of the substance under biological monitoring."[27] As a result, it may be difficult to obtain true measurements of a particular compound when exposure to several substances has occurred. This difficulty has been noted with regard to agricultural workers who generally handle more than one organophosphate

pesticide at a time.[28] The interpretation of results is further complicated by the fact that many of the separate compounds share the
same metabolic end points.[29]

The relationship between exposure and actual uptake of the chemical or its metabolite might be modified by various environmental and
biological factors.[30] The interaction of the chemical "with other environmental and workplace chemicals may stimulate or inhibit its
metabolism and elimination, and thus influence the toxicity of the
chemical in the worker."[31] Another complicating factor in ferreting
out a cause–effect relationship is nonoccupational exposures that
may cause the observed effects.

Third, *multiple factors can cause biological variations in response
among workers exposed to the same substance.* In developing, applying, and interpreting biological analyses, numerous factors must be
considered, including

1. The rate of metabolism, including
   a. individual variations in enzyme complement,
   b. diet,
   c. stimulation or inhibition of enzymes in the metabolic se-
      quences,
   d. dose of the exposure chemical, and
   e. competition for the necessary enzyme;
2. The ratio of bound to free chemical in the blood;
3. Special situations in which excreted levels of the index chemical
   do not indicate current exposure levels;
4. Concentration changes due to volume changes in the bioassay
   material;
5. Nonworkplace occurrence of the index chemical in the body and
   the resulting natural variations in concentration;
6. Age of the worker;
7. Disease;
8. Sex of the worker;
9. Normal range of the index chemical to be expected in the bioassay material;
10. Time required for the index chemical to appear in the bioassay
    material;
11. Analytical methodology; and
12. Route of exposure.[32]

Because multiple factors can cause such variability in response, it
is difficult to determine the "normal" response for an individual. This
makes the interpretation of results difficult, even when they are

accurate. In addition, apparently healthy individuals with the same biological monitoring results may differ greatly in sensitivity.

Fourth, *the parameter of interest for biological monitoring can be altered artificially.* For example, blood lead levels are commonly used to assess lead body burden. These levels can be artificially decreased by a chelating agent, which is a substance that chemically binds lead and makes it biochemically and toxicologically inactive or unavailable.[33] Workers engaging in prophylactic chelation therapy would, therefore, have lower blood lead levels than they would otherwise. It would then appear that the workers might not need to be removed from the workplace because their blood lead levels would be within the limits required by the Occupational Safety and Health Administration (OSHA) (see "Medical Removal Protection" in Chap. 9). The potential risks of this practice differ according to the different chelating agents, but generally the effects of the treatment include nervousness, feelings of pressure in the chest, transient rise in blood pressure, kidney problems, aplastic anemia, and possible increases in the absorption of lead from the gastrointestinal tract if lead exposure continues.[34] The OSHA lead standard does not authorize the use of prophylactic chelation as an alternative to controlling employee exposure. Diagnostic or therapeutic chelation in situations of acute overexposure to lead is, however, approved as long as the employer ensures "that it be done under the supervision of a licensed physician in a clinical setting with thorough and appropriate medical monitoring and that the employee is notified in writing prior to its occurrence."[35]

This limitation may carry with it associated health risks. The practice of prophylactic chelation has the potential for serious misuse. Chelating the workers would keep their blood lead levels below the removal trigger level (see "Medical Removal Protection" in Chap. 9), so employers might also realize an economic advantage in not having to remove workers. For employers who expose employees to lead levels above the permissible OSHA standard, instituting the practice of chelation would be more cost-effective than installing expensive engineering controls to bring ambient lead levels within the regulated level. The installation of engineering controls may then seem unnecessary because of the "acceptable" blood lead levels of the employees. Such employer response is inconsistent with the OSHA policy that requires altering the workplace by instituting engineering controls to control lead exposure rather than altering the worker.

The fifth limitation is intraindividual variability; that is, *changes in a biochemical parameter of interest for an individual worker may be nonspecific and variable.* A trend for a cause–effect relationship is

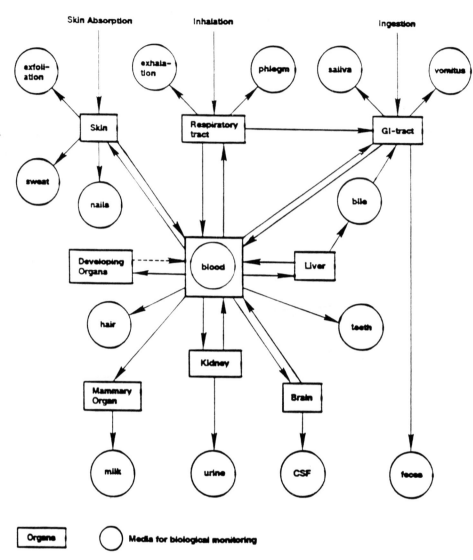

Figure 5. *The possible metabolic pathways of a xenobiotic compound by three routes of exposure and their association with target tissue dosage. GI = gastrointestinal, CSF = cerebrospinal fluid. Reprinted from NRC Committee on Biological Markers, "Biological Markers in Health Research,"* Environmental Health Perspectives *(1987) 74:3– 9, 5. Adapted from C. -G. Elinder, G. Oberdorster, and L. Ger- hardsson, "Overview," in* Biological Monitoring of Toxic Metals, *T. W. Clarkson, L. Frieberg, G. Nordberg, and P. R. Sager, eds. (New York: Plenum Press, 1988).*

possible, however, if results of a working *population* (with baseline parameter determinations) are properly analyzed along with a comparable control population.

Understanding the rate of metabolism relevant to the type of specimen chosen for monitoring is essential in timing biological monitoring. For example, some substances are excreted in the urine very rapidly after exposure (e.g., the metabolite trichloroethanol from trichloroethylene exposure), while others have a longer retention time once exposure has been discontinued (e.g., lead). To best determine the occurrence of exposure or uptake for trichloroethylene, the workers should be monitored 1–3 hours after exposure.[36] Conversely, lead is excreted so slowly via the kidneys that the level of lead found in the urine is not informative as to uptake at any particular time.

The rate of metabolism as it relates to the timing of testing is also linked to the nature of the investigation being conducted. For example in testing for long-term exposures to 1,1,1-trichloroethane (methylchloroform), the preferred biological parameters are trichloroacetic acid and methylchloroform. For short-term exposures, methylchloroform measured directly after exposure is the end-point parameter of choice and trichloroethanol is the biological parameter of choice for a 1- or 2-day exposure assessment.[37]

The most reliable way to quantify the presence of a substance or its metabolite in the body would be to measure the concentration in the adversely affected organ (e.g., biopsy). According to one researcher, "the best indicator of the risk is not necessarily the uptake but the amount of the chemical or its active metabolite at the site of action."[38] This certainly is not a practical large-scale testing scheme for a working population or for promoting worker participation in the program. As a surrogate, biological monitoring usually involves the collection and analysis of urine, blood, and expired air. Other specimens less commonly used are biopsied fat, saliva, breast milk, hair, nails, and feces.[39] Although these specimens may be useful for certain analyses, they produce associated problems of collection, storage, and analysis.[40] Figure 5 depicts the possible media for biological monitoring.[41] A discussion of the three more commonly used specimens follows.

URINE ANALYSIS

Urine is one of the most frequently used biological monitoring specimens.[42] Samples are easy to collect and collection is noninvasive.

Analysis of the samples usually involves measuring a metabolite of the substance of concern (e.g., measurement of urinary phenol resulting from benzene exposure). Criteria listed below have been established for the reliability of urine analysis for a particular organic index chemical. Studies indicate that urine analysis for a particular organic index chemical will be most reliable if:

1. The index chemical has no nonworkplace progenitors;
2. The slope of the dose–response curve is fairly steep;
3. The time needed to eliminate half of the substance from the body (half-life) is no longer than 8 hours and preferably no longer than 4 hours;
4. The method of analysis is *specific* for the exposure substance;
5. The method of analysis is validated in humans at the highest exposure level of interest (dose–response curves should not be extrapolated beyond the highest experimental level);
6. Urine collection times are consistent and appropriate for the excretion half-life time;
7. Urine samples are analyzed shortly after collection;
8. The method and determination of the concentration of the index chemical are first validated for the group of workers of interest before routine application;
9. The worker is not on a diet, has no preexisting disease, and is not taking any medicine that could interfere with the kinetics of the reaction of interest or any procedures;
10. The worker is not being exposed off the job to the index chemical or another progenitor of the index chemical;
11. The urinary level of the index chemical is relatable to the amount of exposure chemical absorbed by all routes;
12. The dose–response equations are shown to apply to both men and women, or separate ones are developed and applied to each sex; and
13. The workdays of the group of interest and the group used to derive the concentration of the index chemical in the urine are the same, if the half-life of elimination is much greater than 8 hours.[43]

As with all methods of biological monitoring, it is necessary to have adequate knowledge of the metabolism of the parent compound, or urinary levels will not be helpful in quantifying exposure.[44] In addition, the indicators of adverse health effects must be carefully selected. For example, the detection of proteinuria with trichloroacetic acid can reveal renal tubular damage in workers exposed to cadmium.[45] However, urine monitoring for low-molecular-weight proteins would reveal the same effect earlier.[46]

Investigation into the type of sample analysis performed is also important. For example, the assay for 4,4'-methylenebis (2-chloroaniline) (MBOCA) measures only parent MBOCA and two types of conjugates.[47] For the conjugates to be measured separately from parent MBOCA, the sample must undergo acid hydrolysis before analysis. Otherwise, the conjugates will be measured as parent MBOCA. The acid hydrolosis procedure, however, is not performed by many laboratories.[48] As a result, only the parent MBOCA without contributions from the conjugates might be measured, giving an incorrect and misleading monitoring result.

Another illustration of analytical problems involves a comparison between the thin layer chromatography (TLC) method, used by commercial laboratories that service most polyurethane companies, and the National Institute for Occupational Safety and Health (NIOSH) recommended method of gas chromatography–electroncapture (GC-EC).[49] An experiment using 15 split samples resulted in 9 out of 11 disagreements because the TLC readings were lower than the GC-EC readings. On the basis of these preliminary results, it is believed that the commercially used TLC method is insufficiently sensitive.[50]

The Occupational Safety and Health Administration has promulgated no standards to date that require urinary biological monitoring on a routine basis. The OSHA benzene standard does contain a provision in the medical surveillance section for monitoring urinary phenol, one of the principal urinary metabolites of benzene.[51] The urinary phenol levels are to be monitored "if an employee is exposed to benzene in an emergency situation . . . at the end of the employee's shift."[52] The biological trigger level is 75 mg of phenol per liter of urine. If the urine level is lower than the trigger level, no further testing is required. If higher, then the employer must provide additional hematology tests at monthly intervals for 3 months following the emergency exposure.[53]

In 1975, NIOSH recommended that urinary fluoride analyses be conducted at least every 3 months among a select group of workers, using postshift urine samples.[54] A preshift urinary fluoride sample would serve as a baseline reference.[55] NIOSH's analysis suggested diet as part of the evaluation. (Diet is a variable to be considered in evaluating the results of biological monitoring tests.)

The *NIOSH/OSHA Occupational Health Guidelines* also makes recommendations for urinary biological monitoring for some substances, although it does not provide trigger levels or guidance on steps to take if the substance or metabolite is found. For example, the medical guidelines for inorganic mercury, tellurium, and manganese state that urinary determinations of the substances "may be helpful" in assessing absorption or exposure.[56]

In view of the previously mentioned factors that must be taken into account in interpreting urinary biological monitoring results, published scientific reports on occupational biological applications give widely varying conclusions. For example, some researchers believe that the measurement of urinary phenol is unreliable as an indicator of benzene exposure, while others believe it to be a good index of workplace exposure. Even though the OSHA benzene standard provides for urinary phenol determinations, researchers have reported that individual determinations may be unreliable because of interindividual variability in metabolism of benzene and differences in nutritional status.[57] Others concluded that urinary phenol levels do not serve as reliable indicators of benzene exposure if such exposure is less than 8 hours at five parts of benzene per million parts (ppm) of air.[58] The current average 8-hour permissible exposure level for benzene is 1 ppm.[59] Thus, in workplaces where benzene exposure is less than 5 ppm averaged over 8 hours, some may consider urinary phenol measurements inappropriate or useless. In addition, ingestion of the recommended dosages of over-the-counter medicines such as Pepto-Bismol® and Chloraseptic® has been reported to cause urinary phenol levels in excess of 75 mg of phenol per liter of urine without exposure to benzene.[60] Except in those cases in which medicines cause elevated urinary phenol levels, other researchers believe that urinary phenol is probably a good index of workplace exposure to phenol or benzene.[61] Although the measurement of urinary phenol may be nonspecific and insensitive for individual assessments of exposure to low levels of benzene in the air, such monitoring conducted among a statistically significant sample of workers may indicate the potential risk for the exposed working population as a whole.[62]

Urinary biological monitoring is also used to discover the uptake of organics like toluene and styrene, as well as metals like lead and cadmium.[63] Concern about worker exposure to cadmium and its known toxic effects on the kidney has prompted the practice of urinary cadmium monitoring.[64] As with benzene, the accuracy of this test to determine the body burden of cadmium has been disputed. Some researchers believe that "cadmium . . . in urine . . . may be used for estimating the internal dosage of cadmium and hence the risk of health impairment."[65] The report in *Assessment of Toxic Agents* concurred.[66] However, others believe that the "body burden of cadmium can be estimated with certainty only by measuring the renal and/or hepatic cadmium concentrations with biopsy or at autopsy. . . . Urinary cadmium concentration may provide some measure of cadmium exposure; however at present, the evidence is only indirect."[67]

Because of the multiple biological and analytical variables that can influence the testing measurements, it may be difficult to interpret the results and know what actions to take on the basis of them. As mentioned previously, the OSHA benzene standard does provide guidance for further actions when urinary phenol results are greater than 75 mg of phenol per liter of urine. Researchers note that the ambiguity and uncertainty in how to interpret the results of urinary monitoring complicate the use of the data for regulatory purposes and possible medical removal actions.[68] They also caution that the limitations of urinary monitoring be kept in mind when interpreting the results. The limitations include realizing that good information may not be available regarding how the results of different analytic techniques compare, that data may not be adequate to establish action levels or trigger levels for medical removal, and that sampling times may not be properly coordinated with the metabolism of the toxin.[69]

Other methods for urinary monitoring have been proposed in an attempt to overcome the inherent limitations previously mentioned. One method proposed is the use of X-ray fluorescence. This technique is said to measure the heavy metal concentration in teeth, bones and soft tissue in situ by providing a simultaneous evaluation of the tissue burden of a number of different heavy metals.[70] It is promoted as a safe, rapid, noninvasive method that is beneficial to workers exposed to a number of toxic metals, because the health effects due to multiple exposures are likely to be greater than those produced by exposure to a single element.[71]

Immunoassays have also been suggested as a method to monitor toxic exposures in the workplace. It is believed that this technique may be helpful in detecting and quantifying organic toxicants in urine. Four potentially useful tests include the free-radical assay technique, the enzyme-mediated immunoassay technique, radioimmunoassay, and hemagluttination inhibition.[72]

EXPIRED AIR ANALYSIS

Analyzing contaminants in expired air is a biological monitoring technique that is increasing in application,[73] yet only 2.3% of the monitoring studies in recent years have focused on expired air as a testing method.[74] Generally, this type of analysis has been limited to chlorinated hydrocarbon solvents[75] and is performed to provide a quantitative evaluation of exposure, dose, or body burden.[76] The chemicals enter the body via the lungs (although some may be absorbed through the skin), then enter the vascular system, equilibrate with the body, and are later excreted in exhaled air. Equilibrium of the contaminants between the body and respired air can be used as "an indication of the concentration of the contaminant in the workroom air to which the individual has been exposed."[77] Experimental inhalation studies also have shown "a good correlation between concentration decrease of the index chemical in post-exposure exhaled air and prior exposure."[78] The concentration of chemicals in the exhaled air decreases exponentially with time, not only when the chemical is inhaled, but also when it is absorbed via the skin and ultimately exhaled unchanged.[79] According to one researcher, "if the concentration of the exposure chemical in exhaled air varies in some regular fashion with body burden, regardless of route of absorption, this would provide a very desirable method for measuring industrial exposure."[80]

As with other types of biological monitoring, careful consideration must be given to the selection of a biological parameter and the timing of testing. For example, monitoring for dichloromethane can be achieved by measuring the amount of the solvent itself in expired air. However, the production of carbon monoxide seems to be the health risk limiting factor, so biological monitoring of carbon monoxide should be preferred.[81] Expired air analysis for trichloroethene also illustrates the interrelationship between the selected parameter and the time of testing. If the solvent itself is the selected parameter and expired air testing occurs a few hours after exposure, then the results indicate recent exposure concentrations.[82] If that same parameter is tested 16 hours after the last exposure (e.g., the following morning before reexposure), the results indicate the time-weighted average concentration of the preceding days.[83] Monitoring for trichloroethanol, a metabolite of trichloroethene, produces results that indicate the time-weighted average during the preceding 1 or 2 days.[84] If the selected parameter is the trichloroethene metabolite, trichloroacetic acid, then sampling time is not crucial because the testing results will reflect the time-weighted average for trichloroethene over the preceding weeks.[85]

Expired air analyses have some advantages over other biological monitoring techniques. These advantages include the following factors:

1. It is a noninvasive method and therefore may more easily be accepted by workers than blood sampling. All an employee has to do is take several breaths and force expired air through a tube into a container.

2. The method is general and can be applied to a large range of compounds.
3. The analysis is simplified as a result of a simpler matrix than blood or urine.
4. For some inert compounds, expired air analysis is the only means of biological monitoring other than analyzing the substance itself in blood.[86]
5. Metabolism usually would not be involved, so all metabolic factors that can affect the rate of appearance of the index chemical would not affect the analysis.
6. The index chemical appears rapidly in exhaled air. Therefore, it is not necessary to wait hours or weeks for the index chemical to appear in the bioassay material.
7. The analysis would be amenable to gas-chromatographic techniques, which can be made quite specific, thereby eliminating interference from nonindex chemicals. This technique also makes it possible to analyze several chemicals at the same time.
8. Several samples can be taken in rapid succession.
9. Usually the subject can be observed while providing the sample, to ensure that he or she follows instructions.
10. Very few nonworkplace progenitors exist for the index chemical. Therefore, the excreted material is more likely to represent workplace exposure than in the analyses of other biological materials (e.g., urine).
11. The technique is noninvasive.
12. The technique measures individual exposure without the bother of a personal monitoring device.[87]

There are also limitations associated with this monitoring method. The first limitation of expired air analysis is that its use is limited to only those substances that are sufficiently volatile to be exhaled in measurable amounts.[88] This limitation is crucial to the issue of the timing of the test. For example, if a substance is highly volatile, the exposed worker needs to be tested shortly after exposure. This limitation may impose inconvenient testing times, depending on the time of the worker's last exposure relative to when he or she is, for example, to go to lunch or to go home.

A second limitation is that although exhaled air is ideally representative of the average exposure, some data suggest that samples taken shortly after exposure represent the latest exposure level and not an average.[89] Also, because chemicals are excreted at different rates, decay curves need to be developed for all chemicals for which exhaled air analysis will be conducted. There is a related need to gather accurate data on exposure time, because that measurement is necessary to calculate exposure from the developed decay curves.[90] Finally, problems remain in determining the appropriate time to sample as well as in developing satisfactory sampling and analytical methods.[91]

The third limitation of expired air analysis is that the results are difficult to interpret because a number of physiological and non-physiological factors influence the test results.

Physiological factors such as blood concentrations and solubility of the index chemical in tissues and fat may affect exhaled air levels of the exposure chemical. Other physiological factors that may affect postexposure air concentrations include (1) the physical workload during exposure (amount of uptake may increase and retention decrease during increased physical exertion), (2) body build (some substances are lipophilic and deposit in adipose tissue, thereby increasing their retention time), (3) fluctuations in exposure during the working day, (4) individual metabolism (e.g., genetic variation or the intake of other toxic substances), and (5) the type of substance (the correlation between blood levels and exhaled air levels may depend on the solubility of the solvent in the blood).[92]

Nonphysiological factors can also affect the index chemical concentration in expired air and therefore cause variability in the results. Nonphysiological factors that can cause variability in the concentration of index chemicals in expired air include (1) nonworkplace progenitors of the index chemical (e.g., perhaps the chemical entered the bloodstream prior to workplace inhalation; also, it is not possible to detect if the breath sample of the chemical came from the bloodstream or the mouth), (2) respiratory rate (until the chemical is in equilibrium in the body, respiratory rate can affect the rate of uptake, e.g., increased uptake with increased respiration when body compartments are not saturated), (3) sex (males and females are reported to have different absorption coefficients), and (4) skin absorption of the exposure chemical (kinetics in the lung for some solvents may differ between skin absorption exposure and exposure via inhalation).[93]

As previously mentioned, expired air analysis is not used routinely as a monitoring technique.[94] Few good sampling and analytical methods exist, and more data are needed before recommendations for biological monitoring for chlorinated hydrocarbon solvents can be proposed.[95] Standardization and development of methodologies are urgently needed in this area.[96] For only a few chlorinated hydrocarbons, a loose correlation between environmental monitoring and group average values can be estimated.[97]

To date, OSHA has promulgated no standards requiring expired air analysis as part of a biological monitoring scheme. Even though the analysis has been used as a biological monitor for benzene,[98] the OSHA benzene standard does not provide for such testing.

BLOOD ANALYSIS

The analysis of blood samples is another biological monitoring practice conducted to determine toxic chemical exposure to a particular substance. For example, this analysis has been employed to measure carbon monoxide exposure using carboxyhemoglobin levels as an index, to measure pesticide exposure using cholinesterase levels as an index, and to test directly for metals such as lead and cadmium. Approximately 50% of the biological monitoring studies conducted in a 5-year period used blood as the biological material of choice.[99]

The principal limitation on this type of biological monitoring is that the procedure for obtaining a specimen is an invasive one. This can make it difficult to obtain full worker participation and to acquire specimens frequently.

In addition, blood containers and collection devices must usually be selected for a *specific* application. For example, some anticoagulants present in collection tubes interfere with the determination of the substance to be measured (e.g., fluoride is a good anticoagulant but it has been observed to inhibit enzymes such as cholinesterase).[100] Also, some blood-drawing tubes are not suitable for blood specimens to be analyzed for metals because the tubes or tube stoppers themselves contain metals.[101]

The OSHA lead standard is the only health standard that specifically requires blood analysis as a biological monitoring tool for the determination of uptake.[102] A blood lead level determination for workers who are or may be exposed to more than 30 μg of lead per cubic foot of air, averaged over 8 hours, is a component of the medical surveillance provisions.[103] The *NIOSH/OSHA Occupational Health Guidelines* recommends biological monitoring blood analysis for substances such as carbon monoxide and pesticides such as endrin and parathion.[104]

Blood analysis as a biological monitoring technique for cadmium also has been studied, but there is no consensus about the goodness of the test as an accurate indicator of uptake. Some observers believe that "in occupationally exposed persons, cadmium levels in blood is [sic] a good indicator of the average intake during recent months but not of body burden nor of the most recent exposure."[105] Others find that cadmium in the blood is a poor index of body burden but hold that blood concentrations reflect recent exposure.[106] The *Assessment of Toxic Agents*, however, concluded that cadmium in the blood is a good biological indicator for estimating both the body burden of cadmium and the risk of health impairment.[107]

APPLICATION OF BIOLOGICAL MONITORING

In 1983, the Committee on Science, Engineering and Public Policy, a joint committee of the National Academy of Sciences (NAS), the National Academy of Engineering, and the Institute of Medicine, identified a further need to develop analyses of expired air, blood, and urine as a means for evaluating exposure.[108] Potential applications for these indicators included use to increase the power of epidemiological studies (see discussion of the first NIOSH survey in the first section of Chap. 7) and use as a tool to assess the consequences of human exposure in industrial settings.[109]

Recently the NAS/National Research Council (NRC) was asked by the Environmental Protection Agency (EPA) and the National Institute of Environmental Health Sciences to conduct a study of the scientific basis, current state of development, validation, and use of biological markers in environmental health research.[110] The project is being conducted by four subcommittees of the Committee on Biological Markers within NRC's Board of Environmental Studies and Toxicology. These groups will evaluate the status of biological markers for specific biological systems: markers of reproductive and developmental effects, with an emphasis on neurodevelopmental effects; pulmonary system markers of exposure, effects, and susceptibilities; markers of immunological changes as they relate to cancer, including childhood cancer; and markers of ecological toxicity, including markers of ecosystem exposure and altered processes.[111] These markers include those that are potentially useful for biological monitoring as well as for genetic monitoring and screening, and for medical surveillance.

The European Communities (EC) has also expressed a serious interest in biological monitoring. In addition to cosponsoring a seminar in 1980 in Luxembourg,[112] the EC has published a series of monographs on specific substances.[113]

The terms "biologic threshold limit values," (BLVs)[114] "biological permissible limits"[115] and "biological exposure indices" (BEIs)[116] (all three terms are used interchangeably in this discussion) are based on the relationship between some measure of internal exposure (i.e., the level of a chemical or its metabolites or both in biological specimens) and the *permissible air limits of exposure*. In contrast, Lowry reported that Lauwerys recommended that the value be based on the relationship between the internal dose and an *adverse health effect*.[117] The American Conference of Governmental Industrial Hygienists (ACGIH) defined BEIs as reference values representing "the levels of determinants which are most likely to be observed in specimens collected from a healthy worker who has been exposed to chemicals to the same extent as a worker with inhalation exposure to the TLV–TWA [threshold limit value–time weighted average]."[118] The rationale for the adoption of BEIs is that

> there are situations where air analyses, in combination with the atmospheric TLV, are not adequate to evaluate precisely the peril of the hazard, since the amount absorbed cannot be predicted from the data obtained by such determinations. In such situations, it is highly desirable to have other means of estimating exposure. With many substances this can be done by analyzing suitable biologic specimens or excretion products for the toxic agent or a metabolite derived therefrom.[119]

The ACGIH cautioned, however, that the BEIs "are not intended for use as a measure of adverse effects or for diagnosis of occupational illness."[120] The ACGIH recommended that BEIs be used as biological monitoring tools that are complementary to air monitoring. The biological specimens recommended for BEIs included urine, exhaled air and blood. Other specimens such as hair and nails were not recommended.[121]

Scientists worldwide point to the need to develop biologically permissible levels for toxic substances.[122] As a result, some are undertaking efforts to develop such levels. For example, participants at the *Assessment of Toxic Agents* conference in Luxembourg identified the need for consistent international biological indicator levels.[123] In a 1980 survey of nine European countries, the seven governments that responded answered affirmatively the question, "Does your department consider to introduce [sic] in the future biological 'standards' for some agents, which will have in your country about the same significance as standards for concentration in air (e.g., mean air concentration, TLV)?"[124] The EC published three review monographs since 1983 in which BEIs are recommended.[125] The World Health Organization is also reported to be developing BEIs for metals and solvents, as well as for pesticides.[126] Biological exposure indices have been approved by the ACGIH for 10 chemicals.[127] BEIs that have been approved by the ACGIH board of directors are listed as "Notice of Intent to Establish BEI's" and those include BEIs for carbon monoxide, ethylbenzene, styrene, toluene, trichloroethylene, xylenes, benzene, hexane, lead, and phenol.[128] According to one researcher, "it is apparent that the table of BEI's and the values quoted for them do not contain sufficient information to effectively utilize BEI's in an occupational health monitoring program."[129] Another 10 BEIs, including 3 for pesticides, are intended to be established, and 16 more are under study.[130]

Although enthusiasm for developing BEIs is growing, some serious issues regarding the development and use of BEIs must be addressed. First, what is a "normal" limit (see discussion of variability in Chap. 8)? "Normal" may be considered as a "statistical expression [of a distribution] of a large number of individual responses."[131] Comparing an individual value with general norms, however, may result in false negative results.[132] Alternatively, a BEI could be set high enough to eliminate all "normal" values, but then some overexposed workers might never reach it.[133] The limit could also be set at a level that included many people who had not been overexposed to the workplace chemical, but this option would require later confirmation that elevated levels were in fact due to workplace exposure.[134]

The problem lies in trying to devise a single value as the dividing line between normal and abnormal test results. Attempts to do so are usually flawed methodologically. One researcher concluded that clinical studies on the relationship between uptake and quantitative changes in the proposed biological parameter are still insufficient, making definition of meaningful BEIs not yet possible.[135] Others found that many workplace substances are not even suitable for BEI determinations.[136]

Two other important considerations are the goodness of the tests and individual variability. Regarding the former, the test's ability to provide accurate, reproducible results with adequate sensitivity, specificity, and predictive value must be demonstrated before any BEIs are determined (see Table 3 in the Introduction to Part II and accompanying text). The latter consideration is one that has received attention from the ACGIH. The ACGIH recognized that individual variability leads to difficulty in interpreting the BEI results and cautioned, "Intraindividual and interindividual differences in tissue levels of determinants occurring at the same exposure conditions must be considered."[137] The variable factors that are the main sources of inconsistency in comparing biological monitoring results with BEIs include the following:[138]

1. The physiological and health status of the worker (e.g., body build, diet, enzymatic activity, body fluid composition, medication, and disease state);

2. Occupational exposure sources, including the intensity of the physical work load and fluctuation of exposure intensity, skin exposure, temperature and humidity, and coexposure to other chemicals;

3. Environmental sources (e.g., community and home air pollutants and water and food contaminants);

4. Individual life-style sources (e.g., working and eating habits, smoking, and alcohol and drug intake); and

5. Methodological sources (e.g., specimen contamination, storage, and analysis).

Making an assessment for an individual on the basis of a test result using a BEI as a reference point is difficult because each factor must be assessed for each individual. Comparison of group testing results with a reference BEI may, however, be more useful as a predictor of adverse health effects than a comparison for an individual. For example, if measurements in specimens obtained from a group of workers at the same workplace exceed the BEI, the exposures should be investigated.[139]

To date, only OSHA's lead and benzene standards require adherence to a biological threshold limit value.[140] The biologically permissible limit for lead in the blood is 50 μg of lead per 100 g of blood, and the benzene standard provides for a urinary BLV of 75 mg of phenol per liter of urine after exposure during an emergency. In addition, NIOSH recommended a urinary BLV for fluoride.[141]

Although the idea of establishing and implementing adherence to BEIs is attractive, the seriousness of the limitations of the concept cannot be ignored. If BEIs are eventually routinely established on the basis of reliable and accurate tests, and factors affecting variability are carefully considered, then BEIs should be used as an adjunct to medical surveillance testing and environmental monitoring, but certainly not in place of either one. One member of the ACGIH BEI Committee concluded that BEIs

> are not a substitute for controlling the workplace environment, and that environmental monitoring is still the method of choice to ensure that the working environment is safe. . . . Prudent practice is that

environmental monitoring should be used to assess the workplace levels of chemicals and thus comply with OSHA regulations, while biological monitoring should be used to assess more accurately the uptake of workplace chemicals by the employee with biological limit values used as guidelines to ensure worker health protection. . . . A final precaution: biological limit values must be utilized with care by a knowledgeable occupational health professional, since the fate of an industrial chemical in man is a dynamic process, and strict attention to the pharmacokinetics is required prior to collection of the sample to interpret properly results using previously established biological limit values.[142]

6. Genetic and Other Sensitivity Screening

An employee undergoes sensitivity screening only once, usually as part of a preemployment or preplacement exam, to determine individual risk from exposure to a certain workplace substance or substances. Preemployment medical examinations to determine individuals' basic capabilities to perform certain tasks have a long history and a legitimate function that in some cases relates to risk.[1] As commentors pointed out, an attribute such as poor and uncorrectable visual acuity in a vehicle operator may place an employee and others at increased risk even under normal circumstances.[2] This objectively and unambiguously measurable characteristic relates to job fitness in such a direct way that policies to select prospective workers on this basis are quite defensible.

Below we examine a number of characteristics that are sometimes measured, or have been proposed for measurement, which generally have a less direct relationship to risk and job fitness. An individual's risk of injury or illness from exposure to a certain workplace substance or substances can be elevated relative to the average because of genetic inheritance, because of acquired characteristics, or (perhaps most frequently) because of a combination of genetic and environmental influences. For example, an allergy to a specific contaminant is always an acquired characteristic, but there are genetic differences in the vigor with which different parts of an individual's immune system respond to different foreign substances. It is convenient to divide our discussion below, however, into subsections on genetic screening and other sensitivity screening, according to the predominant source of variability in characteristics that are thought to affect risk.

GENETIC SCREENING

Genetic screening should not be confused with *genetic monitoring,* which is conducted periodically to determine risk to a *group* of employees who may exhibit chromosomal changes that are not inherited but due possibly to exposure to certain substances in the workplace.

There are numerous human traits for which screening can determine genetic predisposition to occupational disease. The Office of Technology Assessment (OTA), in a broad-ranging study, reviewed only a small percentage of the traits.[3] However, OTA is currently undertaking a second study to be completed in 1990 (see conclusion of Chap. 4). We describe here a small sampling of the traits that have most commonly been mentioned as candidates to form the basis of preemployment screening tests. Our review is based in part on a more extensive discussion by Schulte and Halperin.[4]

Glucose-6-Phosphate-Dehydrogenase Deficiency

People with glucose-6-phosphate dehydrogenase deficiency (G6PD), which is caused by a genetic change on the X chromosome, have a known risk of hemolytic anemia (breaking of red blood cells) if they receive specific drugs.[5] On this basis, it was postulated more than 25 years ago that G6PD-deficient individuals would also be at higher risk when exposed to industrial chemicals (aromatic amines and nitro compounds), and test tube studies of red cells have indeed tended to support this hypothesis. In only one case, however (the explosive TNT), has excess risk been demonstrated in vivo in actual working populations.[6]

Glucose-6-phosphate dehydrogenase deficiency and other genetically determined red cell conditions (sickle cell anemia and thalassemia[7]) tend to be more common in people who trace their ancestry to areas with a historically high incidence of malaria.[8] In those environments, the genes often confer some selective advantage on heterozygotes—individuals who carry one normal copy of the gene and one copy of the gene that, in homozygotes, produces overt disease. The known ethnic associations with these genes have raised the concern that use of tests based on these red cell traits will result in somewhat less occupational opportunity for minority groups that are also disadvantaged in other ways, and therefore may require an unusually strong health and safety justification.

Alpha-1-Antitrypsin Deficiency

Alpha-1-antitrypsin (AAT) deficiency has excited considerable interest in recent years, because it has shed light on the fundamental mechanisms involved in emphysema—a chronic lung disease characterized by the destruction of the walls of the smallest airways in the lungs (respiratory bronchioles) and of the terminal air sacs (alveoli) where gas exchange occurs.[9] Emphysema results from the apparently irreversible destruction of the walls of the alveoli and the smallest airways (the bronchioles). This is now thought to be the result of excessive release of protein-digesting enzymes by specific types of cells (macrophages and neutrophils) involved in defending the lung against bacteria and other foreign particles. Cigarette smoke contributes to this process in part by providing a massive dose of particulate matter that induces the migration and activation of the macrophages, and the release of protein-digesting enzymes that weaken the lung's structural support system (proteins including elastin and collagen). Sometimes the damage is worsened by a genetically determined deficiency of substances, including AAT, that normally inhibit the activity of these protein-digesting enzymes.[10] The rare individuals (1/4,000–1/8,000 in the general population) who have inherited two copies of genes coding for AAT deficiency have approximately an 80% lifetime risk of developing emphysema.[11] The risk to individuals who have inherited only one copy of the deficiency gene (3% of the general population) is less clear, although the fact that they have AAT levels of only 55–60% of normal reasonably suggests the possibility of some increased risk.[12] One researcher reported, "Some heterozygous phenotypes are statistically overrepresented in hospitalized populations and among workers with impaired lung function, suggesting that they are statistically at slightly greater risk for developing lung disease than are homozygous normal individuals. These data suggest that a screen for AAT carriers would be marginally acceptable scientifically, but would pose ethical questions of discrimination and equity in use of disease-detecting resources."[13] After a review of relevant ethical criteria, Lappe concluded "Currently, programs directed at early detection of symptomatic workers coupled with reduction or elimination of offending agents are scientifically and ethically more warranted than full-scale genetic screening for AAT deficiency."[14]

Slow Acetylator Phenotype

Aromatic amines are an important class of occupational bladder carcinogens and are most frequently found used in dyes.[15] In Western
countries, there is about a 50–50 split in the general population of a
genetically determined difference in the rate at which acetyl groups
attach to typical aromatic amines.[16] As it happens, the acetylated
forms of the amines appear to be relatively inactive in carcinogenesis.[17] There is thus a reasonable theoretical basis to suspect that
people who are fast acetylators might be less likely to develop
aromatic-amine-induced bladder cancer.

This hypothesis appears to have been confirmed by observations in
a group of workers who developed bladder cancer after occupational
exposure to benzidine. One researcher found that 22 of 23 such workers (96%) had the "slow acetylator" phenotype, whereas, in contrast, a
sample of 95 persons from a local general population showed that 54
(57%) were "slow acetylators."[18]

Qualitatively, therefore, evidence of some increased susceptibility
in this case is relatively strong. It is not possible from these limited
data to calculate how much greater the risk of a similar aromatic
amine exposure might be for average people with the "slow" phenotype. However, the indicated difference seems likely to be at least
severalfold. Whether this is enough to justify screening programs is a
social policy judgment that needs to be made in the light of the absolute magnitude of the risk indicated for a specific exposed population,
and other opportunities to reduce the risk.

Paroxonase Deficiency

Compared with other sources of individual differences, there are
very wide differences in the human population in the rates at which
the blood of different individuals can detoxify paroxon, the activated
metabolite of the insecticide parathion.[19] These differences are produced by a well-characterized genetic polymorphism.[20] However, it
has not yet been verified that individuals whose serum is low in
paroxonase in fact have slower overall metabolism of paroxonase in
the body as a whole, or are at increased risk of parathion poisoning.
Nevertheless, this hypothesis is worthy of further study.

The general findings of OTA regarding these and other potential
screening techniques are that "while the biological foundations of
the concept of genetic screening to identify predisposition to occupational disease are sound," more epidemiologic investigation is

needed. OTA also cautioned that factors other than genetic status may contribute to observed toxic effects and that

> the identification of genetic factors that may contribute to the occurrence of job-related disease is a science truly in its infancy. . . . Genetic differences may in part explain the variability of responses to chemicals in the workplace. What percentage of the total variability may be explained by genetic factors is uncertain.[21]

Geoffrey M. Karney of OTA testified before a congressional subcommittee that "few data" presently "support the correlation between any of these traits and an increased risk for disease from occupational exposure, mainly because of serious flaws in study design."[22] As with genetic monitoring, genetic screening methods are neither adequately specific nor sufficiently developed for current use in reducing occupational disease.[23] As discussed above, OTA is undertaking a new study/survey to be completed in 1990 (see conclusion of Chap. 4).

Much controversy surrounds the practice of genetic screening, particularly because several years ago 59 corporations informed OTA that they planned to begin genetic screening programs of their workers in the next 5 years,[24] even though the usefulness of such tests had not been confirmed.[25] The one-time nature of sensitivity screening programs, and the adverse consequences for prospective workers who may be "screened out" in error, imposes special burdens on the design and execution of such systems. When a test is done only once, there is no automatic corrective procedure to catch simple laboratory errors. If a test is not very well correlated with future risk, the ratio of unnecessary and unproductive exclusions (and whatever adverse effects may be produced by the test itself) to illness prevented rises.

Another difficulty is that genetic factors do not exist in isolation. Nutritional status, age, preexisting disease, and the interactions of various medications may affect an individual's susceptibility to toxic substances in ways that may be relatively long lasting or only temporary.[26] The overall state of the art for genetic screening has not been developed broadly enough to distinguish genetic factors from these other variables that may cause a response to a toxic substance, or, for environmental causes, temporary from permanent increments to possible susceptibility. For example, during World War I, it was speculated that TNT-induced adverse effects were intensified by inadequate diets.[27]

A substantial amount of evidence exists to support the proposition that some individuals have a genetic predisposition to industrially related disease (e.g., G6PD deficiency related to an increased risk of hemolytic anemia[28]). The principal problem, however, is that the levels of exposure required to cause the response are not usually documented. Therefore, it is difficult to estimate risk or to determine the adequacy of established workplace exposure standards in protecting worker health.

Because of this obvious gap in the scientific data and the inability to distinguish genetic factors from other variables, screening for the purposes of preemployment testing, preplacement testing, job denial, or job transfer seems misguided and unjustified at this time.[29] Speculation on its use as an accurate and reliable tool in the future is difficult, because workers are exposed to thousands of chemicals in industry. One would need to test each of those chemicals for adverse effects in those with heritable traits, take into consideration other variables, and perform statistical analyses on the data before one could ascertain the goodness of the tests.

Those who favor the practice of genetic screening believe that it serves to reduce occupational disease by protecting the employees, particularly the "hypersusceptibles," from workplace hazards.[30] It may be difficult, however, to determine which workers are actually "hypersusceptible" as a result of genetic predisposition. This difficulty is reflected by the fact that of the 92 human disorders for which a genetically determined specific enzyme deficiency has been identified, only 5 meet the prerequisite for a different job assignment.[31]

The National Cancer Institute some time ago awarded a Canadian scientist a contract to "perfect a simple test for identifying cancer-prone individuals."[32] Such a candidate test has serious potential for misuse. From a scientific point of view, the test would have to demonstrate acceptable sensitivity, specificity, predictive value, and reliability. Individual biological variation must be factored in along with variables like age, nutritional status, and preexisting disease. The test must also include appropriate markers that identify disease with certainty and be subject to verification by appropriate statistical analysis and epidemiological evidence. To date, the state of the art for genetic screening has not achieved this.[33]

Some critics contend that genetic screening may lead to discriminatory employment practices (see Chap. 11) against certain ethnic and racial groups by industry.[34] Opponents of genetic screening also contend that such screening practices shift the focus from cleaning up the workplace, so that all workers are protected as much as possible from harmful exposures, to a "blame the worker" attitude resulting in the removal of workers. This removal may create a false sense of security that all of those who will develop cancer have been identified and removed, as well as encourage the employer to divert attention from the detection and removal of chemical and physical workplace hazards that pose a continuing threat to those workers who remain.

Results from genetic screening tests may be interpreted wrongly to mean that some workers will experience responses from exposures to certain chemicals. Such workers who exhibit what is in fact normal variation are inappropriately categorized as "hypersusceptible."[35]

NONGENETIC SENSITIVITY SCREENING

Many of the considerations discussed above also apply to relatively long-lasting acquired characteristics used as a basis for screening workers. Perhaps because it appears less novel, and does not involve characteristics that might stigmatize whole families, there has generally been less controversy about the tests used in nongenetic sensitivity screening.

Commenting on the American Conference of Governmental Industrial Hygienists' traditional design goal of threshold limit values to protect "nearly all workers," one writer offered a rather vague criterion that "the TLV should be low enough to protect any significant subpopulations which may be more susceptible." However, the writer noted that "when a more susceptible subpopulation is very small, it may not be feasible to reduce the TLVs sufficiently to protect it, and that alternative methods such as preemployment screening examinations or refusing employment to certain categories of workers should be used."[36]

Perhaps the most common type of nongenetic preemployment screening relates to allergies or "atopy." According to one researcher,[37]

Atopy denotes the exceptional capacity to produce immunoglobulin [sic] IgE antibody when exposed to common environmental allergens. The characteristic is frequently used for preemployment screening purposes. Too little attention has, however, been paid to the rationale and the consequences of this practice. Atopy is very common, and so decisions made because of atopy probably affect about a third of the working population. Work-related hypersensitivity symptoms cannot be eradicated by weeding out the atopics. The intensity of exposure and/or the sensitizing properties of causative agents are often extremely strong in occupational settings and trigger the production of specific IgE antibodies even in nonatopics. Atopy is probably not sufficiently discriminative for screening purposes even in environments where atopics are known to have a greater risk of developing asthma (e.g., laboratories with animals). Moreover, weeding out atopics may be used instead of hygienic and technical measures to reduce exposure levels. . . . There is an urgent need for prospective studies in various occupational environments.

Recently, increased attention has been focused on workers with "multiple chemical sensitivities," many of which do not seem to be immunoglobulin E mediated and hence are not atopy.[38] A resurgence in workplace chemical sensitivities suggests a reexamination of the observations of clinical ecologists may be in order.[39]

Actual practice in the field in screening for atopy appears to be mixed. Of 163 laboratory animal facilities surveyed in a study, the majority reported the presence of laboratory animal allergy as a workplace disease. Nonetheless, although 103 facilities required pre-employment medical examinations, only 6 reported including hyper-sensitivity screening as part of the examination.[40]

Another study reported results on preemployment testing of a group of 3,407 individuals for atopy before beginning work with enzyme-containing detergents. Positive skin test results from a number of different allergens were obtained for a large number—735. The researcher found that "the proportion of persons . . . positive to a given allergen who had relevant symptoms varied from 7.7 percent to cat fur to 36.1 percent to grass pollens." An important conclusion was that "no relationship exists between atopy and the development of asthma with many occupational allergens."[41]

Finally, other researchers examined the usefulness of a number of criteria for screening prospective laboratory animal workers, includ-ing "a personal history of allergy, chronic rhinitis or asthma, positive direct skin tests, elevated serum immunoglobulin E, abnormal forced expiratory volume in 1 second, and a family history of allergy." They calculated sensitivity, specificity, and positive predictive value for each criterion. They interpreted their results as indicating that "cur-rently, the use of these screening criteria as determinants for hiring persons to work with laboratory animals is unwarranted."[42]

Other authors reported more positive experiences in screening for other types of work. Two administered preemployment medical ex-aminations to 1,916 people in Hong Kong to assess their fitness to work in a compressed air environment. Of these, 367 were dis-qualified, most often by an abnormal chest X-ray (indicating active or inactive tuberculosis). The next most common reasons for dis-qualification were cardiovascular disease and hypertension. Of 1,549 subjects initially judged to be fit, however, 130 were subsequently disqualified, usually on the basis of one or more episodes of decompression sickness during the first five shifts, dysbaric osteonecrosis, and related conditions. It is not clear, of course, what the risk might have been for those workers who were disqualified. However, those authors concluded, "Applying strict medical criteria for preemployment medical examinations and medical surveillance are important factors for preventing decompression sickness and dysbaric osteonecrosis."[43]

As with genetic screening, nongenetic sensitivity screening discussed above is also in its infancy and widespread application does not seem sufficiently scientifically grounded to be warranted at this time.[44]

7. The Frequency and Timing of Examinations

The decision of when in the employment cycle to administer tests to workers is usually determined by Occupational Safety and Health Administration (OSHA) regulations, by management alone, or as a result of an agreement between management and labor. Tests most commonly conducted in the employment cycle include

- preemployment,
- preplacement,
- periodic,
- post-illness or post-injury,
- episodic,
- termination or retirement.

The 24 OSHA health standards provide for testing on some of these occasions, and the *NIOSH/OSHA Occupational Health Guidelines* provides substance-by-substance recommendations on when to test.[1] Table 5 describes categories for the general application of the tests relative to screening and the three types of monitoring.

The decision of when to conduct testing should be made on a substance-by-substance basis. The rate of metabolism of the substance is one factor that must be considered in the decision. Metabolic rates for chemicals vary from individual to individual and from substance to substance. The time between exposure to a certain agent and the appearance of the agent or its metabolite in the urine, for example, may vary from a few hours to days. For instance, not until 42–69 hours after exposure to trichloroethylene does the metabolite trichloroacetic acid peak in the urine.[2] In this case, urinary biological monitoring for the metabolite would not be useful if conducted at the end of a shift on those exposed workers.

Table 5. Temporal Characteristics of Tests for the Four Types of Human Monitoring

Time of examination	Medical surveillance	Genetic monitoring	Biological monitoring	Sensitivity screening
Preemployment	X		X	X
Preplacement	X	X	X	X
Periodic	X	X	X	
Post-illness or -injury	X		X	
Episodic	X	X	X	
Termination/ retirement	X			

The natural history of the disease caused by exposure to that substance must also be factored into the decision of when to conduct testing. For example, asbestos-related pulmonary diseases usually appear no sooner than 15 years after first exposure.[3] Therefore, screening for asbestos disease in the first year of exposure would be highly unlikely to detect an asbestos-related pulmonary illness. This approach is well illustrated by the OSHA standard for asbestos.

The amended 1986 asbestos standard no longer requires annual chest X-rays for all workers—"Given the potential radiation hazards posed by X-rays and given the long latency periods for most asbestos-related diseases, the requirement for annual X-rays has been changed to one that establishes frequencies based on a worker's age, duration of exposure and latency considerations."[4] The standard now requires that X-rays be offered to workers at 5-year intervals during the first 10 years following an employee's first exposure to asbestos and offered subsequently thereafter on the basis of the age of the worker.[5]

Analyzing data gathered from populations for which the latency period (time between exposure and the development of disease) has not yet "ripened" may lead an observer to conclude that no occupationally related disease exists among the workers. This conclusion cannot be adopted with confidence, because the natural history of the disease relative to the exposure substance has not been considered. The workers may in fact have a dormant occupationally related disease that will be detected clinically or symptomatically after the latency period is reached or exceeded.

From 1972 to 1974, data on the percentage of workers in a study population receiving preemployment, preplacement, periodic, post-illness, and termination exams were collected from 5,000 U.S. workplaces for the first National Institute for Occupational Safety and Health (NIOSH) National Occupational Health Survey.[6] The survey included workplaces representing a range of plant sizes and industry types. The data obtained have not been well coordinated or analyzed, either in isolation from or in conjunction with other worker information (e.g., exposure data). According to OSHA, "Most companies have no mechanism (such as a unique identifying number) to permit easy linkage of medical and work history records, job descriptions, exposure data and medical test results."[7] The data should be used for epidemiological (i.e., morbidity and mortality) and biostatistical analyses as well as integrated with industrial hygiene data. According to the Occupational Medical Practice Committee of the American Occupational Medical Association,

> When appropriate, these data should be used to conduct epidemiological studies to assess the effects the workplace may have had or is having on the employees. . . . The occupational health program must maintain occupational medical records on each employee, documenting the reasons for and the results of all physical examinations. . . . These data must be maintained confidentially. . . . Procedures . . . allowing access to those with a bona fide need to know, must be developed.[8]

The data generated from surveillance activities may indicate that occupational illnesses have occurred. In an effort to collect and evaluate the data in a way that allows for the efficient tracking of certain occupational conditions, NIOSH established the Sentinel Event Notification System for Occupational Risks (SENSOR). The SENSOR system is a NIOSH-funded network designed to develop "local capability for the recognition, reporting, follow-up and prevention of selected occupational diseases."[9]

Few OSHA standards provide any guidance on what to do if an abnormal testing result is observed. Only the asbestos, vinyl chloride, cotton dust, lead, ethylene oxide, and benzene standards mention any action to be taken based on abnormal human monitoring results.[10]

The lead standard provides for additional follow-up blood sampling when an employee's blood lead level exceeds the criterion articulated under the medical removal protection (MRP) provisions.[11] The benzene standard articulates two types of action to take if an abnormal testing result is observed. It provides for additional examinations and referrals when certain conditions might exist based on abnormal complete blood counts and for additional blood testing if urinary phenol results reach a certain level when measured at the end of a shift after an emergency exposure.[12]

The ethylene oxide, cotton dust, and amended asbestos standards recognize the possibility of medical removal of the worker, at a physician's discretion, as a means of placing "recommended limitations on the employee." The cotton dust standard is even more specific in implying a medical removal remedy by providing that the physician can recommend to the employer "limitations upon the employee's *exposure*." The ethylene oxide standard provides for testing conducted more frequently than required by the standard, at the physician's discretion. Although the language of the standard does not articulate that the impetus for more frequent testing is abnormal testing results, it could be so interpreted.[13]

The asbestos, vinyl chloride, and cotton dust standards contain provisions for medical removal, and the lead and benzene standards contain provisions for MRP.[14] It is worth repeating that *medical removal* must be distinguished from *MRP,* because even though the two concepts appear almost identical on the surface, they provide for measures that affect workers in very different ways. *Medical removal* involves removing the worker from exposure, possibly without regard for earnings, seniority, and other employment benefits, such as in the vinyl chloride standard. The asbestos and cotton dust standards mention considerations for the same pay and employment benefits. These provisions are distinguishable from MRP provisions, in that the removals for asbestos and cotton dust employees are not triggered by specific results of either medical surveillance or biological monitoring tests. Rather, they are based on an employee's ability to wear a respirator. One could argue, however, that to determine one's ability to wear a respirator, certain pulmonary tests (i.e., medical surveillance) must be conducted—so the removals might under that scenario, in fact, be triggered by medical surveillance testing results.

Medical removal protection under the lead standard is triggered by a specific blood lead level, and removals under benzene are triggered by "abnormal" results (no values are specified) of serum blood counts. MRP, according to OSHA, is

> a protective, preventive health mechanism integrated with the medical surveillance provisions [which include biological monitoring] of the final [lead] standard. [It] provides temporary medical removals for workers *discovered through medical surveillance* to be at risk of sustaining material impairment to health from continued exposure. [It] also provides temporary economic protection for those removed.[15]

MRP benefits include the maintenance of "the earnings, seniority, and other employment rights and benefits of a worker as though the worker had not been removed or otherwise limited."[16] Under MRP, earnings include overtime, shift differentials, incentives, and other compensation regularly earned while working, in addition to base wage.[17]

The maintenance of economic benefits is sometimes referred to as *rate retention*. MRP should be viewed as an entire package that includes temporary removal with accompanying continuation of economic and employment benefits. Rate retention, therefore, is a standard condition in MRP.

The OSHA rule governing access to employee exposure and medical records treats information gathered as part of examinations during the employment cycle as part of the employee's medical record.[18] OSHA defines "employee medical record" as

> a record concerning the health status of an employee which is made or maintained by a physician, nurse, or other health care personnel or technician, including:
>
> (A) Medical and employment questionnaires or histories (including job description and occupational exposures),
> (B) The results of medical examinations (preemployment, preassignment, periodic, or episodic) and laboratory tests (including chest and other X-ray examinations taken for the purpose of establishing a base-line or detecting occupational illness, and all biological monitoring . . .),
> (C) Medical opinions, diagnoses, progress notes, and recommendations,
> (D) First aid records, descriptions of treatments and prescriptions, and
> (E) Employee medical complaints.

The components of the record include data obtained from any and all of the employment cycle testing schemes, as discussed below.[19]

PREEMPLOYMENT EXAMINATION

A preemployment examination is generally a routine procedure (like the familiar checkup examination given by a family doctor), frequently required as a condition of employment, and given before an initial assignment in the workplace. The purposes of conducting a preemployment examination include

1. Establishing a baseline of medical testing results that can be used for comparison against future results,

2. Determining if the individual can physically perform the intended work, and
3. Determining whether there is any health condition that might require special precautionary care or job placement consideration.[20]

A preemployment examination commonly includes a medical history (including any preexisting disease), selected medical information about the worker's parents, a smoking history, a physical examination, and routine medical surveillance tests like blood analysis, urinalysis, and chest X-ray. If appropriate, baseline biological monitoring tests and pulmonary function tests may be conducted.

An occupational history is also a component of a thorough preemployment exam. *The importance of a complete occupational history cannot be stressed enough*; it is considered the cornerstone of an occupational health examination.[21] Unfortunately, the occupational history often is overlooked, or it consists of only the title of the employee's last job. Such incompleteness is not adequate to determine the work-relatedness of disease for either epidemiologic or legal purposes. An occupational health history should include a job profile that contains

1. Workplace name, location, and products manufactured;
2. Job title and description of operation:
    a. chemical (generic) or physical form of agents handled,
    b. operating and cleanup practices,
    c. protective equipment and clothing,
    d. ventilation and other engineering controls,
    e. eating or smoking at job site;
3. Exposure monitoring information;
4. Inclusion of part-time jobs and military service;[22]
5. The timing of symptoms;
6. The occurrence of symptoms or illness among other workers; and
7. Any nonwork exposures and other factors (e.g., alcohol, smoking, location of residence).[23]

Although routine medical surveillance tests can raise suspicion or help confirm that a disease or injury is work related, "ultimately it is information obtained from an occupational history that determines the likelihood that a given medical problem is work-related."[24] A physician is not able to diagnose occupational disease without evidence of exposure, so an occupational history that includes information about current and past jobs is essential.[25]

PREPLACEMENT EXAMINATION

A preplacement examination is conducted when an already employed worker is assigned to a particular job where certain exposures may be new or different from those associated with a current job. In some instances, a preplacement examination can be the same as a pre-employment examination, depending on job assignment. According to the second NIOSH National Occupational Health Survey, 58.8% of workers are required to take preplacement examinations.[26]

A preplacement examination has essentially the same purposes as those outlined above for a preemployment examination.[27] The examination is not, however, to be used as a substitute for the primary prevention or elimination of workplace hazards.[28] According to the Occupational Medical Practice Committee of the American Occupational Medical Association, a preplacement examination is considered to be an essential part of an occupational health program. It should include an assessment of health status and emotional status to ensure that the person can perform a job safely and efficiently without endangering the person's safety or health and that of others.[29]

Other essential components of a complete preplacement exam include

1. An analysis of the job description, which includes the requirements and activities of the work, potential hazards or exposures, and the type of protective equipment to be used. The job description is used to identify the key elements to be included in the physical examination and which laboratory tests to select (i.e., tests should be conducted on those organs or systems that are affected by the certain toxins to which the worker is exposed);

2. An occupational health history, including a job profile (see above), as well as information on home and community exposures that may be contributing to the worker's condition (e.g., proximity of home to a factory, hobbies with potentially hazardous exposures, and use of pesticides in garden);

3. A past medical history and review of systems, in order for the preplacement examination to serve as a complete baseline examination;

4. Life-style activities that may affect the worker's health status or test results, such as cigarette smoking and alcohol consumption;

5. A physical examination; and

6. An optional personal health maintenance program.[30]

The scope of the examination may be influenced not only by the physician's discretion but also by federal or state standards requiring the inclusion of certain physical, laboratory, or epidemiological tests for certain types of exposures.[31]

The recommendations made to management by a physician before job placement of a worker should be based on (1) a medical history, (2) an occupational history (including a complete account of past work performed), (3) an assessment of organ systems likely to be affected by the assignment, and (4) an evaluation of the description and demands of the job under consideration.[32]

The testing components of a preplacement examination must be valid and reliable (see the Introduction to Part II), and any abnormal findings must have a relationship to an adverse health effect. In instances when these two criteria are not met, the tests may be used improperly as a discriminatory tool. Discrimination in this context can be on an individual or group basis. An example of individual discrimination includes low back pain, which is a common complaint among workers from many occupations but is most frequently associated with workers involved with lifting and materials handling. It has not been unusual for a low back X-ray to be included as part of a preplacement examination for workers applying for physically demanding jobs. It was believed that abnormalities detected on X-ray served as predictors of future back injuries. The current view, however, is that defects discovered on X-ray "are not etiologically related to the soft-tissue injuries of the back presented by workers."[33] Because developmental defects have no demonstrated predictability for future back injuries, the procedure served only to expose the job applicant to unnecessary doses of ionizing radiation. In addition, if employers incorrectly believed that any abnormal findings were linked to future back injuries, those workers having defects on their X-rays might not be hired for the job or might be discriminated against for hiring or transfer purposes in order to protect the employer from liability in case of injury.

Sensitivity screening as part of a preplacement examination serves as an illustration of the possibility of discrimination on a group basis. For example, in 1980 it was reported that the DuPont Company, the 13th largest employer in the United States at that time, routinely screened blacks for sickle cell trait.[34] The company believed that sickle cell trait in combination with certain chemical exposures caused workers' blood oxygen levels to decrease.[35] DuPont's corporate medical director disclaimed the practice.[36]

At DuPont's plant in Deepwater, New Jersey, Italian workers were the largest single ethnic group employed.[37] Italians are a group ethnically linked to genetic traits for both beta thalassemia and glucose-6-phosphate dehydrogenase and these genetic traits are believed to surpass the sickle cell trait as health risks. In spite of this fact, the Mediterraneans received no genetic testing. Even though only 0.2 of 1% of American blacks develop sickle cell anemia, the blacks were the only ones tested for genetic traits.[38] This testing approach is inconsistent with the findings of the Office of Technology Assessment, which determined that the state of the art for sensitivity screening is not developed enough at this time to justify such screening in the workplace.

In the future, however, such screening methods may become more scientifically valid and reliable. Even if the technology for sensitivity screening is improved to the point of workplace implementation, the very real and disturbing possibility of more group discrimination seems likely (see Chap. 6).

PERIODIC EXAMINATIONS

Periodic examinations are conducted most commonly on an annual or semiannual basis for workers who are exposed to known health hazards via skin absorption, inhalation, or ingestion.[39] It is estimated that in the years 1981–1983, 40.2% of workers were given periodic medical examinations.[40]

The goals of a periodic medical examination are to

1. Detect evidence of absorption of industrial toxins;
2. Detect the early signs or symptoms of disease;
3. Provide data indicating the need for evaluation of the plant's control measures;
4. Detect any changes in the health of the employee since the time of the preemployment examination or of the last periodic examination that might indicate the need for a change in the work process or in job placement;
5. Detect any patterns of disease in the work force that might indicate any underlying work-related problems; and
6. Provide the option to conduct tests of personal health maintenance.[41]

Periodic examinations may also function to evaluate the effectiveness of preventive measures (e.g., engineering controls) and to establish or revise threshold limit values.[42]

The basic components of a periodic examination include interval occupational and medical histories, biological monitoring if indicated, a review of monitoring results, and a targeted physical examination.[43] These examinations should give special attention to target organs or bodily organ systems that are most likely to be affected by the substances to which the workers are exposed.[44] The testing intervals should be designated on a substance-by-substance basis so as to detect any adverse health effects early enough to permit remedial action and preclude lasting consequences.[45]

Understanding the natural history of an occupationally related disease is absolutely essential in order to best determine the appropriate tests and testing intervals for workers exposed to specific substances. Both should be selected with reference to specific risks associated with certain exposures or occupations. For example, consider a nonsmoking worker who is exposed to chronic low levels of sulfur dioxide (SO_2). Studies show that SO_2 is very irritating to the mucous membranes of the upper respiratory tract, where 90% of the SO_2 is absorbed.[46] There is only slight SO_2 penetration in the lower respiratory tract (i.e., lungs).[47] To date, OSHA has not promulgated a sulfur dioxide rule.[48] Pulmonary response to low-level SO_2 includes bronchoconstriction accompanied by increased pulmonary resistance. Therefore, workers exposed to low-level sulfur dioxide should have a preemployment/preplacement chest X-ray and pulmonary function tests in order to obtain baseline data measurements. Subsequent periodic examinations should continue to include pulmonary function tests, comparing those results with the baseline measurements. Annual chest X-rays, however, for the purpose of detecting occupationally related pulmonary disease related to low-level SO_2 exposure, are not appropriate, because pulmonary function tests better determine the pulmonary pathology induced from sulfur dioxide.[49] Consideration should also be given to smoking habits and exposures to other pulmonary irritants in both preplacement and periodic exams.[50]

In 1979, the Canadian Task Force on the Periodic Health Examination conducted a study on the usefulness of annual health examinations. The task force found insufficient justification to continue conducting annual examinations and recommended that periodic examinations be substituted in their place. Some of the conditions for which there was sufficient scientific evidence to warrant periodic examination include

1. Smoking—workers in asbestos, silica, uranium, coal, and grain industries;
2. Cancer of the bladder—smokers and workers exposed to bladder carcinogens;

3. Cancer of the skin—outdoor workers and others in contact with polycyclic aromatic hydrocarbons; and

4. Tuberculosis—those exposed to the disease through work.[51]

Abnormalities detected in the periodic examination could indicate that the work site and job site need to be evaluated and that industrial hygiene measurements are indicated along with a review of health and safety procedures.[52]

The health status of a worker should be determined after an absence from work because of injury or illness. The logging industry serves as an example of testing after injury. NIOSH recommends that those workers employed in logging (from felling to first haul), who are absent for 5 or more days because of injury, receive a medical examination upon return to determine fitness.[53] The OSHA lead standard serves as an example of testing after illness. The standard contains provisions for blood lead level testing before the return (to former job status) of workers who were removed because of high blood lead levels or other medical determinations.[54] Depending on the blood lead level that caused the employee to be removed, the employee can be returned to former job status after two consecutive blood samples indicate that the employee's blood lead is at or below a specified level. An employee removed on the basis of a medical determination can also be returned when it is medically determined that "the employee no longer has a detected medical condition which places the employee at increased risk of material impairment to health from exposure to lead."[55] Such determinations will ensure that the worker has sufficiently recovered from the illness or injury to perform the job without undue risk to the individual or others, and that the worker is not taking any medication that increases the risk of illness or injury in the workplace.[56]

EPISODIC EXAMINATIONS

For the purposes of this discussion, episodic examinations are those appropriate human monitoring tests that are administered after an emergency exposure, such as an accidental spill. Five OSHA standards, vinyl chloride, 1,2-dibromo-3-chloropropane, ethylene oxide, benzene, and formaldehyde, serve as examples for such testing following an emergency during employment.[57]

TERMINATION OR RETIREMENT EXAMINATION

An employee's health status should be evaluated upon termination of employment or retirement. The employee should be informed concerning his or her health status and advised of any adverse health effects from his or her job.[58] Termination examinations, also referred to as exit examinations, are required by several OSHA health standards. Workers who are covered by the arsenic, coke oven, or acrylonitrile standards and have not received medical exams within 6 months of terminating employment must have such examinations available to them before termination.[59] Employees covered by the asbestos standard are to have exit examinations within 30 calendar days before or after terminating employment.[60] Employees covered by the ethylene oxide standard are to have a medical examination at termination of employment or reassignment to an area that has exposures below the action level for at least 30 days a year.[61] Some NIOSH Criteria Documents provide recommendations, not requirements, for termination or retirement examinations. For example, NIOSH recommends that workers engaged in the manufacture and formulation of pesticides have a comprehensive medical examination within 1 month after the end of employment.[62] A termination examination is recommended for workers exposed to toxicants in coal gasification plants if no comprehensive medical examination was conducted within the preceding calendar year.[63]

It can be argued on health grounds that workers exposed to toxic substances should be monitored after retirement as well, but no legal mechanism currently exists to provide this on a routine basis.[64]

The accuracy, reliability, and predictive value of tests used in human monitoring vary greatly and may be especially sensitive to the timing of the examinations. Because monitoring schedules must reflect the need to track a variety of toxic exposures and health consequences and demonstrate a concern for business or production constraints, an effective, comprehensive industrial program for a workplace with multiple hazards and complex exposure patterns may be a challenge to design, implement, and maintain.

PART III

The Health Implications of Removing Workers on the Basis of Human Monitoring Tests

8. Human Variability and High-Risk Groups

The rationale behind human monitoring is to identify those individuals or working populations that exhibit the early signs of occupational disease or the propensity to develop disease.[1] Individuals differ in their responses to increasing doses of a toxic substance. Those who require relatively lower doses to induce a particular response in a test are said to be more *sensitive* than others who would require relatively higher doses before experiencing the same response.[2] If one plots the cumulative numbers of individuals who exhibit the particular response at a variety of doses, the result is a *population* dose–response curve.[3] If the particular response used to define sensitivity in this way is either identical to or perfectly correlated with the true long-term disease/adverse effect of concern for a specific occupational exposure, then the more sensitive workers identified by the test are also considered to be more susceptible for development of the disease/adverse effect from that exposure.

Employer actions to change the work environment, provide alternative employment, or suggest medical treatment ideally follow from the correct interpretation of monitoring results. The introduction to Part II addressed the adequacy of a wide variety of tests and their interpretation. This chapter discusses the application of monitoring results to the discovery of high-risk workers, the methodological limitations of the discovery process, and the underlying causes of human variability.[4] One general limitation is that a monitoring activity is only a single snapshot that gives a measure of the specific chosen parameter at one time. Unless a sufficient number of successive snapshots are taken, which relates to the timing of the tests (see Chap. 7), an incorrect interpretation and inappropriate remedial action may result.

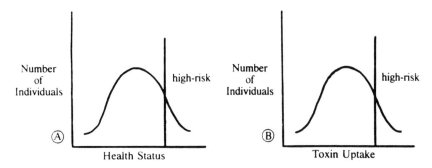

Figure 6. *The two kinds of experimental data yielded by monitoring: distribution of indicators of health status and distribution of toxin uptake.*

THE DISTRIBUTION OF MONITORING RESULTS AND THE DISTINCTION BETWEEN HIGH-RISK AND HYPERSENSITIVE POPULATIONS

Monitoring activities yield one of two kinds of experimental data: a distribution of indicators of health status or a distribution of uptake indicators (see Figure 6). Medical surveillance generally provides the first type of data and biological monitoring the second. Examples are lung function results and lead uptake as reflected by blood lead levels, respectively. In the graph of each distribution in Figure 6, the vertical line represents a somewhat arbitrary fence separating the "high-risk" individuals from the remaining "normal" population. Remedial action concentrating on only the high-risk group is often misguided. Potentially more informative are the *changes* observed over time on an individual basis, because both "normal" and "high-risk" populations may shift over time as a result of continuing exposure (see Figure 7).

Often, remedial action taken for individuals not yet in the high-risk category may reverse or arrest a disease process that later may be difficult to affect significantly, if at all. Therefore, action directed exclusively toward the high-risk workers as defined by one specific cutoff may result in less effective prevention than if measures were taken to reduce exposures of workers at an earlier stage in the disease or toxin accumulation process.

The causes of the differences among workers in health status or toxin uptake that are represented in Figure 6 may include variation

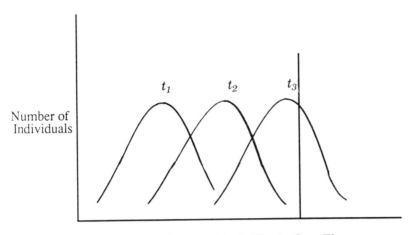

Health Status or Toxin Uptake Over Time

Figure 7. *Population shifts over time as a result of exposure. t_1, t_2, and t_3 indicate progressively later times.*

in current and past exposures, other illnesses/disease processes, and "biological makeup." A hypothetical distribution of "thresholds," the minimal doses necessary to cause different individuals to exceed the cutoff defining "normal" health status or "acceptable" toxin uptake, is shown in Figure 8A. This graph represents the sensitivity distribution mentioned at the beginning of this chapter. Another similar type of distribution can be constructed in terms of the amounts of time required for different individuals to exceed defined cutoffs of health status or toxin uptake, given a particular dose rate (Figure 8B).

Those individuals who cross the "normal" fence for a health status indicator or toxin uptake indicator at lower dose rates or shorter times of exposure than do other individuals have been called sensitive or "hypersensitive" individuals.[5] They may or may not be high-risk workers with respect to the ultimate development of disease. This is because very often the specific health status indicator used for monitoring may be only a proxy for the underlying disease process. The truly high-risk workers may include those with a lower functional reserve capacity in areas not measured by the specific test (e.g., because of prior disease) or a variety of other characteristics, as well as some (but perhaps not all) who are measured to be more sensitive on the specific test.

The vagaries involved in the use of a proxy health status indicator are well illustrated by the case of byssinosis. In many but not all

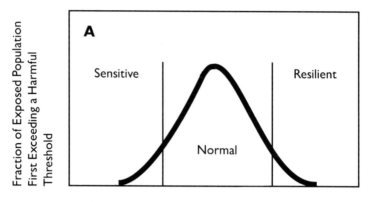

Dose (Exposure) Required to Exceed a Threshold

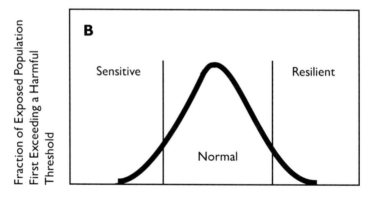

Time Required to Exceed a Threshold at a Given Dose Rate

Figure 8. *A hypothetical distribution of sensitivities as a function of dose (graph A) or time (graph B) needed to cause different individuals to exceed the cutoff separating "normal" health status or toxin uptake from a defined effect.*

workers, some component of cotton dust causes the release of histamine from specialized cells in the lung, and the histamine produces a contraction of small airways in the lung. This can often be directly perceived by the workers as chest tightness or difficulty in breathing, particularly on Monday mornings following a weekend of no exposure, during which time the lungs' stores of histamine have had a chance to build up to their normal levels. The *short-term* response can also be measured as the difference between the amount of air that workers can expel in 1 second (FEV_1) before and after a Monday workshift.

The *long-term* decline in FEV_1 is often used as an indicator of permanent changes in lung function that can advance to disabling levels. In a 10-year prospective study of changes in lung function, researchers found that those workers who gave short-term responses to cotton dust at the beginning of the decade of study suffered an annual permanent decline in FEV_1 of 111 ml per year.[6] Those workers who did not show short-term responsiveness to cotton dust at the beginning of the study, but did develop responsiveness by the time they were examined again at the end of the 10-year period, suffered an annual decline in FEV_1 of 70 ml—less than those who showed short-term sensitivity to begin with, but still appreciable. Both of these rates of decline are greater than the 20–35 ml per year seen in studies of people not exposed to cotton dust.[7]

As will be described more fully below, the underlying causes of variability in sensitivity and variability of high-risk status are complex. In addition, both short-term sensitivity and an individual's position on a monitoring-results distribution can change over time. Hence, the population distributions are dynamic. An individual can be in the sensitive area one month and in the resilient area the next. Furthermore, sensitive populations may or may not comprise a significant portion of the group that is truly at high risk of developing long-term disease. This is because short-term measurements of either proxy health status indicators or toxin uptake may not be strongly correlated in some cases with the relevant human disease processes.

APPROXIMATE AMOUNTS OF HUMAN VARIABILITY IN SENSITIVITY TO TOXIC AGENTS

The potential benefits of human monitoring to detect workers who are more sensitive than average depends not only on the accuracy of the tests used for that purpose but also on the amount of human interindividual variability that actually exists for the tests to detect. This section gives an overview of analyses of quantitative data by Hattis, Erdreich, and Ballew on interindividual variability in different kinds of physiological parameters that may directly affect individual sensitivity to specific chemicals under specific circumstances.[8] It should be stressed at the outset that the data sets reviewed here (with specific exceptions noted below) pertain only to groups of normal healthy people. They therefore implicitly exclude variability that may be present in general population samples as a result of different pathological processes and other factors.

For purposes of quantification, the relevant physiological parameters are divided into three broad groups:

1. *Exposure-determining parameters* that alter the dose taken into the body for a given concentration of chemical present in air, water, or food. These include, for example,
   —differences among people in breathing rates for a given amount of activity; and
   —behavioral differences such as dietary habits (people who eat a great deal of swordfish will tend to get a larger dose of swordfish mercury than people who do not).
2. *Pharmacokinetic parameters* that determine the relationship between the external dose and the concentration and length of time the chemical persists in the blood or at its site of action in the body. Such parameters include the times required for the elimination of half of a chemical from the blood (elimination half-lives), the maximal concentration attained in the blood after an acute dose, and the time-weighted integral of the concentration of the chemical in blood after one dose or a series of doses.
3. *Response parameters* that determine differences in toxic responses after controlling for differences in the first two kinds of parameters, that is, controlling for differences in concentration and time of chemicals in the blood for each unit of the same chemicals in the environment.

On this basis, Table 6 gives the ratios of parameter values that are expected to include 90% of a "normal" population. Figure 9 illustrates the meaning of the numerical terminology used in Table 6 for a hypothetical series of measurements of half-lives for elimination of an average chemical. For example, assume that 5% of the people were found to have elimination half-lives of less than 100 minutes, but that 95% of the people were found to have half lives of less than 230 minutes. These two values are the 5th and 95th percentiles of the distribution of half-lives, and the 2.3-fold range that separates them (230/100 = 2.3) includes 90% of the measured values. All of the calculations on which Table 6 is based assume that the parameters are distributed in a log-normal fashion in the human population (i.e.,

Table 6. Examples of Human Variability in Various Types of Parameters That May Be Related to Susceptibility (Expressed as the Width of the Ranges Expected to Include 90% of Normal Healthy People)[a]

Parameter	Width of the 90% range for an average chemical or test[b]	Width of the 90% range for chemicals with greater interindividual variability[c]
Related to uptake		
Breathing rates	1.8-fold	Not applicable
Skin absorption	2.5-fold	5.9-fold[d]
Systemic pharmacokinetic		
Half-life for elimination (by metabolism and/or excretion)	2.3-fold	5.8-fold
Maximum blood concentration (after a single dose)	2.3-fold	11-fold
Area under a concentration–time curve	3.0-fold	8.1-fold
Potentially related to carcinogenic risks		
Metabolic activation	17-fold	1600-fold
Metabolic detoxification	5.6-fold[e]	Not available
DNA adduct formation (includes metabolic activation)	29-fold[e]	Not available
DNA repair (of damaged induced by UV light only)	2.6-fold	Not available
Preliminary estimate of overall sensitivity (combining relevant parameters)		
Cancer risk from a skin-absorbed metabolically activated chemical	42-fold	Not available
Risk of anticholinesterase death:		
From agents metabolized by plasma cholinesterase	5.5-fold	Not applicable
From parathion (metabolized by paroxonase)	12-fold	Not applicable
Risk of anticholinesterase behavioral symptoms:		
From agents metabolized by plasma cholinesterase	19-fold	Not applicable
From parathion (metabolized by paroxonase)	42-fold	

[a]The numbers are the ratios of the value of each parameter for the 95th percentile individual to the value of the parameter for the 5th percentile individual (see text and Figure 9 for illustration).

(Continued on next page)

Table 6—Continued

[b]The data are from analyses of available information for various numbers of chemicals (see note 8 in Chap. 8): 12–44 in the case of systemic pharmacokinetic paramenters, 6–8 in the case of the parameters putatively related to sensitivity to carcinogenesis in a variety of tissues (generally in tissue culture systems).

[c]Chemicals differ in the degree of spread of the distributions of human interindividual variability exhibited for different parameters. The data in this column are for the 95th percentile of all chemicals studied (i.e., chemicals that, for each parameter, show greater interindividual variability than 19 out of 20 other chemicals).

[d]The calculation of interchemical differences in this case was based on meager data for only two chemicals.

[e]The calculations in these cases were based on patient or other "special" subpopulations that are not necessarily representative of the general population.

the logarithms of the parameter values would have a normal gaussian distribution). This is broadly consistent with most of the available data, and would be expected if the factors causing variability in the population were numerous and interacted multiplicatively with each other.

It can be seen in the middle column of Table 6 that the ranges of variability for some of the parameters involved in the carcinogenic process can be quite large, even for average chemicals. Chemicals differ, of course, in the variability of their processing and other factors affecting sensitivity distributions. It can be seen in the far right

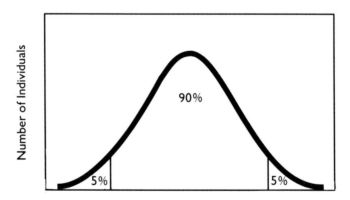

Half-Life for Elimination of the Toxin From the Body

Figure 9. *The width of the ranges expected to include 90% of the population.*

column that chemicals with more variability than 19 out of 20 other chemicals can produce very substantial spreads in sensitivity among groups of normal people. The summary calculations in Table 6 provide some very tentative estimates of the overall spread of sensitivities to carcinogenesis and anticholinesterase toxicity, considering all of the exposure, pharmacokinetic, and response-determining parameters for the estimates of variability, and assuming that each parameter exerts a simple multiplicative effect on overall sensitivity independent of the action of other parameters. Particularly for some of the processes related to carcinogenesis and toxicity to the insecticide paroxonase, the expected spread of individual sensitivities is appreciable. In considering these numbers, it should be remembered that 5% of the population is expected to be even more widely separated on both the high- and low-sensitivity sides of the distributions.

UNDERLYING CAUSES OF HUMAN VARIABILITY

Because of the biological variability described in the previous sections, different workers exposed equally to the same substance will exhibit differences in the results of both medical surveillance and biological monitoring. A number of factors cause the differences in testing results in a homogeneously exposed population, including factors that are determined by natural differences not within the employee's control, such as genetics, age, and sex, life-style factors somewhat in the control of the employee, environmental factors that may be partly under the control of someone other than the employer or the employee, and factors related to preexisting disease or accumulated functional impairment that may be in part attributable to the worker's past and current employers. The following discussion of variability follows these four groups of factors categorized to the extent possible by issues of employee control.

"Stochastic," Genetic, Age, and Sex Variability

Even if all subjects were in fact uniform in their responsiveness, some test and disease variability would occur simply by chance ("stochastic" variability). Imagine a group of soldiers advancing across a field in the face of machine gun fire. Some of the soldiers get hit and some don't, not because of any great inherent differences in susceptibility (although those who present a greater cross-section to the opposing fire are likely to be at somewhat greater risk) but because some just happen to be in the wrong place at the wrong time. Similarly, a group of workers exposed to radiation or some other genetically acting carcinogen may exhibit some inherent differences in susceptibility (see Table 6 in this chapter), but the fact that some get cancer and others do not may reflect stochastic variability.

Of course, true interindividual differences in susceptibility may contribute to different test results and disease risk among individuals. Even though the amount, route, and duration of exposure can be controlled, "there is still likely to be a great deal of variation in the response of individual members of a population to a specific toxic agent. . . . Some of this variation can be attributed to factors that influence the absorption, distribution, metabolism or excretion of the toxic agent."[9]

The concept of biochemical individuality may also account for variability in testing results. According to one researcher, "Overwhelming biochemical evidence has shown that each person has his/her own characteristic metabolic pattern, identifiable and recognizable by the activities of the enzymes involved. . . . Each . . . responds in an individualistic fashion to various toxic agents."[10]

Certain easily recognized genetic traits may cause a variation in response to toxic agents.[11] Genetic factors may also play a role in infectious resistance as well as adaptation to climate and high altitude in certain populations.[12] The mechanism accounting for the biological variation may be the inherited structure of protein receptors, which causes abnormal reactivity to toxic agents or drugs.[13]

It is often difficult to distinguish genetic from environmental contributions to variability. According to one researcher, "A major problem in man is that most populations are markedly heterogeneous with respect both to environmental and genetic factors" and "many environmental factors that alter rates of drug disposition do so by affecting genetic mechanisms."[14] Pharmacokinetic factors that control the results of clearance and metabolism of solvents are probably both genetically and environmentally determined.[15]

Approximately 150 genetic diseases have been identified in humans, and 26 of those have been identified as having a "theoretical basis for causing enhanced susceptibility to toxicants."[16] One researcher reported that only five genetically determined specific enzymes should be used to predict increased susceptibility to toxicants in industrial settings.[17] The Office of Technology Assessment reviewed genetic traits for screening, but the extent to which these traits are responsible for occupational disease is unknown.[18] It is believed, however, that enhanced susceptibility to stressor agents due to simple genetic differences at specific locations (loci) in the genome usually affects only minor subsegments of the population.[19] Other genetic differences are likely to take the form of numerous small quantitative influences on susceptibility, but these may generally be more difficult to recognize in an occupational medical setting.

Persons may be more susceptible to adverse effects from environmental agents at certain ages.[20] Studies using laboratory animals of different ages have shown that "differences in the rate of drug metabolism have been shown in senescent animals and thus metabolic and excretion patterns may be contributing to toxicity variation at both extremes of the life-span rather than simply in the newborn."[21] Although at least one researcher found that "age plays a small role in controlling the rate of elimination of certain drugs,"[22] others believe that the blood level and excretion rate following a given dose of a medicine change with age. Because the metabolism and excretion of industrial chemicals use the same enzymes and excretion mechanisms, similar changes could be expected for industrial chemicals.[23]

Other changes occur with age. Blood pressure increases,[24] and individuals above the age of 50 may have a greater tendency to retain pollutants such as fluoride.[25] After adolescence, the immune system progressively degenerates, possibly increasing sensitivity to carcinogens and respiratory irritants.[26]

The sex of a person is a factor that might affect chemical concentration in expired air analysis (see discussion of physiological factors affecting exhaled air levels of an exposure chemical in "Expired Air Analysis" in Chap. 5). Some differences result from variations in total blood volume and extracellular fluid, affecting the rate at which the chemical accumulates in the body and the maximal concentration it attains after an acute dose.[27] Another source of sex-related differences is that sex hormones sometimes influence the enzymatic biotransformation of an agent.[28]

Life-style and Behavioral Factors

Moving out of the area in which variables are controlled by nature and into an area in which the worker may be able to exert more control, we now consider exposures to life-style and other environmental factors. These are numerous and complex, making it "exceedingly difficult to attribute quantitatively different portions of the total interindividual variation to specific single environmental factors."[29] Environmental factors can cause variability in biological response, toxin uptake, or both.

Nutritional deficiencies may exacerbate the toxic effects of certain pollutants.[30] Dietary factors can influence toxicity by producing changes in body composition, physiological and biochemical functions, and nutritional status.[31] Diet, particularly an unbalanced one, could alter enzymatic activities, leading to changes in both metabolism and excretion of workplace chemicals.[32] Diets low in vitamin E can enhance toxicity to environmental agents, especially ozone, nitrous oxide, and lead.[33] A vitamin E deficiency coupled with a glucose-6-phosphate-dehydrogenase deficiency may markedly enhance the toxicity of ozone to red blood cells.[34] Vitamin C deficiencies may enhance the toxicity of agents like carbon monoxide, arsenic, lead, and mercury.[35] Persons deficient in riboflavin (30% of women and 10% of men aged 30–60 ingest less than two-thirds of the recommended daily allowance) may exhibit enhanced toxicity to lead, ozone, and hydrocarbon carcinogens.[36]

Alcohol is the most widely used and abused liver-damaging agent in the United States across all age ranges.[37] In addition, people who ingest large quantities of alcohol frequently have otherwise inadequate diets, particularly in B vitamins, which are necessary for the maintenance of normal liver functions.[38] Alcohol intake may also affect the absorption, metabolism, or excretion of some nutrients.[39] Alcohol, metabolized in the liver, may damage that organ and thereby reduce the ability of the liver to deactivate toxins. For employees who drink alcohol and work with various chemicals like lead or pesticides, toxicity may be enhanced.[40] Thus, alcohol may not only contribute to nutritional deficiencies but also potentially cause damage to the liver, decreasing the body's ability to detoxify workplace chemicals.

Adverse health conditions related to cigarette smoking, such as lung cancer, cardiovascular disease, chronic bronchitis, and emphysema are well known. Cigarette smoking coupled with certain occupational exposures places workers at an even greater risk of developing disease. For example, significant exposure to cigarette smoke is associated with a risk of death from lung cancer that is 11 times greater than that of nonsmoking members of the general population.[41] Smokers working in occupations with asbestos exposures, however, have a risk 55 times as great.[42]

Workers may develop airway obstruction as a result of occupation alone (e.g., coal miners, firefighters, and cotton textile workers). Those who smoke tend to develop an even greater degree of airway obstruction than nonsmokers.[43] In addition, cigarettes may facilitate oral entry of some substances, such as lead, simply by contamination. Some substances that enter the body by cigarette contamination are chemically transformed by the heat of the cigarette, and workers may become ill after inhaling the combination of the transformed substance and cigarette smoke.[44]

Environmental Factors

A multitude of nonoccupational agents may also contribute to variability in observed responses and testing results. Those more or less under the direct control of the worker have already been mentioned. Environmental chemicals may alter the receptor for the toxic agent in the biological test system, or the absorption, distribution, and excretion of the toxic agent.[45] Some of these environmental factors include outdoor and indoor air pollutants, drinking water contaminants, and consumer products like household cleaning agents and cosmetics.[46] Exposures to these agents may cause allergic sensitization,[47] possibly resulting in exacerbated responses to workplace chemicals among some workers.[48] Chemical sensitivity may also occur by nonallergic mechanisms not mediated by immunoglobulin E (see "Nongenetic Sensitivity Screening" in Chap. 6).

Aside from causing sensitization, environmental exposures may also burden the body with the same substance that the worker is being exposed to at work. For example, a particular blood lead level measurement will generally reflect lead exposure from work, ambient air exposure to lead in gasoline, and dietary lead exposure. The most recent documented decrease in blood lead levels among workers in lead-producing and lead-using industries appears to have resulted as much from decreases in ambient air lead concentrations caused by lowered lead content of gasoline as from decreases in occupational exposure.[49]

The influence of other less studied environmental factors on human responses to toxins is beginning to receive more attention. For example, some believe that emotional factors may "influence the susceptibility of man to toxic agents in his environment [and] epidemiologists increasingly include consideration of such effects as urbanization, noise, adaptive response to change, and other social and economic pressure in the etiology of disease states associated with air and water pollution."[50] Increasing experimental data indicate that environmental factors such as vibration, acceleration, and magnetism may influence biological responses in both experimental animals and humans.[51] Increasing exercise can cause a considerable increase in solvent uptake simply by increasing the respiratory rate and volume of contaminated air inhaled.[52]

Some environmental exposures may lead not only to allergic sensitization but also to increased risk of disease or exacerbation of existing disease. For example, living near a hazardous waste site could conceivably increase the risk of certain diseases for local residents.[53] In atmospheres where there is a significant concentration of cigarette smoke coupled with poor ventilation, enough carbon monoxide may build up to exacerbate symptoms of angina pectoris (cardiac-related chest pain) and chronic obstructive pulmonary disease.[54] Quite substantial peak levels of nitrous oxide have been observed in homes using gas stoves for cooking purposes.[55] This exposure could contribute to adverse health effects in sensitive persons.[56]

Preexisting Disease

Preexisting disease can result from nonoccupational origins as well as from past or current occupational exposures. Regardless of the origin, poor health, varying degrees of organ pathology, and various disease conditions are likely to influence the toxic response in the exposed individual.[57] Disease states may also significantly alter and conceal genetically controlled drug (and perhaps toxin) elimination.[58]

Persons with certain preexisting diseases of nonoccupational origin may increase the severity or frequency of their symptoms when exposed to certain workplace agents. For example, those with chronic respiratory disease or asthma may have their symptoms aggravated by respiratory irritants like ozone or sulfates.[59] Persons with coronary artery disease may find the condition exacerbated by stress or exposure to carbon monoxide, fluoride, or respiratory irritants.[60]

Medical surveillance measures not only the effects of current occupational exposure but also the deterioration of health status from occupational disease induced by prior employment. For example, a worker currently exposed to cotton dust may exhibit reduced lung function as a result of both current exposures and prior impairment caused by exposure to asbestos associated with work in construction or to coal dust from work in underground coal mines.

9. Consequences to the Worker of Medical Removal

The decision to remove a worker from a job is linked to the results of biological monitoring tests, medical surveillance tests, or a combination of the two. Because the very serious decision to remove a worker depends strongly on these results, one must assess again the appropriateness and validity of the test for the substance of concern (see the Introduction to Part II and Chap. 8). For example, in a situation in which testing may give false positive results, workers incorrectly diagnosed as sick may be inappropriately removed. Conversely, asymptomatic workers who have false negative results may remain on the job when, in fact, they should be removed.

MEDICAL REMOVAL DISTINGUISHED FROM MEDICAL REMOVAL PROTECTION

Medical removal (MR) must be distinguished from medical removal protection (MRP), because each provides measures that affect workers in very different ways. *Medical removal* involves removing the worker from exposure, possibly without regard for earnings, seniority, and other employment benefits. Medical removal benefits include the maintenance of "the earnings, seniority and other employment rights and benefits of a worker as though the worker had not been removed or otherwise limited."[1]

Medical removal protection is defined by the Occupational Safety and Health Administration (OSHA) as

> a protective, preventive health mechanism integrated with the medical surveillance provisions [which include biological monitoring] of the

final [lead] standard. [It] provides temporary medical removals for workers *discovered through medical surveillance* to be at risk of sustaining material impairment to health from continued exposure. . . . [It] also provides temporary economic protection for those removed.[2]

Under MRP, earnings include base wage, overtime, shift differentials, incentives, and other compensation regularly earned while working.[3]

The maintenance of economic benefits is sometimes also referred to as *rate retention*. MRP should be viewed as an entire package that includes temporary removal with accompanying continuation of economic and employment benefits. Rate retention, therefore, is a standard condition in MRP.

STANDARDS REQUIRING REMOVAL BASED ON MEDICAL SURVEILLANCE AND BIOLOGICAL MONITORING TRIGGERS

Medical Removal

The OSHA vinyl chloride standard, promulgated in 1974, provides for medical removal. In the medical surveillance requirements, the standard states, "If any employee's health would be materially impaired by continuous exposure, such employee shall be withdrawn from possible contact with vinyl chloride."[4] The rule does not provide the employee with either job or economic security after removal. Employees might choose, therefore, not to consent to medical examinations for fear of abnormal findings that would lead to job loss, temporary layoff, or transfer to a lower paying position.

Medical Removal Protection

The OSHA lead standard, promulgated in 1978, contains specific and stringent MRP provisions.[5] These MRP requirements are contained in a separate MRP section of the standard and are triggered by results of biological monitoring, not medical surveillance alone. Any employee whose blood lead level exceeds 40 μg per 100 g of whole blood must be notified both of the blood lead level and that temporary removal with MRP benefits is available when the blood lead level exceeds the measurements articulated under the MRP provisions.[6] An employee showing a blood lead level of 80 μg or more per 100 g of whole blood will be given a written warning notice and be advised that his or her blood lead level must be returned to a level below 80 μg within the next 90 days. The employee's blood lead level will be checked each 30 days, and he or she will be advised of the results. If at the end of the 90-day period the employee's blood level is not less than 80 μg, excepting extraordinary mitigating circumstances, he or she will be discharged.

The lead standard does not specify where a removed worker must be placed and states, "Practically any action is permissible provided the worker is not exposed to lead at or above the action level [30 μg of lead per cubic meter of air]."[7] Removal options include a reduction in the number of hours worked, transfer to a job with reduced or no lead exposure, or temporary layoff. No matter which option is selected, the standard requires that a removed worker receive MRP benefits: "The employer shall maintain the earnings, seniority, and other employment rights and benefits of an employee as though the employee had not been removed from normal exposure to lead or otherwise limited."[8] The employer must provide these MRP benefits for up to 18 months *each time* the employee is removed from lead exposure.[9]

The maintenance of economic and employment benefits during removal is an attractive feature for workers. The employee does not risk continued exposure, and the guarantee of benefits encourages workers to participate in medical examinations and biological monitoring. This incentive is one reason OSHA included MRP in the lead standard.[10]

Aside from lead, benzene is the only other OSHA health standard that specifically provides for a MRP plan. Removal based on benzene exposure can occur in two circumstances. The first circumstance is based on the objective results of blood tests. If abnormal blood counts are observed, the plant physician can trigger the removal when he or she believes that referral to a hematologist or internist is necessary while waiting for the report from the same.[11] The second circumstance for removal is based on the findings of the hematologist or internist.[12]

Workers who are removed are to be provided a follow-up examination, and the physician along with the hematologist or internist is to decide within 6 months of removal whether the employee can return to his or her job or should be removed permanently.[13]

Under any of these scenarios, it is important to note that the trigger for removal in the benzene standard is medical surveillance testing results, not biological monitoring results reflecting the amount of uptake, as in the lead standard. For example, an abnormal blood count that could trigger additional testing and possible subsequent removal of a benzene-exposed worker includes a hemoglobin or thrombocyte count that falls outside a 95% confidence interval. This testing result does not indicate the amount of benzene *uptake,* but rather that benzene *exposure* has occurred and has resulted in abnormal hematological findings that are not specific for only benzene. If the trigger for removal was benzene uptake, then the test would reflect biological monitoring instead of medical surveillance.

Employees exposed to benzene above certain levels are to be removed to comparable jobs for which the employee is qualified or can be trained in a short period of time and where exposures are as low as possible but not higher than the action level.[14] If an employee is removed on the basis of one of the two circumstances mentioned above and no job is available, then the employer is to provide MRP benefits until a job is available or for 6 months, whichever comes first.[15] If permanent removal is based on the consultation of the physician with the hematologist or internist, the employee shall be given the opportunity to transfer to an available position, or one that later becomes available, for which he or she is qualified or can be trained for in a short period.[16] In such circumstances, the employer "shall assure [sic] that such employee suffers no reduction in current wage rate, seniority or other benefits as a result of the transfer."[17]

The employer must provide 6 months of MRP benefits immediately after each time an employee is removed from benzene exposure because of hematological findings, unless the employee has been transferred to a comparable job with exposures below the action level.[18] These benefits include maintenance of the current wage rate, seniority, and other benefits of an employee as though the employee had not been removed.[19] These MRP benefits are reduced to the extent that the employee receives contributions for lost earnings during the removal period from a compensation program or from employment with another employer by virtue of the employee's removal.[20]

An interesting distinction between the MRP provision of the lead and benzene standards and that of the asbestos standard (see "Traditional Chronic Toxicity" in this chapter) involves the availability of a transfer to a comparable job. Whereas the MRP benefits for workers exposed to asbestos are contingent on the availability of a comparable position, OSHA promulgated more stringent requirements in the final lead and benzene standards.[21] Regarding the lead standard, the agency stated, "The standard by implication rejects industry suggestions that the provision of MRP benefits should be contingent upon the employer's ability to locate an available transfer position. Such an available position precondition would end MRP's role as a means of effectuating meaningful participation in medical surveillance."[22]

The removal provisions of the lead standard take individual variability into account and thereby recognize individual risk. The standard (as of March 2, 1983) provides a blood lead trigger level for removal of 50 μg of lead per 100 g of blood, but not all workers will necessarily be safe at this blood lead level. The standard provides for removing a worker whose lead levels remain *below* the threshold if a physician determines that, for medical reasons, the worker should have reduced or no lead exposure.[23] In such instances, removal would be triggered not necessarily or exclusively by biological monitoring results but also by results of medical surveillance testing. Workers so removed are still entitled to full MRP benefits.[24]

The removal provisions in the benzene standard emphasize the desirability of transferring a worker to a job where the action level is not exceeded. If test results indicate that an employee must be permanently removed from an area where action levels are exceeded, the employer is to transfer the employee to an available job or one that becomes available for which the employee is qualified or can be trained for a short period.[25] This is the first OSHA standard to require retraining of an employee in the event of removal. The standard does not, however, quantify the term "short period" as it relates to such training.

Removal Based on the Discretion of the Physician When No Medical Removal Protection Plan Is Provided in the Standard

Several health standards do not contain specific MRP plans but do imply removal based on the physician's recommendation. The ethylene oxide, cotton dust, and amended asbestos standards recognize the possibility of removal of a worker for medical reasons as a means of placing "recommended limitations on the employee."[26] The cotton dust standard is even more specific by providing that the physician can recommend to the employer "limitations upon the employee's *exposure*."[27] In each of these standards, this provision appears in the Physician's Written Opinion subpart of the Medical Surveillance section. As an element of that subpart, "any recommended limitations on the employee" is required to include such recommendations for removal based on the findings of the employee's medical examination.

STANDARDS REQUIRING REMOVAL BASED ON RESPIRATOR USAGE

The OSHA asbestos standard, repromulgated in 1986, contains an MRP provision in the Personal Protective Equipment section, not the Medical Surveillance section, for employees who cannot wear respirators, provided that a different job is available. The provision states,

> No employee shall be assigned to tasks requiring the use of respirators if, based upon his most recent examination, an examining physician determines that the employee will be unable to function normally wearing a respirator, or that the safety or health of the employee or other employees will be impaired by his use of a respirator. Such an employee shall be assigned to another job or given the opportunity to transfer to a different position whose duties he or she is able to perform with the same employer, in the same geographical area and with the same seniority, status, and rate of pay the employee had just prior to such transfer, *if such a different position is available.*[28]

This provision for rate and benefit retention seems to be a hybrid between medical removal for vinyl chloride and the very detailed MRP plans for benzene and lead exposures. The removal is triggered at the discretion of the physician and the regulation does not clarify what happens to a worker who is unable to wear a respirator when no alternative position exists. In such a case, the worker may be limited to medical removal only, with no opportunity to retain wages or employment benefits.

The asbestos standard does not specify what types of medical surveillance results trigger removal, where the removed worker is to be reassigned, what the allowable exposure limits in the different job are, when the worker can return, or whether he or she can return at all.

The respirator section of the OSHA cotton dust standard, repromulgated in 1985, includes the same hybrid MRP provisions as well. That provision states,

> Whenever a physician determines that an employee . . . is unable to wear any form of respirator . . . the employee shall be given the opportunity to transfer to another position *which is available* or which later becomes available having a dust level at or below the PEL [permissible exposure limit]. The employer shall assure that an employee who is tranferred . . . due to an inability to wear a respirator suffers no reduction in current wage rate or other benefits as a result of the transfer.[29]

As with asbestos, these MRP provisions depend solely on the worker's inability to wear a respirator, as determined by an examining physician; provide no articulated connection with the medical surveillance provisions; and provide no criteria for removal.

It could be argued that the removal provisions for asbestos and cotton dust exposures do not encompass MRP because MRP involves not only the retention of employment rights and benefits but also a removal trigger based on medical surveillance or biological monitoring test results. The lead standard states that MRP is a mechanism "integrated with the medical surveillance provisions."[30] The benzene standard states that MRP is a preventive health mechanism that is particularly appropriate "when a worker's body may be biologically monitored for adverse health effects caused by exposures when the health effects are reversible."[31] Because the removal provisions for asbestos and cotton dust are linked to personal protective equipment and respirator provisions, respectively, and not medical surveillance or biological monitoring provisions, some may consider the removal provisions not to fall within the scope of MRP.

Conversely, while the removal may not be triggered by specific elements required in the medical surveillance provisions, the findings that an employee is unable to wear a respirator logically are made from some type of medical examination. The elements of a preplacement or initial examination for the asbestos and cotton dust standards provide the minimum of what the examination is to include and no maximum for testing is articulated.[32] Both standards require that pulmonary function testing be conducted, and the results from these tests, which are medical surveillance methods, may provide the basis for the physician's determination that an employee is unable to wear a respirator and should be removed from that particular work area.

NATIONAL INSTITUTE FOR OCCUPATIONAL SAFETY AND HEALTH/OCCUPATIONAL SAFETY AND HEALTH ADMINISTRATION GUIDELINES ON REMOVAL

The *NIOSH/OSHA Occupational Health Guidelines* provides substance-by-substance recommendations, not requirements, for the type and timing of medical surveillance and biological monitoring tests (see "National Institute for Occupational Safety and Health" in Chap. 2). In following the *Guidelines*, employers may, on their own initiative, choose to remove workers from exposure on the basis of test results. The *Guidelines* provides no recommendations for MRP (see discussion of the *Guidelines* under "Medical Surveillance" in Chap. 1). Two proposed generic standards on medical surveillance programs and on exposure monitoring following the proposed updating of section 6(a) standards are also silent on medical removal or MRP.[33]

POTENTIAL BENEFITS AND LIMITATIONS OF MEDICAL REMOVAL

It is important to recognize from the outset that removing certain workers[34] may only remove the "sensitive canaries."[35] Certain sensitive workers may simply exhibit symptoms or suspicious monitoring results earlier than the rest of the working population. "Like the proverbial canary in a coal mine, the most sensitive worker may herald dangers that will ultimately affect all workers."[36] Removing particular employees may therefore give a false sense of security to remaining and replacement workers. In addition, a false sense of security may develop from the unwarranted conclusion that because the risk to the removed individual is reduced, the risk to the work group as a whole is lessened.

Before considering a medical removal strategy, it is important to identify both the toxic substance of concern and the effects of exposure to given levels. The shape of the dose–response relationship for the agent and the effect in question will determine whether redistributing dosage among an exposed worker group will increase, decrease or leave unchanged the total harm done to the aggregate of all exposed workers.[37] Consider, for example, a simple linear no-threshhold dose–response relationship, as may be expected for a risk such as radiation-induced cancers. In this type of case, redistributing a specific exposure among a larger population of exposed workers—for example, twice as many workers—will cut in half the individual risk but double the total number of workers who bear the risk, leaving the number of workers expected to develop cancer from the exposure unchanged.

Official requirements for operators of nuclear power plants and other facilities now require workers to be removed if they exceed a specific amount of radiation within a 3-month period. For relatively "dirty" jobs involving relatively high dose rates, this has led to the practice of hiring temporary workers, allowing them to receive their quarter-year allotment of radiation exposure in a few hours, and then hiring new workers to continue the task as needed. This process tends to limit the risk that is permitted to be imposed on/accepted by any individual worker (which may be considered a desirable goal on equity grounds), but clearly this removal/rotation process can be expected to do nothing to reduce the aggregate exposure that is permitted for the working population as a whole. If workers are implicitly given the impression that the removal process will ensure that their radiation exposures are "safe" (implying a low-dose threshold for radiation-induced carcinogenesis, contrary to current thinking), then the medical removal system may be falsely reassuring to some workers.

Removal systems that have the effect of redistributing dose can in fact reduce aggregate risk to the working population if the dose–response relationship has a threshold, or at least has an increasing slope at low doses. This kind of dose–response relationship can be expected for many "traditional" acute and chronic toxic agents, as described below. On the other hand, if the dose–response relationship bends the other way (showing, e.g., saturation behavior), then spreading the dose among a larger population will tend to increase the harm done to the working population as a whole. This appears to be the case for chronic noise-induced hearing loss.[38]

Determining dose–response relationships (especially at low doses), however, is an area of much debate. Frequently, human data are unavailable, and scientific studies on the substances involve only animals.

One of the authors has developed a classification system for the fundamental mechanisms that produce adverse effects (see Table 7) that is helpful both for making preliminary inferences about the likely forms of dose–response relationships and for structuring the questions that should be asked in considering a medical removal/MRP system.[39]

The primary division in the system between processes within the "traditional toxicological" category located in the upper part of Table 7 and those in the lower part of Table 7 depends on the nature of the processes that the hazardous agent is contributing to at *preclinical stages* of the disease process or *subclinical doses* of the agent that do not produce overtly detectable signs or symptoms. If what is going on is basically reversible with a period of no exposure—for example, as in most enzyme inhibition, the deaths of cells can be easily replaced by the reproduction of other similar cells (e.g., skin cells), and temporary buildup of a toxicant in a body compartment—then the process belongs in the upper part of Table 7 and is appropriately treatable within the paradigm of traditional toxicology. On the other hand, if what is going on at low doses or preclinical stages of the disease process is essentially irreversible—for example, changes in information coded in DNA, the deaths of nonreplicating types of cells (e.g.,

Table 7. Types of Health Hazards Requiring Fundamentally Different Approaches for Assessing Risks and Designing Medical Removal Protection Systems

---

"Traditional" toxicity—Proceeds by overwhelming body's compensatory processes; below some threshold, in individuals who are not already beyond the limits of normal function without exposure, response is reversible.

- *Traditional acute toxicity*—Toxic action is completely reversible or proceeds to long-term damage within about 3 days of exposure (e.g., lung damage from inhalation of chlorine; probably many teratogenic effects).
- *Traditional chronic toxicity*—Toxic process typically proceeds to permanent damage over a time period from several days to several months, due to either reversible accumulation of a toxic agent (e.g., lead) or accumulation of a slowly reversible toxic response (e.g., cholinesterase inhibition).

"Nontraditional" toxicity—Effects resulting from insidious processes that are irreversible or poorly reversible, even at low doses or early stages of causation.

- *Molecular biological (stochastic process) effects*—Occur as a result of one or a small number of irreversible changes in information coded in DNA—mutagenesis, most carcinogenesis, and some teratogenesis.
- *Chronic cumulative effects*—Occur as a result of a chronic accumulation of many small-scale damage events (e.g., emphysema, coal miners' and other pneumoconioses, noise-induced hearing loss, atherosclerosis, probably hypertension, and depletion of resting oocytes by cigarette smoke).

---

neurons), or the destruction of physical structures that do not regrow (e.g., alevolar septa, the divisions between air sacs in the lung, or nephrons, the functional units of the kidney)—then the process belongs in the "nontraditional" categories represented in the lower part of Table 7. We will now consider the merits and limitations of medical removal programs for diseases within each of the four categories in turn.

Traditional Acute Toxicity

As indicated in Table 7, the traditional acute toxicity category includes any toxic action that either is completely reversible or proceeds to overtly detectable damage within hours to a few days. In this case, the primary potential role of an MRP program would have to come after a worker receives a high enough short-term exposure to do damage that is readily apparent. The acute toxic event itself must signal both the need for removal from exposure and the initiation of medical monitoring. Depending on the nature of the toxic response, the contaminant concentration, and the duration of exposure, the physiological damage may or may not be reversible. At short-term exposures of less than 90 mg per cubic meter of air of cyanide salts, for example, most workers will completely recover from the tissue-damaging anoxia caused by inhibition of enzymes involved in the production of available chemical energy used by cells.[40] Such recovery might be followed either by the excretion of cyanide metabolites or by some physiological index. In the case of acute lung damage from chlorine or methyl isocyanate, lung function parameters might be followed.

Traditional Chronic Toxicity

As defined, traditional chronic toxicity is any toxic process that, at preliminary stages, is reversible over several days to several months. Where there is a risk that some workers may have long-term exposure to concentrations of a contaminant that exceed the amount that their metabolic, excretory, and repair processes can eliminate without functional impairment, an MRP program may be used to bring about presymptomatic removal and subsequent monitoring of the workers' return toward their baseline (unexposed) status. Traditional chronic toxic processes can be subclassified into those characterized by a gradual buildup of the contaminant in the body (e.g., lead) and those characterized by gradual increments in a given toxicological response (e.g., cholinesterase inhibition, and processes that could ultimately lead to peripheral neuropathy in workers exposed to acrylamide).

For contaminants that are poorly excreted and tend to be reversibly stored in specific organs or other systemic locations, medical surveillance or biological monitoring, as appropriate, should be conducted on the entire exposed workforce at intervals short enough to ensure presymptomatic identification of workers undergoing the maximal rate of toxicant accumulation likely with foreseeable exposures. The length of the removal period should depend on the rate of toxicant excretion; often, as in the lead standard, a worker may be rotated to a low-exposure position during the removal period.[41] An important consideration for this type of MRP is the possibility that rotation will gradually increase the biological exposure levels for all members of the affected population to near the biological threshold triggering removal. Such an outcome may be averted by considering several characteristics of the affected worker population when designing the MRP program, including the worker turnover rates for each job category, the projected retirement rates for exposed workers, and the profile of prior exposure to the contaminant of concern for "new hires."

For a traditional toxic process characterized by chronic accumulation of a toxic *response* (rather than toxin buildup), the basic considerations for developing an MRP system would be similar, except that a biological response or some other physiological indicator would commonly be used to monitor recovery. In general, such a physiological indicator should be designed to detect toxic response before the development of overt symptoms. Neuropathy due to organophosphate poisoning, for example, may be prevented by monitoring plasma cholinesterase levels.

Molecular Biological Diseases

Molecular biological diseases consist of adverse effects that occur as a result of one or a small number of irreversible changes in information coded in DNA. It is now clear that changes in either the content or the sequence of information in DNA is the basis of carcinogenic transformation.[42]

Existing cancer detection techniques provide for diagnosis only after macroscopic tumor development. In general, this may be years after cancer initiation. For those cancers for which there is reason to believe that early detection and treatment will lead to a more favorable prognosis, regular medical *surveillance* of populations suspected to have elevated risks from occupational exposure is certainly indicated. However, for cancer initiators there is a real possibility that medical *removal* programs may be of limited or no benefit to removed workers while creating appreciable additional risks to replacement workers. It is possible, however, that there are some cases in which an overt toxic response contributes to the carcinogenic process by encouraging cell division in target tissues.[43] For such cases, the removal of workers who show evidence of subclinical toxic response may well have significant preventive value.

Designing appropriate surveillance and removal programs for protection against teratogenic and mutagenic hazards is a very delicate and controversial subject. Many women, in particular, are justifiably fearful that (1) newly won employment opportunities may be eroded, and (2) attempts to eliminate women with childbearing potential from employment in specific jobs will result in discriminatory employment practices. Instances of real abuse in company medical removal policy have been alleged in some cases in which women felt forced to choose between keeping their jobs and undergoing sterilization operations.[44] Adding to women's concern over unequal treatment has been the fact that mutagenic risks from exposure, which are expected to occur in reproductively active males, have not received the same level of attention with respect to medical removal as have teratogenic risks.[45]

With care and sensitivity to these issues, it is possible to design MRP programs that may reduce teratogenic and mutagenic risks without infringing on individual rights or other social values. A reasonable general approach includes (1) a full and frank disclosure to all exposed workers of the known and suspected mutagenic and teratogenic risks of the substances with which they work; and (2) removal, with economic protection at the worker's option and triggered by the intention of the worker to have children, sufficiently in advance of conception to allow the substance(s) of concern to be adequately eliminated from the body before the critical events that occur in either sex from exposure.[46]

Chronic Cumulative Functional Impairment

Chronic cumulative functional impairments are the result of a chronic accumulation of individual insignificant, but irreversible, changes at a micro level. The loss of terminal neural elements in the organs of corti in chronic noise-induced hearing impairment and the accumulation of fibrotic lesions in the lungs of victims of silicosis are examples of this type of process.

The application of medical removal protection to this class of conditions has precedent in the Coal Mine Health and Safety Act of 1969, which provides that workers suffering from coal miners' pneumoconiosis may elect to be transferred from high-exposure to low-exposure jobs while retaining the pay rate of their high-exposure job. The actual experience with this provision in the first several years after its enactment was, unfortunately, that even though large numbers of workers had appreciable respiratory impairment from past exposures, few elected to be transferred. This was apparently because although transferred workers retained the rate of pay and benefits of their old positions, their compensation was not thereafter upgraded in step with the old position when pay was increased under new industry–labor contracts.[47] Thus in times of appreciable inflation, the earnings protection tended to erode. Clearly, inflation escalators should be included in serious MRP programs where the removals must necessarily be long term.

The long-term removals required for this category of conditions make them generally more costly, both to the worker and to the society, than the removals for traditional chronic toxic effects. A long-term removal with earnings protection does serve the function, however, of providing the removed worker with sufficient time to secure acceptable employment elsewhere. With this protection, economic and physiological disruption to the worker and his or her family may be less severe than it would be otherwise.

A general limitation of medical removal programs is that rotating workers may tend to divert attention from the primary prevention measure of "cleaning up the workplace." Instead, attention is placed on the affected worker. Such action may reinforce a "blame the worker" attitude, as though the worker were responsible for his or her condition. By removing those workers who exhibit illness or toxin uptake (particularly with no MRP), an employer may have less economic motivation to install more stringent engineering controls. The incentives of employers to remain lax persist. If the conditions of the workplace remain unaltered, it is likely that a removed worker will again be affected when returned to the same environment and that remaining or replacement workers will also be affected. If workers are frequently removed, then environmental exposures should be decreased to ensure that preventive actions yield real results.

PART IV
Legal and Ethical Considerations

10. Limitations on the Authority to Require Human Monitoring

The employer who intends to implement a program of human monitoring should be conscious of two related sets of constraints. First, the imposition of human monitoring will be subject to limitations on the employer's authority to *compel* the employee to submit to the monitoring procedures. Second, the employer's authority to *use* the information obtained through monitoring will be limited. This chapter addresses the issues raised by the first set of constraints: the limits on compulsion, the kinds of monitoring procedures that may be used, and the conditions of administration. Chapter 11 discusses access to and limitations on the use of monitoring information.

PERSONAL PRIVACY

In the abstract sense, an employee may always refuse to be the subject of human monitoring. The Occupational Safety and Health Administration (OSHA), the National Institute for Occupational Safety and Health (NIOSH), and the employer have no legal authority to compel employees to cooperate.[1] Refusal to participate, however, may well mean the loss of a job. Thus, the relevant inquiry is the extent to which the employer may condition employment on such cooperation. For example, may an employer require a prospective employee to submit to genetic or biological screening as a precondition to employment? May he or she require a current employee to submit to periodic biological monitoring or medical surveillance? These questions raise important issues of confidentiality and discrimination. Apart from these issues, however, there remains a question as to whether the employer has general authority to require human monitoring of his or her employees.

Monitoring in Response to Agency Directive

At the outset, a distinction must be made between human monitoring that OSHA, NIOSH, or the Environmental Protection Agency (EPA) requires and monitoring that the employer implements on his or her own initiative. In the first case, in which a federal agency requires monitoring, the worker will have a valid objection only if (1) the requirement exceeds the agency's statutory authority, or (2) the requirement violates the Constitution. The scope of OSHA and NIOSH authority to require monitoring under the Occupational Safety and Health Act (OSHAct), and of EPA authority to require monitoring under the Toxic Substances Control Act, is discussed in Chapter 2. This chapter addresses the limitations imposed by the Constitution.

Congress was mindful of constitutional considerations in drafting the OSHAct. For example, it specifically acknowledged the need for a balancing of interests where an employee asserted a religious objection to a monitoring procedure.[2] Human monitoring can also impinge on the worker's constitutional right to privacy.[3] In the case of human monitoring, the privacy right may be articulated in two ways: the right to *physical integrity*, and the right to *withhold information* likely to prove detrimental to one's self-interest.

If an employee does not wish to comply with a monitoring procedure required by agency regulation, imposing that procedure as a condition of employment may invade that employee's constitutional right to physical integrity. It may, depending on the nature of the procedure, infringe upon the right to be free from unwelcome physical intrusions and/or on the right to make decisions regarding one's own body. Although these rights are obviously related, they are derived from separate constitutional doctrines. The former is grounded in the Fourth Amendment's proscription against unreasonable search and seizure,[4] whereas the latter is closely associated with the rights of personal privacy commonly identified with the Ninth and Tenth amendments.[5] Although protected by the Constitution, these privacy interests are not inviolate. The Supreme Court has followed a general policy of balancing the privacy interests of the individual with the public health interests of society. In some situations, the former will be deemed to outweigh the latter, but in others intrusion will be permitted in the name of public health.[6]

The public health significance of human monitoring, when properly used, is difficult to deny. Gathering information through human monitoring to develop standards for the protection of worker health, or for the enforcement or evaluation of existing standards, serves an important public health purpose. Furthermore, although the Constitution places limits on governmental paternalism,[7] the fact that this public health interest parallels the affected worker's own interest in a healthy workplace may make monitoring of this nature a less onerous invasion of privacy than it would otherwise be. To the extent that monitoring serves a legitimate public health purpose, a limited intrusion of physical privacy appears constitutionally permissible. The less the accuracy, reliability, or predictability of a particular intrusion, however, the weaker the case for violating physical privacy.[8]

The scope of permissible intrusion depends on the nature of the monitoring. The insertion of a urethral tube, for example, involves a greater invasion of personal privacy than does the taking of a blood sample. Some monitoring procedures also involve greater risk than others. A program of periodic lung X-rays, for instance, poses a greater risk than a program of periodic lung function tests. At some point, the degree of risk or intrusiveness may become sufficiently compelling to outweigh the public health interests. Indeed, some forms of human monitoring may simply be too risky or too intrusive to be constitutionally permissible. Furthermore, the worker may well have a right to insist on an alternate, less intrusive procedure that adequately fulfills public health purposes. To survive constitutional challenge, then, a regulation requiring human monitoring should not only be reasonably related to an important public health goal, but should also impose the least intrusive method necessary to achieve that goal.

The employee's privacy interest in refusing to participate in a program of agency-directed monitoring is heightened where the resulting information may be used as a basis for termination, transfer, or demotion. For example, the worker who suffers reduced lung capacity as a result of workplace particulate exposure may fear that a program of medical surveillance will reveal this condition to the employer and thus induce removal. In this sense, participation in a monitoring program can be tantamount to self-incrimination.[9] Presumably, the fact that a compulsory monitoring program may cause employees to lose their jobs in this manner will have an effect on the nature of the "balance" to be struck under the Fourth Amendment.[10] If the public health need for the monitoring in question is not clear and compelling, or if the program is drawn more broadly than necessary, the underlying regulation may not survive constitutional challenge.

The Supreme Court held in a 1989 decision that Federal Railroad

Administration regulations requiring compulsory drug and alcohol testing of railroad workers are permissible under the Fourth Amendment, even though such testing could result in job loss or criminal sanctions for individual employees.[11] However, it would require a substantial conceptual leap to extend the reasoning of this case to the more general issue of compulsory health and exposure monitoring. In upholding the railroad worker testing requirements, the Court acknowledged that Fourth Amendment considerations were at stake. In permitting this invasion of worker privacy, the Court was careful to point out that (1) the monitoring in question was designed to reveal the presence of substances associated with criminal activity (drinking and drug taking on the job), (2) the targeted activity had an undeniable relationship to public safety, and (3) the testing was required only after the occurence of events that raised public safety concerns (major train accidents and the violation of certain safety rules).[12] Industrywide programs of health and exposure monitoring do not fit easily into this framework. Simply put, a testing program that results in the discharge of employees in a safety-sensitive profession whose illegal on-the-job behavior has put innocent third parties at grave risk is one thing. A program that results in the discharge of employees merely because they have had the misfortunate of being exposed to toxic chemicals, and thus might themselves become sick, is quite another.

In developing human monitoring requirements, an agency should seriously consider the constitutional dimensions of the issue. To avoid a challenge on a "self-incrimination" basis, OSHA might consider including mandatory medical removal protection (MRP) programs as part of its monitoring requirements.[13] Properly used, an MRP program would safeguard the employment rights of employees whose health was damaged or threatened by workplace exposure and would help ensure employee cooperation.[14]

Monitoring in the Absence of Agency Directive

As discussed in Chapter 2, employers have general authority at common law to require their employees to comply with reasonable programs of human monitoring. Congress did not intend the OSHAct to "preempt the field" by authorizing the implementation of human monitoring requirements. One of the OSHAct's express purposes is to "stimulate employers . . . to institute new and to perfect existing programs for providing safe and healthful working conditions."[15] Congress intended that employers take the initiative on a number of fronts, including human monitoring, in developing health and safety programs. As long as it promotes "safe and healthful working conditions," employer-initiated human monitoring appears to be welcome. Similarly, nothing in the act precludes employers who are subject to OSHA monitoring requirements from implementing additional programs.

If an employer institutes a human monitoring program in the absence of agency directive, he or she is still subject to applicable restrictions under state common law, state statute, and federal labor law. Common law requires that human monitoring be implemented in a "reasonable" fashion (see Chap. 2). Determining reasonableness involves balancing the benefits gained by monitoring against the risk, discomfort, and intrusiveness of the monitoring procedure. In a given jurisdiction, the balance might be affected by a state statute defining a right of personal privacy. Further, employees may be able to impose limitations on human monitoring through the collective bargaining process authorized by federal labor law.[16]

INFORMED CONSENT

Assuming that a human monitoring program is permissible, there will be limitations on the manner in which an employer implements the program. In general, one who undertakes the performance of monitoring procedures will have a duty to perform those procedures properly and will face liability for damages caused by the negligent administration of a monitoring procedure.[17]

An interesting question arises, however, with regard to the applicability of the doctrine of informed consent. Strictly speaking, "informed consent" is a medical–legal concept, and grows out of a belief that persons have a right to make decisions governing their own bodies and health.[18] Thus, a medical professional is said to have a duty to inform the patient honestly and accurately of the potential risks and benefits of a proposed medical procedure so that the patient can make an informed choice about the advisability of consenting to that procedure. All human monitoring procedures are medical or quasi-medical in nature. Most commonly, they will be performed by medical professionals: physicians, physician assistants, nurses, or nurse practitioners. Thus, the concept of informed consent appears at first glance to be applicable. The differences between human monitoring and medical treatment, however, are not insignificant, and they raise serious questions about the applicability of the traditional doctrine of informed consent to the occupational setting.

An initial question is whether the relationship between the worker and the medical professional who administers the monitoring procedure can be characterized as a physician–patient relationship. Quite often, neither the employee (nor his or her union, if there is one) selects the occupational physician. Rather, the employer selects and often directly employs the physician. Accordingly, some courts have held that the performance of a physical examination, which would clearly establish a physician–patient relationship in a purely medical context, does not create that relationship if it is a preemployment examination requested by the prospective employer.[19] To the extent that the physician–patient relationship does not exist in the occupational setting, traditional notions of informed consent may not be applicable to human monitoring.[20]

Similarly, the doctrine of informed consent is closely tied to the concept of medical *treatment*. It assumes not only that the patient is being requested to submit to a procedure designed for his or her own benefit, but also that the patient is in a position to make a voluntary choice to participate . Workplace monitoring calls both these assumptions into question. In many cases, monitoring benefits the employer more than the employee. Monitoring may not be "treatment" in the conventional sense of the word. Furthermore, monitoring is usually compulsory in that it is a condition of continued employment. It may be meaningless to speak of "informed consent" if the worker/patient is not free to reject the procedure without jeopardizing his or her job. In this light, the applicability of informed consent appears particularly dubious in the case of agency-directed monitoring, where neither the employee nor the employer has the discretion to discontinue monitoring.[21]

Regardless of the applicability of informed consent in the traditional sense, a complete and accurate disclosure of risks seems an advisable adjunct to a program of human monitoring. Whether or not a physician–patient relationship exists, imposing a medical procedure on a person not fully informed of the risks of that procedure may still be a battery and may give rise to liability in tort. In addition, prudent social policy requires full disclosure of risks. If the employer is required to disclose all risks inherent in a program of human monitoring, employee and union scrutiny will act as an incentive to the employer to develop programs that use the safest and least intrusive techniques possible. Indeed, unions probably have a right to demand such information as a part of the collective bargaining process (see "The National Labor Relations Act" in Chap. 11). Recognition of a duty to disclose material risks seems as appropriate in the area of human monitoring as it is in the area of medical treatment.

A final question concerns the scope of the required disclosure. The employer should, of course, disclose all material physical risks. The most significant risk of all, however, may be dismissal from employment. Should employers or occupational physicians be required to warn employees that one of the risks of submitting to a program of human monitoring may be a loss of his or her job? The "Code of Ethical Conduct" adopted by the American Occupational Medical Association and the American Academy of Occupational Medicine states that physicians should

> treat as confidential whatever is learned about individuals served, releasing information only when required by law or by over-riding public health considerations, or to other physicians at the request of the individual according to traditional medical ethical practice; and should recognize that employers are entitled to counsel about the medical fitness of individuals in relation to work, but are not entitled to diagnoses or details of a specific nature.[22]

This leaves the employee's job security in jeopardy. For, even though the physician may not disclose to the employer the specific results of human monitoring, the employer is "entitled to counsel about the medical fitness of individuals in relation to work." A preferable alternative practice may be to involve the worker in such discussions between the physician and the employer.[23]

II. The Use of Monitoring Results

What may be done with monitoring information once it is created? Who has access to the data, and how may the data be used?

EMPLOYEES' RIGHT OF ACCESS

The Occupational Safety and Health Administration Access Rule

A private employer may not limit or deny an employee access to his or her own medical or exposure records.[1] The current Occupational Safety and Health Administration (OSHA) regulation,[2] promulgated in 1980 and revised in 1988,[3] grants employees a general right of access to medical and exposure records kept by their employer. Furthermore, it requires the employer to preserve and maintain these records for an extended period of time. As defined in the regulation, both "medical" and "exposure" records may include the results of biological monitoring. The former, however, are generally defined as those pertaining to "the health status of an employee," while the latter are defined as those pertaining to employee exposure to "a toxic substance or harmful physical agent."[4]

The employer's duty to make these records available is a broad one. The regulation provides that upon any employee request for access to a medical or exposure record, "the employer *shall* assure that access is provided in a reasonable time, place, and manner." If the employer "cannot reasonably provide access to the record within fifteen (15) working days," the employer is required to notify the employee of "the reason for the delay and the earliest date when the record can be made available."[5] Although this may appear at first glance to be rather open ended, OSHA has made it clear that it expects "the vast majority" of requests "to be satisfied within fifteen days."[6]

Because the regulation defines "access" as including the right to make copies of records, the employer appears to have an affirmative duty to maintain such procedures as are necessary to ensure that, in most circumstances, the employee will have a copy of the records in his or her possession within 15 days after the request.[7] The employer cannot escape this duty by contracting with others to maintain the records. Although the regulation does not specifically require a physician, health maintenance organization, or other health care provider to permit employee access to records, it does require the employer to "assure that the preservation and access requirements of this section are complied with *regardless of the manner in which records are made or maintained.*"[8] Thus, any employer contract with a third party must provide for the disclosure of those records.[9]

An employee's right of access to *medical* records is limited to records pertaining specifically to that employee.[10] The regulation allows physicians some discretion as well in limiting employee access. The physician is permitted to "recommend" to the employee requesting access that the employee (1) review and discuss the records with the physician, (2) accept a summary rather than the records themselves, or (3) allow the records to be released instead to another physician.[11] Further, where information in a record pertains to a "specific diagnosis of a terminal illness or a psychiatric condition," the physician is authorized to direct that such information be provided only to the employee's designated representative.[12] Although these provisions were apparently intended to respect the physician–patient relationship and do not limit the employee's ultimate right of access, they could be abused.[13] In situations in which the physician feels loyalty to the employer rather than the employee, the physician could use these provisions to discourage the employee from seeking access to his or her records.

Similar constraints do not apply to employee access to exposure records. In the first instance, the employee is assured access to records of his or her own exposure to toxic substances. To the extent that those records fail to detail the amount and nature of the substances to which the employee has been exposed, however, the employee is also granted access to the exposure records of other employees "with past or present job duties or working conditions related to or similar to those of the employee."[14] In addition, the employee enjoys access to all general exposure information pertaining to the employee's workplace or working conditions and to any workplace or working condition to which he or she is to be transferred.[15]

Employers are only required to preserve records of employee exposure to substances defined as "toxic." The regulation defines this term with appropriate breadth and includes as "toxic" all chemicals identified as potential human toxicants in the "Registry of Toxic Effects of Chemical Substances" compiled by the National Institute for Occupational Safety and Health (NIOSH).[16] During the Reagan administration, OSHA had proposed to narrow this definition significantly and to include only those chemicals that have already been shown to be toxic in humans or toxic at specified significant levels in animals.[17] As the agency noted at the time, the proposed redefinition would have resulted in "a greater than 90 percent decrease in the number of chemicals specified."[18]

Not only would the proposed definition have excluded certain human and animal mutagens and certain chemicals that display mutagenic potential in short-term, in vitro tests, but it also would have discouraged epidemiological research on chemicals not already known to be toxic. One major purpose of occupational epidemiology is to determine the toxic effects of substances not presently known to be toxic to humans, so that employers can take the steps necessary to reduce workplace exposure. The OSHAct was intended to facilitate that process. The value of epidemiological research in this area, however, depends in large part on the availability of reliable data regarding employee exposure to substances not already proved toxic. Appropriately, the revised OSHA access rule continues to apply to the compilation of data on a wide variety of substances.

One criticism of the OSHA regulation is that it does not require the employer to compile medical or exposure information but merely requires employee access to such information if it is compiled. The scope of the regulation, however, should not be underestimated. The term "record" is meant to be "all-encompassing," and the access requirement appears to extend to all information gathered on employee health or exposure, no matter how it is measured or recorded.[19] Thus, if an employer embarks upon any program of human monitoring, no matter how conducted, he or she must provide the subjects access to the results. Any record keeping required under the Toxic Substances Control Act (TSCA), for example, presumably is available to workers under the OSHA rule (see "Authority of the Environmental Protection Agency under the Toxic Substances Control Act" in Chap. 2). It is conceivable, however, that the access requirement may serve as a disincentive for an employer to monitor employee exposure or health voluntarily where it is not clearly in the employer's interest to do so.

The access rule does not prevent employers from denying employees the benefit of having health or exposure data for a number of substances simply by failing to record such data if not otherwise required to do so by law.

The trade-secret interest of employers places a limitation on employee access. Section 15 of the OSHAct requires OSHA to be sensitive to employer trade secrets in its collection and use of occupational safety and health information.[20] OSHA originally read this section as requiring the agency to *balance* employee safety and health against competing economic interests of the employer,[21] and proposed during the Reagan administration to significantly expand the protections given to trade secrets under the access rule.[22] This interpretation did not survive court review. Responding to a challenge to the definition of "trade secret" in OSHA's hazard communication standard,[23] the Third Circuit Court of Appeals held in a 1985 decision that neither section 15 nor any other part of the OSHAct permits OSHA to provide trade-secret protection beyond that which is afforded by state law. Further, the court noted that section 15 "deals only with what the agency and its employees may disclose, not with what disclosures the agency may compel in the interest of safety in the workplace."[24]

The trade-secret provisions in the revised OSHA access rule appear to have been drafted with the Third Circuit's admonition in mind.[25] Nonetheless, these provisions do provide for somewhat greater protection of trade secrets than had been afforded under the original rule. The revised regulation permits the employer to deny access to "trade secret data which discloses manufacturing processes . . . or . . . the percentage of a chemical substance in a mixture," provided that the employer

1. Notifies the party requesting access of the denial, and
2. If relevant, provides alternative information sufficient to permit identification of when and where exposure occurred.[26]

To this extent, the revised rule follows the language of its predecessor. The original rule, however, ensured employee access to the precise identities of chemicals and physical agents, whether or not the employer claimed this information as a trade secret.[27] This access is especially critical for chemical exposures. Within each "generic" class of chemicals there are a variety of specific chemical compounds, each of which may have its own particular effect on human health. The health effects can vary widely within a given family of chemicals.[28] Accordingly, the medical and scientific literature on chemical properties and toxicity is indexed by specific chemical name, not by generic chemical class.[29] To discern any meaningful correlation between a chemical exposure and a known or potential health effect, an employee must know the precise chemical identity of that exposure.[30] Furthermore, in the case of biological monitoring, the identity of the toxic substance or its metabolite is itself the information monitored.

The revised rule places barriers on the disclosure of such information. The rule permits the employer to delete from an exposure record "the specific chemical identity, including the chemical name and other specific identification of a toxic substance," so long as the employer

1. Notifies the requesting party of the deletion;
2. Can support the claim that the information is a trade secret;
3. Gives the requesting party "all other available information on the properties and effects" of the toxic substance in question; and
4. Provides the specific chemical identity of the substance to a treating physisian or nurse if such information is "necessary for emergency or first-aid treatment."[31]

Were the trade-secret protections to end here, they would defeat much of the public health purpose of granting employee access to exposure information and would make it difficult to establish necessary baseline information on the relationship of various substances to various health outcomes. Sensibly, however, the revised rule establishes additional procedures that should make specific chemical identity information available to interested employees in most circumstances.

If the employee is not satisfied with exposure records from which specific chemical identities have been deleted, the employee may file a written request with the employer for such information. This request must contain

1. A description, in "reasonable detail," of one or more "occupational health needs" for which the information is being sought;
2. An explanation, "in detail," as to why certain enumerated kinds of other information would not be adequate to meet the occupational health needs in question;
3. A description of "the procedures to be used to maintain the confidentiality of the disclosed information"; and
4. An indication of the employee's willingness to be bound by a written confidentiality agreement.[32]

The "occupational health needs" for which disclosure may be sought under this section are rather broadly defined and include "studies to determine the health effects of exposure."[33] Further, the rule includes provisions designed to discourage employers from using the mantle of trade secrecy as a ruse for denying legitimate requests.

The employer must respond to the request for chemical identity information within 30 days. If the request is denied, the employer must provide a written response that includes "evidence to support the claim that the chemical identity is a trade secret," states "the specific reason why the request is being denied," and explains "in detail" how the occupational health needs in question can be met without the requested information.[34] Upon such a denial, the requesting party may refer the matter to OSHA for resolution. If OSHA determines that the claim of trade secrecy is not bona fide, or that the information can be disclosed to the requesting party for a legitimate public health need without jeopardizing the employer's proprietary interest, "the employer will be subject to citation by OSHA."[35] Finally, if the employer demonstrates that a confidentiality agreement would not be sufficient to protect a bona fide trade secret, OSHA "may issue such orders or impose such additional information as may be appropriate to assure [sic] that the occupational health needs are met without an undue risk of harm to the employer."[36]

The revised rule gives employers somewhat greater freedom in fashioning the "confidentiality agreements" that may be required as a condition of the disclosure of specific chemical identities. The original rule also permitted such agreements, but the explanatory comments to the rule made it clear that they could not be used "as a pretext for more onerous requirements such as the posting of penalty bonds, liquidated or punitive damages clauses, or other preconditions."[37] The revised rule softens this approach, and specifically permits the "reasonable pre-estimate of likely damages" in the event of a breach of confidentiality.[38] However, the prohibition against the use of penalty bonds continues in effect.[39] This would appear to strike an appropriate balance between legitimate competing interests. By specifying that any liquidated damage provision must be "reasonable," this section should help ensure that such provisions are used as a legitimate means of guarding against disclosure, and not as a means of discouraging employees from following through on their request for information. Further, by specifically disallowing the penalty bond—which presumably would have to be purchased by the requesting party prior to the reciept of the information—the rule helps keep the costs of such requests to a minimum.

The Toxic Substances Control Act

In addition to requiring the creation of information that becomes subject to the OSHA access rule, TSCA gives workers certain rights to obtain monitoring information that has been submitted to the Environmental Protection Agency (EPA). Section 14(b) of TSCA gives EPA the authority to disclose from health and safety studies all data pertaining to chemical identities, except for the proportion of chemicals in a mixture.[40] In addition, EPA may disclose information, otherwise classified as a trade secret, "if the Administration determines it necessary to protect . . . against an unreasonable risk of injury to health."[41] Monitoring data thus seem subject to full disclosure.

The National Labor Relations Act

In addition to the access provided by OSHA regulations, individual employees may have a limited right of access to medical and exposure records under federal labor law. The National Labor Relations Act (NLRA) covers the majority of workers in the manufacturing sector. Arguably, the right to refuse hazardous work inherent in the NLRA carries with it the right of access to the information necessary to determine whether or not a particular condition is hazardous.[42] In the case of toxic substance exposure, this may mean a right of access to all information relevant to the health effects of the exposure and may include access to both medical and exposure records. This clearly is not an adequate substitute for the OSHA access rule, however, because there is presently no systematic mechanism for enforcing this right.

Collective employee access, however, is available to unionized employees through the collective bargaining process. The National Labor Relations Board (NLRB) has ruled that unions have a right of access to exposure and medical records so that they may bargain effectively with the employer regarding conditions of employment.[43] Citing the general proposition that employers are required to bargain on health and safety conditions when requested to do so,[44] the NLRB adopted a broad policy favoring union access. "Few matters can be of greater legitimate concern to individuals in the workplace, and thus to the bargaining agent representing them, than exposure to conditions potentially threatening their health, well-being, or their very lives."[45] The Board's decision was upheld on all issues by the District of Columbia Circuit Court of Appeals.[46]

Nonetheless, the NLRB did not grant an unlimited right of access.

As discussed later in this chapter, the union's right of access is constrained by the individual employee's right of personal privacy. Furthermore, the NLRB acknowledged an employer's interest in protecting trade secrets. While ordering the employer to disclose the chemical identities of substances to which the employer did not assert a trade-secret defense, the NLRB indicated that employers are entitled to take reasonable steps to safeguard "legitimate" trade-secret information.[47] The NLRB did not delineate a specific mechanism for achieving the balance between union access and trade secret disclosure. Instead, it ordered the parties to attempt to resolve the issue through collective bargaining. Given the complexity of this issue and the potential for abuse in the name of "trade-secret protection," the NLRB may find it necessary in some circumstances to provide further specificity before a workable industrywide mechanism can be achieved.[48]

EMPLOYEES' RIGHT TO CONFIDENTIALITY: ACCESS TO EMPLOYEE RECORDS BY AGENCIES, UNIONS, AND EMPLOYERS

Of all of the issues raised by human monitoring, employee confidentiality may have received the most attention.[49] An employee's right to maintain the confidentiality of information regarding his or her body and health places a significant limitation on the ways in which others can use that information. As programs of human monitoring are developed, mechanisms must be found that maximize both the employee's interest in privacy and society's interest in promoting general workplace health and safety. In the final analysis, this may be more a technological challenge than a legal or ethical one.

In a broad sense, private citizens do have a right to protect the confidentiality of their personal health information. With regard to *governmental* invasions of privacy, this right is created by the Bill of Rights and is one component of the constitutional right of personal privacy discussed above (see "Monitoring in Response to Agency Directive" in Chap. 10). With regard to *private* intrusions, the right is grounded in statute and common law.[50] In the medical setting, it grows out of the confidential nature of the physician–patient relationship, although rights of confidentiality exist outside this relationship as well. In essence, the recognition of a right of privacy reflects an ongoing societal belief in the need to protect the integrity of the individual.

Although the right to privacy is not absolute, courts nonetheless remain sensitive to society's concern for individual confidentiality.[51] They generally look for a reasonable middle ground when faced with legitimate interests on both sides of the confidentiality question. They prefer an approach that permits both the use of health information for a socially useful purpose and the protection of the privacy of the individual.[52] The key is the development of technology that will make that approach more readily available.

Developing such technology will be especially important in protecting the confidentiality of information generated by human monitoring. Both medical and exposure records contain health information of a confidential nature, and the employee has a legitimate interest in limiting its disclosure. At the same time, public agencies, unions, and employers have a legitimate interest in using this information. From a technical point of view, the solution will lie in mechanisms that allow third parties to use meaningfully health information that is not tied by name or other common identifier (such as a social security number) to any one individual, and that allow data relevant to toxic substances exposure to be separated from other health information. When disclosure is limited to relevant medical and exposure information[53] that cannot be traced to any worker by name, any detrimental effect of disclosure will be held to a minimum.

Proper development of the necessary technology, however, will not follow from piecemeal solutions devised by reviewing courts. Rather, what is needed is a concerted, comprehensive, multidisciplinary approach. OSHA, NIOSH, and the EPA could pursue such technology either as an agency research and development project or through cooperation with private industry. This technology, once developed, could then be made available to employers at the cost of installation and equipment. No system will resolve completely the conflict between confidentiality and disclosure, and the potential for abuse will always be present. However, methods of record keeping that permit the effective use of relevant health information without requiring the disclosure of other personal data would eliminate much of that conflict. Presently, the conflict remains substantial, especially regarding medical records prepared under methods that are ill adapted to protective disclosure.

Agency Access

In addition to the limitations it places on the government's authority to compel an employee to submit to monitoring procedures (see "Monitoring in Response to Agency Directive" in Chap. 10), the Constitution imposes limitations on federal agency *access* to monitoring information once it has been compiled.[54] The Supreme Court has outlined a number of important issues in this general area in *Whalen v. Roe,* a case involving a New York law that required physicians to provide the state with the names of persons receiving prescriptions for certain controlled drugs.[55] The Court upheld the statute against privacy claims raised by both patients and physicians because the law was narrowly drawn to apply only to a limited class of arguably dangerous drugs and New York had a legitimate public health interest in controlling the dissemination and use of those drugs.[56] In doing so, the Court indicated the broad framework within which questions of constitutional privacy rights must be decided. On the one hand, the right to confidentiality clearly can be limited when such limitation is necessary to meet a legitimate public health purpose:

> Disclosures of private medical information to doctors, to hospital personnel, to insurance companies, and to *public health agencies* are often an essential part of modern medical practice even where the disclosure may reflect unfavorably on the patient. Requiring such disclosures to representatives of the State having responsibility for the health of the community does not automatically amount to an impermissible invasion of privacy.[57]

On the other hand, the Court also indicated that the disclosure of confidential information should be no broader than necessary to meet the desired public health purpose: "The right to collect and use such data for public purposes is typically accompanied by a concomitant statutory or regulatory duty to avoid *unwarranted* disclosures."[58] As with the protection of physical privacy, the Constitution demands a careful balancing of the individual's right to confidentiality and the legitimate interests of society.

Both OSHA and NIOSH have sought to achieve this balance. They have, however, taken markedly different paths toward this end. OSHA access to medical records is secured by a regulation designed to protect employee confidentiality.[59] In general, records obtained under this regulation must be secured through a specific, written access order; must be used only for the purposes indicated on the order; and must be destroyed or returned after OSHA has completed such use.[60] A significant flaw in this regulation is the fact that it applies only to "personally identifiable employee *medical* information."[61] By its terms, it is inapplicable to "*exposure* records, including biological monitoring records."[62] Instead, OSHA access to exposure records is governed by the OSHA access rule discussed at the beginning of this chapter. A provision of this rule grants OSHA "prompt" entry to such records, without any mechanism for limiting the use to which the agency may put such information.[63] To the extent that these records contain constitutionally protected health data, this lack of privacy protection may violate the doctrine enunciated in *Whalen v. Roe.*

The National Institute for Occupational Safety and Health, on the other hand, has not promulgated access regulations. Instead, it has sought access on a case-by-case basis by using its subpoena power. Employers have resisted the subpoena on the basis of the employees' constitutional rights to privacy. As a result, decisions of various federal courts have developed limitations on NIOSH access.[64]

In general, the courts have applied the *Whalen v. Roe* doctrine and have conditioned access by NIOSH upon the development of procedures designed to limit the intrusion on individual worker privacy. The Court of Appeals for the Sixth Circuit, for example, noted that there should be "no public disclosure of the medical information" beyond the agency itself.[65] Significantly, the court also recognized that the conflict between confidentiality and public health grows more out of practical than philsophical considerations. It "[did] not believe that the parties' interests . . . were mutually exclusive. With proper security administration, [NIOSH] should be able to complete [its health studies] without jeopardizing the constitutional rights of the individuals involved."[66] This recognition of practical constraints underscores the need for a creative approach to medical and exposure information storage and transfer.

Union Access

Although a union is usually presumed to be acting on behalf of its members, at times the union's assertion of access to medical or exposure records will conflict with an employee's interest in keeping those results confidential. All employees have an interest in ensuring that the union's right of access is not unchecked, but rather is limited to legitimate purposes.

Where the union seeks medical and exposure information from an employer as a part of the collective bargaining process, employee privacy interests will be balanced against the union's interest in securing disclosure.[67] In two cases before the NLRB, the *employer* asserted the physician–patient privilege as a defense to a union's request for access to medical records.[68] In striking the balance between disclosure and privacy, the NLRB ordered the employer to provide access "to the extent that such data do not include medical records from which identifying data have not been removed."[69] But the

NLRB did indicate in both of these decisions that the union's interest in securing health and safety information could be satisfied without disclosure of personal identifiers. It thus did not foreclose the possibility that a broader right of access might be appropriate if the union establishes a legitimate need for such data. In upholding the NLRB's decision, however, the District of Columbia Circuit Court of Appeals noted, "Employers may have a legitimate and substantial interest in protecting the confidentiality of employees' medical records [and] the mere deletion of names may not sufficiently ensure employees' confidentiality."[70] The precise nature of the appropriate balance, then, is not altogether clear.

Nor is it clear whether more exacting employee protection might be required when the employee, rather than the employer, asserts the right to confidentiality. The additional protection, if any, available to dissenting union employees has not yet been delineated. As a matter of policy, it seems that the rationale for protecting personal privacy is as compelling in the case of union access as it is in the case of agency access and that the union's interest in collective bargaining should be accommodated in a manner that respects the confidentiality of the individual employee.

Unions also have a right of access to employee records under the OSHA access rule. Where a union has been recognized as the bargaining representative for a certain group of employees under federal labor law, it is authorized to secure access to their exposure records under the OSHA rule as their "designated representative."[71] In general, the union has the same right of access to exposure records as do the employees themselves. The union is not required to secure individual employee authorization before it is entitled to such access. Noting that "there are occupational health benefits to be gained by permitting [unrestricted] union access to records,"[72] OSHA in 1988 turned down a request by employers that the rule be revised to require individual authorization as a prerequisite to union access. In response to employer complaints that union access requests were often burdensome, however, the agency revised the rule to require designated representatives to "specify with reasonable particularity" the records requested and the "occupational health need" for disclosure.[73] The OSHA rule also grants designated representatives a right of access to employee medical records. In recognition of the more confidential nature of medical information, however, the rule requires "specific written consent" from each affected employee before such access may be secured.[74]

Employer Access

Perhaps the most obvious threat to employee confidentiality is that posed by employer access. Of all parties seeking access to employee health information, the employer has the most direct economic incentive to use that information in ways detrimental to the employee. On the other hand, human monitoring data are essential for those employers who strive in good faith to eliminate workplace hazards.

By accepting or seeking employment, the employee implicitly consents to certain limitations on his or her expectations of confidentiality. To the extent that individual employee information—even information of a personal nature—is relevant to a legitimate employer interest, the employer may condition employment on its disclosure.[75] In general, employers are entitled to information that bears upon the employee's ability to perform his or her job, and to information that indicates the levels of toxic substance exposure in the workplace. Although not all information gathered through health and exposure monitoring meets these criteria, much of it does. In the absence of protective statutes, employers will have a right of access to such data. Health and personal information that is not reasonably related to the work environment, however, arguably is protected either by the physician–patient relationship[76] or by tort concepts of personal privacy.[77] In theory, it should be unavailable to the employer.

In practice, however, this may not be the case. Testimony taken by OSHA in 1980, for example, indicates that many employers routinely gain access to an employee's complete medical file. According to OSHA, the following statement by a member of the United Auto Workers was representative of the testimony received:

> I have been in medical . . . trying to talk to the company doctor. A member of [management] would come down and just, you know, hi, doc, and then go through the records, the medical records, and pull a particular individual's medical record and without even consulting the doctor first or a nurse or anybody as far as that goes, just directly [go] to the cabinet and pull an individual's record. . . . They will just go directly down and pull the file themselves. So there is no confidentiality.[78]

There is little reason to believe that this does not remain the practice in many workplaces.

The Occupational Safety and Health Administration has acknowledged that this is a "serious problem" but has thus far declined to take any specific remedial action.[79] It did not discuss the issue when it revised the employee access rule in 1988. Some form of protective action may be necessary. Where the information in question was gathered pursuant to a monitoring program that was required or expressly permitted by OSHA regulation, the agency may well have a constitutional obligation to protect employee privacy. Indeed, even where the information is related to a legitimate employer interest, the doctrine of *Whalen v. Roe* may require the agency to protect the employee's confidentiality in such a situation.[80]

As a practical matter, much of the problem might be alleviated if human monitoring and the maintenance of medical and exposure records were undertaken by a third-party health care provider, such as a health maintenance organization.[81] Much of the abuse inherent in employer access to employee health information arises from simple proximity. The employer is often the keeper of the information to which claims of confidentiality attach. If this information were held by a third party, such as a health maintenance organization, that party would be in a better practical position to ensure that all those with legitimate rights of access—the employee, the agency, the union, and the employer—exercise those rights in full compliance with the law.

LIMITATIONS ON EMPLOYERS' USE OF MONITORING DATA

Even if an employer obtains human monitoring data through a legitimate exercise of his or her right of access, the right to use such data is not absolute. Employers may not use health information to discriminate against employees on a basis deemed impermissible by federal or state law. Beyond discrimination, a more essential, and perhaps more difficult, question arises: To what extent may employers use health and exposure information to limit or terminate the employment status of individual employees or to deny employment to a prospective employee?

Limitations under Common Law

At early common law, an employer had the right to take an employee's health into account in determining whether to continue to employ that person. If the employment contract was "open," with no definite term, the employee could be discharged for any reason, including health status, at the will of the employer.[82] If the contract of employment was for a definite term, the employee could be discharged for "just cause." Typically, significant illness or disability constituted "just cause."[83] Although federal labor law, workers' compensation, and recent common law limitations on the doctrine of "employment at will"[84] have profoundly affected the nature of employee–employer relations in this century, courts continue to recognize an employer's interest in discharging employees who cannot perform their work safely.[85] Thus, if the worker has no statutory or contractual protection, an employer likely retains a presumptive common law right to discharge the worker whose health status makes continued employment dangerous or whose health status prevents him or her from performing his or her job.[86]

Medical and exposure monitoring, however, places the issue in a somewhat different light. In a broad sense, monitoring is designed to reveal whether an employee has been, or in the future may be, harmed by the workplace itself. When the employer seeks to discharge an employee on the basis of such data, it will be because the employee was, or may be, harmed by a situation created by the employer. The right of the employer to discharge the employee is not as clear here as in the general case.

Suppose that an employer is complying with an existing OSHA standard for a particular toxic exposure and monitoring reveals that one of the firm's employees is likely to suffer serious and irreparable health damage unless he or she is removed from the workplace. In this situation, the employer is complying with public policy as enunciated by OSHA and, absent a mandatory medical removal protection (MRP) provision, arguably is free to discharge the employee. If an employer fails to comply with applicable OSHA standards, however, or if no standard exists and the employer permits workplace exposure levels that violate state and federal requirements to maintain a safe place of employment, the employer is violating public policy.[87] Arguably, to permit the employer to take advantage of that violation by discharging the employee is to permit a further violation of public policy. The courts would be loath to allow the employer who negligently breaks the arm of an employee subsequently to fire that employee because of a resultant inability to do heavy lifting. Although the analogy is not perfect, one who subjects employees to toxic substances commits substantially the same act.[88] An employer's use of human monitoring data to discharge employees in such a circumstance may well be impermissible as a matter of public policy. The employer may be obliged at common law to find safe assignments for the workers at comparable pay or bear the cost of their removal as part of doing business.[89]

Limitations under the Occupational Safety and Health Act, General Duty Clause

The use of monitoring data to limit or deny employment opportunities also raises issues under the general duty clause of the Occupational Safety and Health Act (OSHAct).[90] When monitoring information reveals that an employee risks serious health damage from continued exposure to a workplace toxicant, it may also indicate that the employer is in violation of the general duty clause. When a workplace exposure constitutes a "recognized hazard" likely to cause death or serious physical harm, an employer violates the general duty clause if he or she does not take appropriate steps to eliminate the hazard.[91] When an employer asserts that an employee cannot work without injury to health, the employer admits that the workplace is unsafe. That admission triggers the remedial provisions of the OSHAct. In the case of toxic substances, this may well require reduction of the exposure itself, not mere removal of presumptively sensitive employees from the site of exposure.[92]

Section 11(c)(1) of the OSHAct prohibits employers from discharging or otherwise discriminating against any employee "because of the exercise by such employee on behalf of himself or others of any right afforded by this chapter."[93] If an employee insists on retaining his or her job in the face of medical data indicating that continued exposure to a workplace chemical will likely pose a danger to health, the employee may well be asserting a "right" afforded by the general duty clause. That is, in insisting on retaining employment, the employee is asserting a right to a workplace that comports with the requirements of the general duty clause.[94] Accordingly, an employer who discharges or otherwise discriminates against a worker because of perceived susceptibility to a toxic exposure arguably violates the section 11(c) prohibition.[95]

Support for this position is found in an OSHA regulation issued under section 11(c) and upheld in a unanimous 1980 Supreme Court decision.[96] The regulation gives individual workers a limited right to leave the workplace when they face a situation likely to cause "serious injury or death."[97] Where an employee exercises this right to refuse hazardous work, the employer may not take discriminatory action against the employee by discharging the employee or by issuing a reprimand to be included in the employment file.[98] According to the district court to which the issue was remanded for consideration, withholding the employee's pay during the period in which the employee exercises the right is also prohibited.[99] Since a worker may absent him- or herself from a hazardous work assignment under certain conditions without loss of pay or job security, it would be anomalous to allow an employer to discharge or remove the employee without pay because of the same hazardous condition. This would make the result depend on whether the employee asserted a right to refuse hazardous work before the employer took action to discharge him or her from employment.

The issue has not yet been faced directly by a court. In a 1984 decision, however, the District of Columbia Circuit Court of Appeals did suggest that a general duty clause violation might exist if an employer removed susceptible employees "in an attempt to pass on to its employees the cost of maintaining a circum-ambient [toxic substance] concentration higher than that permitted by law," or in an attempt to avoid the cost of reducing concentrations "to a level that posed an acceptable risk."[100] The best approach may be a regulatory solution. The implementation of mandatory MRP for toxic substances exposure in general, as OSHA has done for lead, might be accomplished by a generic MRP standard.[101] An employer's compliance with a mandatory MRP provision for a particular exposure would remove the threat of a general duty clause citation.

Limitations under Antidiscrimination Laws

In addition to potential liability under the common law and the OSHAct general duty clause, an employer who uses monitoring information to limit employment opportunities may also face liability under antidiscrimination laws. Although not all workplace discrimination is prohibited, state and federal laws forbid certain bases for discrimination.[102] Many of these may apply to an employer's use of human monitoring information. A detailed discussion of the relevant discrimination laws is beyond the scope of this book, but an outline of their potential impact on human monitoring is set forth below.[103]

Handicap Discrimination

Congress and most states have passed laws barring discrimination against handicapped individuals in certain employment situations.[104] The laws, which vary widely among the jurisdictions, all place potential limitations on the use of human monitoring data. Although the courts have adopted a case-by-case approach,[105] the worker who is denied employment opportunities on the basis of monitoring results often falls within the literal terms of many handicap discrimination statutes. In general, two issues will be determinative:

whether the workplace in question is covered by a state or federal handicap act and, if so, whether the worker in question is "handicapped" under that act.

The Federal Rehabilitation Act provides handicapped persons with two potential avenues of protection against job discrimination. Section 503 prohibits private employers with federal contracts of $2,500 or more from discriminating against a present or prospective employee on the basis of handicap.[106] Courts have generally held, however, that section 503 does not create a private right of action on the part of the aggrieved individual.[107] A private right of action *is* available under a companion provision, section 504.[108] Nonetheless, the scope of the federal act is far from all inclusive.[109] The various state acts offer a potential for more extensive coverage. Most extend beyond public contractors and apply to most of the major employers within the state.[110]

A worker excluded from a workplace or job assignment because of the results of human monitoring has been removed because he or she is ostensibly at higher risk of injury or illness than the majority of workers. The worker is perceived as having a physical condition that sets him or her apart from others. Although this clearly is discrimination on the basis of physical status, an applicable handicap discrimination statute will not prohibit the action unless the relevant definitional criteria are met. The stated criteria do not differ widely among most jurisdictions,[111] but judicial interpretations of these criteria have varied substantially. Some state courts have interpreted handicap discrimination laws broadly, taking positions that appear to limit significantly the use of monitoring data for employee exclusion.[112] Others have taken much more restrictive positions.[113] Some federal courts have adopted a middle-ground approach, as will be illustrated shortly in the discussion of *E. E. Black, Ltd. v. Marshall.*

At present, the general applicability of handicap discrimination statutes to the use of human monitoring information is unclear. Examining the definitional criteria in the federal act, on which many of the state statutes are based, will illustrate the issues facing courts— and the potential range of logical interpretations. The Rehabilitation Act of 1973 defines a "handicapped" individual as "any person who (i) has a physical or mental impairment which substantially limits one or more of such person's major life activities, (ii) has a record of such an impairment, or (iii) is regarded as having such an impairment."[114]

In the great majority of cases, the persons facing reduced employment opportunity as a result of human monitoring data do not *presently* have a substantially debilitating medical condition and thus do not satisfy either the first or second clauses of the federal definition.

Rather, they are *perceived* as having an increased risk of developing such a condition in the future. Are they, then, "regarded" as having a substantial impairment under the third clause? A narrow reading of the statute might lead to a negative conclusion. In a literal sense, such persons are regarded only as being *at risk* of an impairment, and cannot be said to be regarded as having the impairment itself.[115] Arguably, however, they are being treated as if they had a substantial impairment by being denied employment opportunities normally extended to those without such a disability. In this sense, they are regarded as substantially impaired. This latter interpretation finds support in the Senate committee report presented before the insertion of this language into the act.[116] The Senate report explained that the third clause of the definition applies both to "persons who do not in fact have the condition which they are perceived as having" and to "persons whose mental or physical condition does not substantially limit their life activities."[117] This second provision appears broad enough to cover persons excluded on the basis of monitoring information.

The one federal district court that directly examined the issue has affirmed the applicability of the 1973 Rehabilitation Act to pre-employment screening of perceived high-risk individuals. In *E. E. Black, Ltd. v. Marshall,* the federal district court for Hawaii held that a 29-year-old who had been denied employment as a carpenter's apprentice as a result of positive findings in lower back X-rays was protected by section 503.[118] The court rejected the suggestion that employers may avoid the act's proscriptions merely by establishing that they have discriminated against a worker on the basis of an insubstantial physical disability. In this regard, the opinion noted that the purpose of the act is not to permit an employer to "be rewarded if his reason for rejecting the applicant were ridiculous enough."[119]

Nonetheless, the court in *E. E. Black, Ltd. v. Marshall* also emphasized that not all high-risk individuals would be treated as "handicapped" under the act. Addressing the requirement that the actual or perceived disability must "substantially limit" a major life activity, the court read into the Act a requirement that the actual or perceived impairment be "a substantial handicap *to employment.*"[120] In determining whether a particular condition meets this criterion, the court indicated that one must first assume that all similar employers within the relevant geographic area use the disputed pre-employment screen (or other discriminatory practice) and then weigh that against the physical and mental capabilities of the particular applicant. If the resultant employment limitations appear "substantial," the person will be deemed "handicapped."[121]

Although perhaps not wholly consistent with the literal terms of the act, this construction of the statute appears to be an attempt to fashion a viable framework for evaluating the treatment of perceived high-risk individuals within the context of "handicap" discrimination. The act seems designed primarily to protect the seriously handicapped, but its language is broad enough to cover discriminatory practices based on data obtained through human monitoring.[122] The middle ground adopted in *E. E. Black, Ltd. v. Marshall* imposes a reasonable limitation on an employer's use of monitoring data.

Even in cases in which handicap discrimination is established, an employer may escape liability if the discriminatory practice is reasonably necessary for efficient operation of the business. The Rehabilitation Act provides employers with no affirmative defense, but does require the handicapped individual to prove that he or she is "qualified" for the job.[123] Thus, if a handicap prevents a worker from safely or effectively performing the job, an exclusionary practice may be permissible under the act.[124] Most state handicap statutes include some form of affirmative defense.[125] Although these vary among jurisdictions, many appear analogous to the familiar defenses that have developed under Title VII of the Civil Rights Act.[126]

Civil Rights and Age Discrimination

Employers who exclude workers on the basis of monitoring information may also run afoul of the more general laws against discrimination. Title VII of the federal Civil Rights Act prohibits employment discrimination on the basis of race, color, religion, sex, or national origin.[127] The scope of the act is substantially broader than that of the federal handicap discrimination act, and it affords protection for the great majority of the nation's employees. In addition, many states extend similar protection to employees not covered by the federal act.[128] The Age Discrimination in Employment Act and some state acts provide protection of comparable breadth against discrimination on the basis of age.[129]

As with handicap discrimination, the applicability of these laws to the use of human monitoring information is not yet clear. In the ordinary case, exclusionary practices based on monitoring data will not be per se discriminatory on the basis of race, sex, national origin, or age.[130] Nor are they likely to involve *disparate treatment* of one of these protected classes. That is, they will not be part of a policy that, while neutral on its face, masks a specific employer intent to discriminate on one or more of these impermissible bases.[131] The practical impact of an exclusionary practice, however, may fall disproportionately on a particular race, sex, ethnic or age group.

The Supreme Court has long held that a claim of *disparate impact* states a viable cause of action under the Civil Rights Act.[132] A similar rationale has been applied in the area of age discrimination.[133] In a 1975 decision, the Court held that job applicants denied employment on the basis of a preemployment screen establish a prima facie case of racial discrimination when they demonstrate that "the tests in question select applicants for hire or promotion in a racial pattern significantly different from that of the pool of applicants."[134] Proof of disparate impact thus requires statistical analysis demonstrating a "significantly" disproportionate effect on a protected class. The cases provide no clear guidance, however, as to the level of disproportion that is required before an effect is deemed "significant."[135]

The potential for disparate impact inheres in many uses of human monitoring data. A genetic screen for sickle cell anemia, for example, will disproportionally exclude blacks and certain ethnic groups because they have a much higher incidence of this trait than does the general population.[136] Similarly, tests that consistently yield a higher percentage of positive results in one sex than in the other may give rise to exclusionary practices that discriminate on the basis of sex.[137] Finally, a wide variety of exclusionary practices based on monitoring data may have a disparate impact on older workers. Older workers have been in the work force longer and usually have been exposed to hazardous work environments much more often than their younger colleagues. Their prior exposure may have impaired their health or left them more vulnerable to current workplace hazards. They may, for example, have a preexisting illness as a result of previous workplace exposures (see "Preexisting Disease" in Chap. 8). Their age alone may account for a certain degree of body deterioration (see "'Stochastic,' Genetic, Age, and Sex Variability" in Chap. 8).

When the employee establishes a prima facie case of disparate impact, the employer will have an opportunity to produce evidence indicating that the exclusionary practice constitutes a business necessity.[138] If such proof is offered, the employee must carry the burden of proving that the practice is not a business necessity.[139] The Supreme Court has characterized "business necessity" as requiring "a manifest relation to the employment in question."[140] In the words of an often cited Fourth Circuit Court of Appeals opinion, this means

that the practice must be "necessary to the safe and efficient operation of the business."[141] Further, if the employee can establish that
another, less discriminatory practice "would be equally as effective
as the challenged practice in serving the [employer's] legitimate business goals," the business necessity defense will not stand.[142]

There are two principal reasons why business necessity may be
difficult to establish for exclusionary practices based on human monitoring data. The first is that the great majority of these practices are
not designed to protect the health and safety of the public or of other
workers. Instead, their "business purpose" is the protection of the
excluded worker and, not incidentally, the protection of the employer
from the anticipated costs associated with the potential illness of
that worker.[143] The Supreme Court has indicated that employer cost
is a factor to be considered in the evaluation of disparate impact
cases.[144]. Nonetheless, as noted in one analysis, "the courts are usually skeptical of an employer's argument that it refuses to hire
qualified applicants for their own good, and they often require a
higher level of justification in these cases than in cases in which
public safety is at stake."[145]

Another, and probably more serious, obstacle to the successful assertion of a business necessity defense is the unreliability of the
screening procedures themselves. If the exclusion of susceptible (i.e.,
high-risk) individuals truly is a business necessity, its rationale dis-
appears if the test used as the basis for such exclusion cannot provide
reasonable assurance that those excluded actually are susceptible
(i.e., at high risk). Indeed, without such assurance, the test becomes
little more than an instrument for arbitrariness and only adds to the
discriminatory nature of the exclusionary practice. To the extent that
the tests in question are not reliable (see the Introduction to Part II),
the availability of the business necessity defense is questionable.

The foregoing discussion of discrimination has presupposed that
the "screened" worker will be excluded from the workplace. As suggested throughout this book, however, employers may have another
option. In many cases, the employer will be in a position to provide
these workers with other jobs in workplaces that do not involve exposures to the substances from which they may suffer adverse health
effects. If such alternative positions were supplied, at benefit levels
comparable to those of the positions from which exclusion was
sought, employers might avoid the proscriptions of the various discrimination laws. Providing an alternative position would certainly
remove much of the incentive for filing a discrimination claim. Further, if such a claim were filed by employees who had already been

hired, courts might find that an adequate MRP program obviated the charge of discrimination.[146] This could be one area where good law and good social policy coincide.

THE USE OF MONITORING DATA IN TORT AND WORKERS' COMPENSATION CASES

From a legal perspective, the most important impact of human monitoring information may be its use as evidence in tort and workers' compensation cases. Although its potential in this area is still to be realized, the science of biological markers may eventually serve to answer the evidentiary question that has plagued most compensation cases involving human exposure to toxic substances: How do we know whether a particular exposure caused a particular person's medical condition? At present, the problem remains a major one.

The Causation Requirement in Compensation Cases

To appreciate the importance of the causation requirement, it is helpful to have an understanding of the role of the workers' compensation and tort systems in providing compensation to injured workers. In most cases, the only route of recovery open to the worker seeking compensation for occupational disease—beyond any available benefits from health or disability insurance—is workers' compensation. Every state has a workers' compensation statute.[147] Although scope of coverage, benefit levels, and other aspects vary among the state programs, all of these programs share two important features.[148]

First, all programs provide compensation for the same general categories of employee loss. Typically, the worker suffering from occupational illness incurs three types of damages: medical expenses; wage loss (including loss of future earning capacity); and physical pain and emotional suffering ("pain and suffering"). Worker compensation is designed to provide compensation (up to certain statutory limits) for the first two of these, but compensation for the third—pain and suffering—is specifically precluded. Compensation for pain and suffering is available under the common law tort system. However, the second feature shared by all the state workers' compensation statutes is an explicit limitation on tort remedies. Under workers' compensation, the employee need not prove that the employer was negligent, only that the injury or disease was job related. In this sense, workers' compensation is a "strict liability" system.[149] In all states, the quid pro quo for this relaxing of the liability requirement is a statutory ban on worker tort suits against the employer based on allegations of employer negligence. Cases of this nature must be brought within the workers' compensation system.

However, in cases of serious disability, such as occupational cancer, the amount available under this system is likely to be well below the worker's true loss. In 1980, the U.S. Department of Labor estimated that, among those cases of occupational disease in this country that received workers' compensation, the average award represented only 13% of the employee's actual wage loss.[150] Workers thus have strong incentive to find ways to pursue compensation within the tort system, where there is no prescribed limit on wage loss recovery and where recovery for pain and suffering is allowed.[151] They have met with some success. A few state courts have allowed workers to bring tort suits against their employers—in spite of the ban against suits for negligence—for having *intentionally* exposed them to toxic substances.[152] Perhaps more important, workers remain free in all states to sue the manufacturers of products that cause workplace injuries. Accordingly, workers have in some instances been successful in bringing products liability claims against the manufacturers of toxic substances used in the workplace.[153]

Regardless of whether the case is brought in tort or under workers' compensation, the worker must satisfy a causation requirement in order to prevail. In a common law tort action, the plaintiff must prove, by a preponderance of the evidence, that the defendant's actions were the *proximate cause* of the injury in question. In its simplest terms, this means that a worker must be able to demonstrate that it is *more likely than not* that his or her disease was caused by a workplace condition and not by some other factor. The burden in a workers' compensation case is essentially the same. As noted, the worker must prove that the injury was job related. Here again, this requires proof that it is more likely than not that a workplace condition led to the disease in question.

Although this does not require scientific certainty, it does require particularity. In situations of toxic substance exposure, it will not be sufficient to estabish that it is more probable than not that the chemical in question causes a disease. Rather, the worker must prove by a greater than 50% probability that the chemical caused his or her particular case of that disease. Even in the best-prepared cases, this is a difficult and often insurmountable burden. The chief reasons for this difficulty are by now all too familiar.

In the first place, the probability that exposure to a toxic substance, especially at the relatively low levels commonly encountered, will produce disease or other long-term cellular damage in any given exposed person is usually quite low. It thus is likely that many actual correlations between medical effects and chemical exposure simply go undetected. Further, there commonly are a number of other (so-called confounding) factors, beyond the suspect toxic exposure itself, that also can cause the injury in question. The statistical probability that any given exposed person who contracts the condition did so as a result of the exposure, then, usually is less than 50%. Finally, many of the results of toxic substance exposure (including most cancers) have long latency periods, and do not become manifest until many years after exposure. Accordingly, an already difficult proof problem is exacerbated by the vagaries of time, distance, and memory.

Not surprisingly, the indications are that most cases of serious disease caused by workplace chemical exposure receive no compensation within either the tort or workers' compensation systems. In its 1980 study, the Department of Labor estimated that only 5% of all cases of serious occupational disease receive any benefits through the worker compensation system.[154] The figures on occupational cancer are even bleaker. Using the Doll and Peto estimate that approximately 4% of all cancer deaths in the United States are caused by workplace exposures (thought by many to be an extreme underestimate),[155] one of the authors of this text has estimated that less than 2% of all occupational cancer fatalities in this country receive workers' compensation benefits.[156]

The Promise of Biomarkers

Obviously, to the extent that increased use of human monitoring adds to the existing data base on the observed correlations between particular diseases and particular chemicals, it will provide increased evidence for use in compensation proceedings generally. More than this, though, human monitoring has the potential to bring about a change in the nature of the evidence used in these cases.

Typically, the evidence offered to prove causation in chemical exposure cases is premised on a *statistical* correlation between disease and exposure. Whether the underlying data are from epidemiological studies, from toxicological experiments, or from the results of a complicated risk assessment model, they usually are *population* based. This places the plaintiff at the mercy of the attributable risk (expressed as the percentage of cases of the disease attributable to the exposure) for the study population. Unless the attributable risk is greater than 50%—that is, unless the incidence rate among those exposed to the chemical is more than double the backgound rate—the plaintiff cannot prove *on the basis of the available statistical evidence,* that more likely than not his or her particular case of the disease was caused by the chemical exposure.

The following matrix, representing a hypothetical population of 200 workers, illustrates the point.

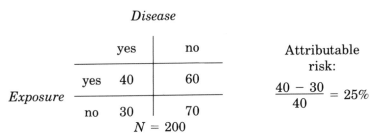

Disease

		yes	no	Attributable risk:
Exposure	yes	40	60	$\dfrac{40 - 30}{40} = 25\%$
	no	30	70	

$$N = 200$$

In this case, 40 of the workers who were exposed to the chemical contracted the disease. Of those, there is a statistical probability that 10 (25%) contracted the disease as a result of the exposure. On the basis of this evidence alone, however, there is no way of identifying which 10 of the 40 are in that category. Without additional evidence, none of the 40 diseased workers who were exposed to the chemical can prove that more likely than not his or her case of the disease was caused by the exposure. Accordingly, even though it is likely that 10 of the 40 are entitled to compensation, the causation requirement will prevent them from receiving it under either the tort or workers' compensation system.[157]

The developing science of human monitoring may offer a way to distinguish individual claimants from the pack. Conceivably, the data generated by various human monitoring procedures will

- Increase our knowledge of the "subclinical" effects of toxic substances, thus permitting us to track the effect of a chemical exposure over time, and also expanding the universe of "medical conditions" for which compensation may be provided;
- Eventually enable us to establish that a particular person has been exposed to a particular chemical (or class of chemicals); and
- Eventually enable us to establish that a particular person's medical condition (or subclinical effect) was caused by exposure to a particular chemical (or class of chemicals).

Already, human monitoring data are being used in some situations to show subclinical changes thought to be associated with particular chemical exposures.[158] This can have many applications in toxic substance compensation cases. In the long term, evidence of subclinical changes occurring between the time of exposure and the time of disease may be a way of distinguishing those whose disease was caused by the exposure from those who contracted the disease because of other factors. Such evidence may also give rise to more immediate legal relief. There is a growing trend toward allowing those who can establish that they have been exposed to a toxic substance—and that they thus have been placed at increased risk of future harm—to recover the costs of medical surveillance from the responsible party.[159] Proof of certain subclinical effects, such as DNA damage, would tend to support an allegation of increased risk and would make the claim for medical surveillance all the more compelling. Further, such evidence may support a separate claim for damages *for having been put at increased risk of future harm,* although it is not clear that such a claim would be viable in most states.[160]

Finally, some evidence of subclinical effects may give rise to a right to recover compensation *for those effects themselves.* For example, human monitoring can detect certain changes in the immune system. There is a body of literature suggesting that chemical exposures can harm the immune system,[161] and evidence of immune system damage has been offered in recent cases involving toxic substance exposure.[162] Thus far, allegations of immune system damage have met with mixed success in the courts, both because the relationship between chemical exposure and immune system damage is not yet clear, and because the evidence of immune system damage was not always considered persuasive. Although human monitoring may not be able to tie particular immune system deficiencies to particular exposures, it should be able to establish with greater certainty whether immune system damage has, in fact, occurred.

Looking to the future, it is quite possible that further developments in the science of biomarkers will permit the identification of "chemical fingerprints"—a distinctive change in the DNA that can be tied to a particular chemical or class of chemicals. At the very least, this should make it much easier to distinguish those who have been exposed to a particular chemical in the workplace from those who have not, and to identify which of the many potential defendants was responsible. More important, it should eventually permit the correlation of particular cases of diseases such as cancer with exposure to particular chemicals (or classes of chemicals). To the extent that this happens, it will narrow the scope of the evidence from the population to the individual and will place the deliberations in these cases on firmer scientific footing.

12. Policy and Ethical Considerations

THE GOALS OF HUMAN MONITORING

As discussed in the Introduction, human monitoring activities have a number of sometimes conflicting goals: (1) to discover an increased harm or risk of harm in a population of workers, (2) to encourage the removal of especially sensitive workers or workers who are in a high-risk group, (3) to reduce actual harm to workers and subsequent employer liability, and (4) to relieve the employer of costs that would otherwise be expended for cleaning up the workplace.

Both workers and employers tend to be risk averse, that is, to err on the side of caution to avoid human and economic costs each might otherwise have to bear. The worker, however, would prefer to have the workplace as hazard free as possible, whereas the employer would prefer to minimize legal and financial liability by removing "problems" (workers) before they arise. The resolution of conflicts between these goals fundamentally depends on one's sense of fairness about where the costs of preventing harm should lie.

RECOMMENDATIONS FOR THE PROPER USE OF HUMAN MONITORING

Each type of monitoring has certain advantages and limitations. Strategies for coordinating the several activities that constitute human monitoring with environmental monitoring must be designed to optimize the reduction of risk from workplace hazards. Considering

159

the various advantages and limitations for each type of monitoring, an optimal combination could include environmental monitoring (ambient and personal), medical surveillance, and, where appropriate, biological monitoring.

Environmental monitoring can, in theory, detect the presence of a toxic substance prior to significant exposure. Thus, the most preventive strategy is the early elimination of a potential hazard from the workplace. If medical surveillance is used as the sole monitoring mechanism, many physiological effects may not be detected until late in the progression of a disease. This limitation has significant negative impact for those diseases that are serious, or reversible only in early stages.

Biological monitoring falls between environmental monitoring and medical surveillance in preventive potential. Biological monitoring ideally occurs before any significant health impact. Genetic monitoring may detect an early, preclinical disease state resulting from exposure. Further development of this type of monitoring may at some point lead to confirmation of exposure and suggest possible health consequences.

The strategies used for human monitoring must be fashioned on a toxic substance-specific basis because the state-of-the-art techniques differ from substance to substance. In general, medical surveillance and biological monitoring for populations should be used only in combination with environmental monitoring. In a case in which a specific harmful substance cannot be identified, however, and the workplace is suspected of being unsafe, medical surveillance may indicate whether a problem exists. In the future, genetic monitoring may also serve as an early indicator that exposure to certain chemicals has occurred in a worker *population*. Genetic screening focuses on removal of the worker before exposure and is preventive *for that worker only*.

In sum, human monitoring should be used only if (1) given the specific workplace problem, monitoring serves as an appropriate preventive tool; (2) it is used in conjunction with environmental monitoring; (3) the tests are accurate and reliable and the predictive values are high; (4) it is not used to divert resources from reducing the presence of toxic substances in the workplace or from redesigning technology; and (5) medical removal protection for earnings and job security is provided.

New solutions involving both technological innovation and job redesign may obviate the necessity of human monitoring. Conflicts now arise only because, under existing technology, workers continue to be exposed to toxic substances.

Discriminatory practices and consequential tort suits, anti-discrimination suits, deterioration of labor–management relations, and agency sanctions may follow poorly conceived and poorly executed human monitoring programs. The weaker the scientific foundation for the tests, the less secure are the legal grounds and defenses available to the employer. In light of the sometimes preliminary, unreliable, and nonspecific nature of the techniques used in human monitoring, the practice is a problematic activity itself in most instances.

If the courts in the future do excuse discriminatory practices by employers who remove workers "for their own good," then expansion of the worker's right to refuse hazardous work should follow. It seems likely that the employer will either pay for medical removal protection or the worker will be inclined to "remove himself or herself," with the consequence that he or she will demand pay to exercise fully the right to refuse hazardous work. The economic burden of removal will then have to be weighed against the cost of hazard reduction by the employer. We believe that when costs of removal are fully internalized in the costs of production, human monitoring as a primary control strategy will not be as economically attractive as early proponents have argued.

TOWARD AN ETHICAL THEORY FOR HUMAN MONITORING

The moral and legal enquiry in the area of human monitoring addresses the behavior of particular actors engaged in the conduct of monitoring tests, the dissemination of the test results, and the use of the information in the context of the employment relationship. Ladd argued that it is important to distinguish ethics from law, custom, institutional practices, and positive morality (the body of accepted popular beliefs of a society about morality): Ethics is concerned with what ought to be.[1] Moral problems emanating from conflicts concerning human monitoring may be categorized as conflicts of interest, conflicts of moral demands (e.g., conflicts of duties), and conflicts in perceptions of what is right or wrong, fair or unfair. Certain rights are possessed by individuals, and those rights impose (moral) obligations on others. Rights and obligations must be viewed together in the context of particular relationships.[2] Ladd and others have argued that people have a general duty to support the fulfillment of the moral requirements of relationships, whether their own or those of others. Some of what is necessary to carry out this duty is embodied in rights and obligations. These rights and obligations may sometimes be given the force of law.

> The concept of rights, as a cluster of claims on society and its institutions on the part of the individual, derives its principal moral warrant from the concept of moral integrity. This concept, unlike the concept of simple self-determination, focuses on the integrity of personal relationships, concerns, and responsibilities. Everyone in society has a duty, individually and collectively, to defend, support, and nourish these moral relationships both personally and in others. The concept of rights provides an effective social and conceptual instrument for carrying out this general duty.[3]

The delineation of rights and duties gives rise to certain expectations or hopes on the part of society concerning human behavior. In imposing rules or legal principles on individuals and institutions, the law often embodies societal attitudes, values, and expectations.[4] This sometimes, but not always, occurs when a significant societal consensus has been reached on a particular moral question derived from human conflicts.[5] The law establishes legal rights, whose violation may be illegal, and provides remedies to correct their violation. But the law also recognizes that conflicts of legitimate interests, conflicts of legal duties, and differences in perception of what is right or wrong, fair or unfair, require a balancing in the fashioning of remedies. Indeed, there are both legal remedies (usually of statutory origin) and equitable remedies that give great discretionary power to the courts or adjudicating institutions, such as the Equal Employment Opportunity Commission. Rules are embodied in legislation and regulations; legal principles guide, but do not unequivocally settle, other conflicts. In examining the conflict questions, the law does indeed view behavior in the context of relationships. Justifiable expectations one party has of another are translated into the legal concept of reliance. Thus, the law will sometimes find a physician–patient relationship between worker and company physician when none was intended by the physician, because it was reasonable that the worker expected certain behavior or transmission of information from the physician. Similarly, although the legal construct of the modern corporation bestows limited personal liability on corporate officers or employees,[6] the courts will "pierce the corporate veil" when corporate behavior violates the ethical norm.[7] Discrimination law is replete with discretionary justice.[8]

The law, of course, does not always serve the ethical interests of the society so nobly. Legislation and legal institutions can be compromised by powerful special interests. In addition, if there is a lack of societal consensus or interest about a moral issue, the law may either not address that issue or fail to give helpful guidance concerning the boundaries of fair or equitable behavior.[9] Thus, it is important to engage in both legal and ethical enquiry concerning human and institutional behavior.

In the context of the transfer of medical information resulting from workplace monitoring and discrimination resulting from its use, the legal and ethical norms are in a great state of flux.[10] Conflicts of interest and conflicts of duty (e.g., for the company physician or governmental official) abound. Moreover, given the weak scientific validity of many of the screening tests and resulting data, questions of what actions to take or not take reflect differences in perceptions of fairness and risk averseness. The worker would rather be safe and keep his or her job; the employer wants to limit his or her legal and economic liability. In the face of great uncertainty, the actors prefer to take few chances and very divergent solutions are pursued concerning both the transmission of uncertain information and its use.

On the other hand, some employers may be motivated to undertake medical screening solely out of a sincere concern for the health of their employees and may even feel a moral obligation to do so. In this case, there may be no conflict if care is taken concerning the dissemination and use of the monitoring results.

The extensive discussion in Chapter 11 reveals the complexity and difficulty with which the law balances competing interests and equities. In some cases, the law embodies the belief that de facto discrimination against certain protected classes of people (e.g., a minority race) is to be affirmatively avoided and cannot be justified by resulting health benefits. In other cases, such as those involving workers who are perceived to be handicapped, the burdens to industry of providing protection may be relevant in deciding how much employment security to require. Discrimination law necessarily involves the exercise of discretion by courts and adjudicating institutions—with its attendant inconsistency and unpredictability.

With legal and ethical norms in flux, it is important to examine the policy options for dealing with future and continuing ethical dilemmas. The possible strategies that deserve consideration include

1. Encouragement of ethical enquiry into the conduct and use of medical screening, that is, educating workers, management, and health professionals to think more seriously about the problems. Perhaps ethicists should be consulted in designing the screening programs;
2. Use of legislative and regulatory means to clarify rights and du-

ties, such as encouraging the Occupational Safety and Health Administration to promulgate a generic earnings and job security protection (medical removal protection) requirement for all medical removal or enacting legislation that requires workers to be notified of occupational risks and prohibits discrimination outright;

3. Encouragement of the use of self-help techniques by workers, such as the right to refuse hazardous work, union bargaining, and the filing of discrimination complaints; and

4. Encouragement of better disposition of conflicts by improving procedural fairness in conflict resolution, such as full and complete disclosure of information to workers, the better maintenance of confidentiality of worker records, or the use of corporate ombudspersons.

These options differ in the extent to which the rights and freedoms of some are diminished to protect those of others. Regulatory or legislative fiats define acceptable behavior and in the process decrease freedom of choice.[11] On the other hand, freedom from harm and discrimination is preserved. Sharpening self-help mechanisms preserves choice but fosters an adversarial solution. Education can persuade and enlighten; it can also sensitize those discriminated against to assert their rights. Procedural fairness tends to right the imbalance of access to legal and political institutions.

The choice of options at any one time reflects the seriousness with which society wishes to address the moral and legal dilemmas. Thinking about these problems is a first and necessary step.[12]

Notes

Introduction

1. See *Hearings on Genetic Screening of Workers before the Subcommittee on Investigations and Oversight of the House Committee on Science and Technology*, 97th Cong., 1st and 2nd Sess. (1981–1982); Office of Technology Assessment, *The Role of Genetic Testing in the Prevention of Occupational Disease* (Washington, D.C.: U.S. Government Printing Office, 1983) (hereafter cited as *OTA Report*). See also the discussion of a second OTA study in progress in Chapter 4.

2. 29 C.F.R. § 1910.1025 (1988).

3. A. Berlin, R. E. Yodaiken, and B. A. Henman, eds., *Assessment of Toxic Agents at the Workplace: Roles of Ambient and Biological Monitoring* (Boston: Martinus Nijoff, 1984).

4. See "Protection of the Sensitive Individual," *Annals of the American Conference of Governmental Industrial Hygienists* (1982), 3.

5. N. A. Ashford, C. J. Spadafor, and C. C. Caldart, "Human Monitoring: Scientific, Legal and Ethical Considerations," *Harvard Environmental Law Review* (1984) 8(2):263–363.

6. See Berlin, Yodaiken, and Henman, eds., *Assessment of Toxic Agents*.

7. W. E. Halperin, P. A. Schulte, and D. G. Greathouse, eds., "Conference on Medical Screening and Biological Monitoring for the Effects of Exposure in the Workplace, Part I," *Journal of Occupational Medicine* (1986) 28(8); T. J. Mason, P. C. Prorok, and R. D. Costlow, eds., "Conference on Medical Screening and Biological Monitoring for the Effects of Exposure in the Workplace, Part II," *Journal of Occupational Medicine* (1986) 28(10).

8. V. Foa, E. A. Emmett, M. Maroni, and A. Colombi, eds., *Occupational and Environmental Chemical Hazards: Cellular and Biochemical Indices for Monitoring Toxicity* (Chichester: Ellis Hornwood, 1987).

9. Though the proceedings was assigned a publication date of 1987, we were unable to obtain a copy in 1989 when this writing was completed.

10. B. S. Hulka and T. Wilcosky, "Biological Markers in Epidemiologic Research," *Archives of Environmental Health* (1988) 43(2):83–89; P. A. Schulte, "Methodologic Issues in the Use of Biologic Markers in Epidemiologic Research," *American Journal of Epidemiology* (1987) 126(6):1006–1016.

11. Committee on Biological Markers of the National Research Council, "Biological Markers in Environmental Health Research," *Environmental Health Perspectives* (1987) 74:3–9, 3–4, emphasis added.

12. Ibid., 3.

13. The Occupational Safety and Health Act authorizes the Secretary of Health and Human Services to require employers to address the problems of susceptible employees [29 U.S.C. § 669(a)(5) (1985)] and aging adults [29 U.S.C. § 669(a)(7) (1985)]. See R. Beliles, "OSHA Occupational Health Standards and the Sensitive Worker," *Annals of the American Conference of Governmental Industrial Hygienists* (1982) 3:71–75. For a description of sensitive populations in general under various environmental legislation, see R. Friedman, *Sensitive Populations and Environmental Standards* (Washington, D.C.: Conservation Foundation, 1981).

14. T. McGarity and C. Schroeder, "Risk-Oriented Employment Screening," *Texas Law Review* (1981) 59(6):999; M. Rothstein, "Employee Selection Based on Susceptibility to Occupational Illness," *Michigan Law Review* (1983) 81:1379; M. Rothstein, *Medical Screening of Workers* (Washington, D.C.: Bureau of National Affairs, 1984).

Chapter 1. Overview and Definitions: Monitoring, Surveillance, and Screening

1. J. R. Goldsmith, S. M. Scharf, and R. Israeli, "Pulmonary Function Screening and Monitoring in Occupational Health," *Journal of Occupational Medicine* (1986) 28(8):657.

2. Ibid.

3. B. S. Hulka, "Screening for Cancer: Lessons Learned," *Journal of Occupational Medicine* (1986) 28(8):687.

4. J. K. Frost, W. C. Ball, M. L. Levin, M. S. Tockman, Y. S. Erozan, P. B. Gupta, J. C. Eggleston, N. J. Pressman, M. P. Donithan, and A. W. Kimball, "Sputum Cytopathology: Use and Potential in Monitoring the Workplace Environment by Screening for Biological Effects of Exposure," *Journal of Occupational Medicine* (1986) 28(8):692.

5. J. D. Millar, "Screening and Monitoring: Tools for Prevention," *Journal of Occupational Medicine* (1986) 28(8):546.

6. Ibid. The optimal prevention of work-related disease depends on the elimination or control of etiological agents through methods such as substitution, process redesign, and improved methods to decrease exposures. See R. S. F. Schilling, "The Role of Medical Examination in Protecting Worker Health," *Journal of Occupational Medicine* (1986) 28(8):553.

7. W. E. Halperin, J. Ratcliffe, T. M. Frazier, L. Wilson, S. P. Becker, and P. A. Schulte, "Medical Screening in the Workplace: Proposed Principles," *Journal of Occupational Medicine* (1986) 28(8):547–548.

8. Millar, "Screening and Monitoring," 546.

9. Hulka, "Screening for Cancer," 687.

10. Ibid., 688.

11. See Hulka and Wilcosky, "Biological Markers in Epidemiologic Research," 83–89, and Schulte, "Methodologic Issues," 1006–1016.

12. Halperin, Ratcliffe, Frazier, et al., "Medical Screening in the Workplace," 551.

13. Frost, Ball, Levin, et al., "Sputum Cytopathology," 692.

14. Hulka, "Screening for Cancer," 687.

15. Ibid.

16. Ibid.

17. Frost, Ball, Levin, et al., "Sputum Cytopathology," 692.

18. Ibid.; Hulka, "Screening for Cancer," 687. For a discussion of these terms, see the Introduction to Part II.

19. Hulka, "Screening for Cancer," 687.

20. Ibid.

21. Ibid.; Halperin, Ratcliffe, Frazier, et al., "Medical Screening in the Workplace," 549.

22. Hulka, "Screening for Cancer," 687.

23. Halperin, Ratcliffe, Frazier, et al., "Medical Screening in the Workplace," 549.

24. Ibid., 548.

25. Ibid., 549.

26. Ibid., 548.

27. Ibid., 550.

28. 29 C.F.R. § 1910.20(c) (1988).

29. Berlin, Yodaiken, and Henman, eds., *Assessment of Toxic Agents,* XII–XIII.

30. D. Hattis, E. Rothenberg, and N. A. Ashford, *Some Considerations for the Design of OSHA Policy on Medical Surveillance and Removal Provisions in Occupational Health Standards,* CPA/WP-79-9 (1979), 2 (submitted to the U.S. Department of Labor by the Massachusetts Institute of Technology, Center for Policy Alternatives).

31. See note 45 in Chapter 2.

32. Berlin, Yodaiken, and Henman, eds., *Assessment of Toxic Agents,* XII–XIII.

33. R. E. Yodaiken, "Surveillance, Monitoring and Regulatory Concerns," *Journal of Occupational Medicine* (1986) 28(8):570.

34. For example, the ethylene oxide standard requires that in addition to a medical history and physical examination, workers are to be given a complete blood count, including at least white cell, red cell, hematocrit, and hemoglobin determinations, as well as any other laboratory tests that the physician deems necessary by sound medical practice [29 C.F.R. § 1910.1047(i)(ii)(3)and(4) (1989)]. This is the extent of the guidance by OSHA to examining physicians, even though OSHA recognizes that exposure to ethylene oxide could severely affect the hematologic system [49 *Fed. Reg.* 25,763 (June 22, 1984)].

In addition to hematological changes that result from ethylene oxide exposure, changes in fertility are also known to occur. Medical examinations for pregnancy testing or a laboratory evaluation of fertility will be conducted *"if requested by the employee and* deemed appropriate by the physician" [29 C.F.R. § 1910.1047(i)(ii)(B) (1989), emphasis added]. This testing scheme leaves too much discretion to the examining physician, who, as the regulation is written, is not obligated to provide such testing unless it is requested by the employee. The employee should not be burdened with the duty of having to ask for such testing, because such inquiries require employees to be aware of infertility problems associated with ethylene oxide exposures and know that in order to be tested for the same, they must initiate the request. In contrast, the benzene standard, also concerned with the effects of exposure on the hematological system, provides much more detailed guidance for examining physicians. The guidance in that standard includes, for example, questions to be asked about exposure to other hematological toxins as well as more specific laboratory tests to be performed, focusing on blood indices [52 *Fed. Reg.* 34,565 (September 11, 1987)].

35. Yodaiken, "Regulatory Concerns," 570.

36. National Institute for Occupational Safety and Health, *NIOSH/OSHA Occupational Health Guidelines for Chemical Hazards,* Pub. No. 81-123, F. Mackison, R. Stricoff, and L. Partridge, eds. (Washington, D.C.: U.S. Department of Health and Human Services, 1981).

37. Occupational Safety and Health Act of 1970, 29 U.S.C. § 655(a) (1985). See also "The Authority to Require Medical Surveillance on Consensus Standards" in Chapter 2.

38. 53 *Fed. Reg.* 20,960–21,263 (June 7, 1988).

39. 53 *Fed. Reg.* 37,591; 37,595 (September 27, 1988).

40. See P. A. Schulte and W. E. Halperin, "Genetic Screening and Monitoring for Workers," in *Recent Advances in Occupational Health,* No. 3, J. M. Harrington, ed. (New York: Churchill Livingston, 1987), 135–154, 140; F. P. Perera, "The Potential Usefulness of Biological Markers in Risk Assessment," *Environmental Health Perspectives* (1987) 76:141–145; F. P. Perera, "Molecular Cancer Epidemiology: A New Tool in Cancer Prevention," *Journal of the National Cancer Institute* (1987) 78(5):887–898; F. P. Perera, "The Significance of DNA and Protein Adducts in Human Biomonitoring Studies," *Mutation Research* (1988) 205:255–269.

41. Proponents of genetic monitoring believe that a relatively high number of environmentally induced alterations in chromosomes (above background incidence) may indicate that a worker is predisposed to certain occupational illnesses, particularly cancer. See C. Holden, "Looking at Genes in the Workplace," *Science* (1982) 217:336–337; see also Perera, "Potential Usefulness" and "Molecular Cancer Epidemiology"; M. S. Legator and J. B. Ward, Jr., "Animal and Human Studies in Genetic Toxicology," in *Pregnant Women at Work,* G. Chamberlain, ed. (London: Royal Society of Medicine and Macmillan, 1984), 167–188, esp. 182–185; J. D. Fabricant and M. S. Legator, "Etiology, Role and Detection of Chromosomal Aberrations in Man," *Journal of Occupational Medicine* (1981) 23(9):624.

42. Berlin, Yodaiken, and Henman, eds., *Assessment of Toxic Agents,* XII, emphasis added.

43. Perera, "Molecular Cancer Epidemiology," 887–898.

44. R. R. Lauwerys, *Industrial Chemical Exposure: Guidelines for Biological Monitoring* (Davis, Cal.: Biomedical Publications, 1983), 5.

45. R. L. Zielhuis and P. Th. Henderson, "Definitions of Monitoring Activities and Their Relevance for the Practice of Occupational Health," *International Archives of Occupational and Environmental Health* (1986) 57(4):250.

46. R. L. Zielhuis, "Biological Monitoring: Confusion in Terminology," *American Journal of Industrial Medicine* (1985) 8(6):515–516.

47. Ibid.

48. H. J. Dunster, "Current Trends in Occupational Health and Hygiene—General Considerations II," in *Assessment of Toxic Agents at the Workplace: Roles of Ambient and Biological Monitoring,* A. Berlin, R. E. Yodaiken, and B. A. Henman, eds. (Boston: Martinus Nijoff, 1984), 12; C. B. Monroe, "The Role of Biological Monitoring in Medical and Environmental Surveillance," in *Chemical Hazards in the Workplace: Measurement and Control,* G. Choudhary, ed. (Washington, D.C.: American Chemical Society, 1981), 5.

49. D. Gompertz, "Solvents—The Relationship between Biological Monitoring Strategies and Metabolic Handling: A Review," *Annals of Occupational Hygiene* (1980) 23(4):410, emphasis added.

50. D. Gompertz, "Assessment of Risk by Biological Monitoring," *British Journal of Industrial Medicine* (1981) 38(2):201.

51. Hattis, Rothenberg, and Ashford, *OSHA Policy on Medical Surveillance and Removal Provisions,* 9.

52. Berlin, Yodaiken, and Henman, eds., *Assessment of Toxic Agents,* XIII.

53. Zielhuis and Henderson, "Definitions," 255.

54. Frost, Ball, Levin, et al., "Sputum Cytopathology," 692.

55. A. L. Linch, *Evaluation of Ambient Air Quality by Personnel Monitoring,* Vol. 1, 2nd ed. (Boca Raton, Florida: CRC Press, 1981), preface.

56. Ibid. The participants at the Luxembourg seminar agreed that personal breathing zone sampling provides a better measure of an employee's daily exposure than area ambient sampling [Berlin, Yodaiken, and Henman, eds., *Assessment of Toxic Agents,* XIV].

57. Berlin, Yodaiken, and Henman, eds., *Assessment of Toxic Agents,* XII.

58. L. Boden, "Impact of Workplace Characteristics on Costs and Benefits of Medical Screening," *Journal of Occupational Medicine* (1986) 28(8):751.

59. E. D. Janus, N. T. Phillips, and R. W. Carrell, "Smoking, Lung Function, and Alpha-1 Antitrypsin Deficiency," *Lancet* (1985) 152–154; R. W. Carrell, "Alpha-1 Antitrypsin, Emphysema, and Smoking," *New Zealand Medical Journal* (1984) 97:327–328.

Chapter 2. Legal Authority for Human Monitoring

1. 29 U.S.C. § 655(b)(7) (1985).

2. 29 C.F.R. § 1910.1001(l)(1)(i) (1988) states that an employer "shall institute a medical surveillance program" for certain employees.

3. 29 C.F.R. § 1910.1017(k) (1988) states, "A program for medical surveillance shall be instituted. . . . The program shall provide each such employee with an opportunity for examinations and tests."

4. 29 C.F.R. § 1910.1003–.1016(g) (1988) states, "A program of medical surveillance shall be established and implemented" and a "(1)(i) . . . physical examination by a physician shall be provided."

5. 29 C.F.R. § 1910.1029 (1988).

6. Ibid., § 1910.1029(j)(iii).

7. 43 *Fed. Reg.* 52,996 (November 14, 1978).

8. Ibid., 52,973–52,974.

9. B. Mintz, *OSHA: History, Law and Policy* (Washington, D.C.: Bureau of National Affairs, 1984), 135.

10. Ibid., 135–136

11. Ibid., 135.

12. Ibid., 136.

13. 29 U.S.C. § 655(b)(7) (1985), emphasis added.

14. Ibid., § 657(c)(1), emphasis added.

15. Ibid., § 657(c)(3), emphasis added.

16. Senate Report 4404, 91st Cong., 2nd Sess. (1970).

17. Subcommittee on Labor of the Senate Committee on Labor and Public Welfare, *Legislative History of the Occupational Safety and Health Act of 1970,* Senate Report 2193, 92nd Cong., 1st Sess. (1971), 368–369.

18. For a comparison of the Nixon administration's substitute bill on this point with the Senate bill, and additional remarks by Senator Dominick, compare Subcommittee on Labor, *Legislative History,* 436–441, with 29 U.S.C. § 655(b)(7) (1985).

19. These previously existing health standards include national consensus standards and established federal standards. According to 29 U.S.C. § 652 (9) (1985), a national consensus standard is a standard or modification that has been "adopted and promulgated by a nationally recognized standards producing organization [e.g., the American National Standards Institute and the National Fire Protection Association]" by a method that resulted in "substantial agreement on its adoption [and]

formulated in a manner that afforded diverse views to be considered." Subsection 10 of the same provision defines an established federal standard as "any operative occupational safety and health standard established by any agency of the United States and presently in effect, or contained in any Act of Congress in force on December 29, 1970."

20. 29 U.S.C. § 655(b)(7) (1985), emphasis added.

21. 29 C.F.R. § 1910.1025 (1988).

22. 29 U.S.C. § 655(a) (1985) addresses the adoption of national consensus standards and established federal standards that are codified in 29 C.F.R. § 1910.1000 (1988). See National Institute for Occupational Safety and Health, *NIOSH/OSHA Guidelines.*

23. National Institute for Occupational Safety and Health, *NIOSH/OSHA Guidelines,* 1, emphasis added.

24. 53 *Fed. Reg.* 37,591 (September 27, 1988).

25. 20 C.F.R. § 1910.20(c)(4) (1988), emphasis added.

26. Ibid., § 1910.20(c)(4)(ii), emphasis added.

27. Ibid., § 1910.20(c)(6)(i)(B). See also Chapter 7 and Table 5.

28. 29 C.F.R. § 1904 (1988). A log is maintained on occupational accidents as well. Because our focus in this book is on occupational health, not safety, only those illnesses and injuries that relate to health standards are discussed.

29. Ibid., § 1904.2(a)(1)and(2), emphasis added.

30. Ibid., §§ 1904.6 and 1904.7(b)(1). Regarding the length of time the employer must retain the log, compare the OSHA Medical Access Rule discussed in Chapter 11.

31. Ibid., § 1904.12(c)(1)–(3). The guidance provided to the record keeper by OSHA in order to determine whether a case is reportable includes this caveat: "Recording an injury or illness under the OSHA system does not necessarily imply that management was at fault, that the worker was at fault, that a violation of an OSHA standard has occurred, or that the injury or illness is compensable under workers' compensation or other systems" [U.S. Department of Labor, Bureau of Labor Statistics, *A Brief Guide to Recordkeeping Requirements for Occupational Injuries and Illnesses,* O.M.B. No. 1220-0029 (Washington, D.C.: U.S. Department of Labor, 1986), 6].

32. Bureau of Labor Statistics, *Log and Summary of Occupational Injuries and Illnesses,* OSHA Form No. 200, Instruction VI (Washington, D.C.: U.S. Government Printing Office, 1986).

33. Ibid. Assuming this exposure is in excess of the OSHA ceiling limit, the question is raised whether all exposed workers are to be tested when overexposed to any toxin and any abnormal results are recorded, or whether testing is to be conducted only on those exposed workers who are covered by the few OSHA health standards that require medical testing after an emergency exposure.

34. Bureau of Labor Statistics, *Brief Guide to Recordkeeping Requirements,* 8.

35. The distinction between first aid and medical treatment depends on both the type of treatment provided and the severity of the injury. Medical treatment includes treatment provided by a physician or other health professional under the standing orders of a physician. First aid treatment is one-time treatment and subsequent observation of minor injuries [Bureau of Labor Statistics, *Log and Summary,* Instruction VI]. Nonminor injuries that are recordable and involve medical and biological testing include those that impair bodily function and those that result in damage to the physical structure of a nonsuperficial nature [Bureau of Labor Statistics, *Brief Guide to Recordkeeping Requirements,* 10], which, arguably, includes chromosomal aberrations.

36. Bureau of Labor Statistics, *Log and Summary,* Instruction VI.

37. Ibid.

38. Bureau of Labor Statistics, *Brief Guide to Recordkeeping Requirements*, 9.

39. Ibid., 10.

40. Ibid., 8.

41. It is important to note that these substances are accompanied by medical surveillance *guidelines* and not regulations. Therefore, industry has no legal responsibility for instituting the medical surveillance provisions suggested in the document, but may implement such medical guidelines voluntarily.

42. R. Severo, "59 Top U.S. Companies Plan Genetic Screening," *New York Times*, June 23, 1982, Sec. 1, A12 (morning edition).

43. See paragraph (g)(1)(i) of each section in 29 C.F.R. § 1910.1003–.1016 (1988). See also note 44 in this chapter.

44. In February 1980, Dr. Eula Bingham, then Assistant Secretary of Labor for OSHA, issued a news release responding to an article in the *New York Times* reporting that there was "a Government regulation mandating genetic screening in industry" [R. Severo, "Federal Mandate for Gene Tests Disturbs U.S. Job Safety Official," *New York Times*, February 6, 1980, Sec. 1, A1 (last of a four-article series entitled "The Genetic Barrier: Job Benefit or Job Bias?")]. Dr. Bingham corrected this statement, which implied that genetic testing was a mandatory component of OSHA medical surveillance provisions, and commented, "There is absolutely no OSHA standard that requires genetic testing of any employee" [U.S. Department of Labor, Office of Information, News 80-107 (February 20, 1980)]. The OSHA Office of Compliance Programming followed this announcement by issuing an interpretive directive to the OSHA enforcement staff in August 1980. The interpretation applied to all OSHA standards that required a medical exam (including a personal history of employees, their family, or both, and occupational background, including genetic and environmental factors) as part of the medical surveillance provisions [OSHA Office of Compliance Programming, *OSHA Medical Surveillance Regulations—Genetic Testing*, Instruction STD 1-23.4 (August 1980)]. The standards affected by this interpretation included 29 C.F.R. § 1910.1003–.1016 (the 13 carcinogen standards), specifically paragraph (g)(1)(i) in each, and 29 C.F.R. § 1990.151 (the OSHA cancer policy—"model standard"). According to Dr. Bingham, such a personal history is "a routine part of standard medical practice. To read into [this] a 'mandate for genetic screening' is a gross distortion" [*New York Times*, March 22, 1980, Sec. 1, A20, (letter to the editor submitted by Dr. Bingham, then Assistant Secretary for Occupational Safety and Health)]. The interpretive directive specifically states, "These provisions do not require genetic testing of any employee" [OSHA Office of Compliance Programming, *OSHA Medical Surveillance Regulations*].

Consistent with its policy on genetic monitoring, OSHA has not authorized the use of genetic screening as part of any OSHA standard to date. There were hints, however, that OSHA temporarily reconsidered its position on genetic testing. On April 21, 1983, the agency published in the *Federal Register* a proposed rule for ethylene oxide. "Screening for chromosome damage" was suggested in the proposal but not required. This suggestion could have been interpreted as recommending the practice of not only genetic screening but also genetic monitoring (periodic testing at the physician's discretion rather than one-time testing), because the proposal stated that "the employer [was] required to make any prescribed tests available *more often than specified* if recommended by the examining physician" [48 *Fed. Reg.* 17,315 (April 21, 1983), emphasis added]. In the final rule, OSHA decided to delete the suggested test for chromosomal damage "because the results of such tests, as applied to an individual rather than a group, cannot be interpreted" [49 *Fed. Reg.* 25,784 (June 22, 1984)].

45. As with the definitions of medical surveillance and biological monitoring, the

terms *medical removal* and *medical removal protection* (MRP) are used inconsistently. Because of the apparent state of confusion of these and the related term *rate retention,* we offer the following definitions, which are consistent with OSHA standards.

According to OSHA,

> MRP is a protective, preventive health mechanism integrated with the medical surveillance provisions [which include biological monitoring] of the final [lead] standard. [It] provides temporary medical removals for workers discovered through medical surveillance to be at risk of sustaining material impairment to health from continued exposure. . . . [It] also provides *temporary economic protection* for those removed. [43 *Fed. Reg.* 52,972 (November 14, 1978), emphasis added.]

Medical removal protection benefits include the maintenance of "the earnings, seniority and other employment rights and benefits of a worker as though the worker had not been removed or otherwise limited" [43 *Fed. Reg.* 52,976 (November 14, 1978)]. Under MRP, earnings include base wage, overtime, shift differentials, incentives, and other compensation regularly earned while working [29 C.F.R. § 1910.1025, App. B, Par. IX (1988)]. This maintenance of economic benefits is sometimes also referred to as rate retention. We view MRP as an entire package that includes temporary removal with accompanying continuation of economic and employment benefits. Rate retention, therefore, is a standard condition in MRP.

Medical removal, to be distinguished from MRP, involves removing the worker from exposure without regard for earnings, seniority, and other employment benefits.

46. OSHA considers MRP to be a protective, preventive health mechanism for the purposes of (1) maximizing meaningful participation in a medical surveillance program under the standard, (2) facilitating the use of temporary medical removals, and (3) appropriately allocating the costs of temporary medical removals [see 43 *Fed. Reg.* 52,972–52,973 (November 14, 1978)].

47. 29 U.S.C. § 651(b) (1985). As stated in the preamble of the final lead standard, "OSHA's adoption of MRP is a direct result of the proven value of this protective mechanism, and by adopting MRP, OSHA is following the Congressional mandate in section 2(b)(4)" [43 *Fed. Reg.* 52,977 (November 14, 1978)].

48. 29 U.S.C. §§ 652(8), 655(b)(5)and(7), and 657(g)(2). Medical removal provisions and economic provisions are provided in the Black Lung Medical Surveillance and Transfer Program, part of the Federal Coal Mine Health and Safety Act of 1969. Although the Supreme Court has not yet spoken directly on the issue, OSHA's authority to include a mandatory MRP provision in a section 6(b) standard has been upheld by the Court of Appeals for the District of Columbia Circuit. The court upheld OSHA's general authority to require MRP programs in appropriate circumstances, and specifically approved the MRP provision in the lead standard [*United Steelworkers of America v. Marshall,* 647 F.2d 1189, 1230 (D.C. Cir.), *cert. denied,* 453 U.S. 913 (1980)]. Pending the denial of certiorari, the Supreme Court stayed all portions of the lead standard *except* the MRP provision. In *American Textile Manufacturers Institute v. Donovan,* 452 U.S. 490 (1981), the Supreme Court invalidated an MRP provision for cotton dust, noting that OSHA had failed to make a record for the connection between such a provision and a "safe and healthful working environment" [*American Textile Manufacturers Institute v. Donovan,* 520]. Nonetheless, the Court noted that justification for an MRP program "very well may" exist [*American Textile Manufacturers Institute v. Donovan,* 539]. In dicta, the Court noted that one such justification may be the usefulness of an MRP provision as an inducement to employees to cooperate with human monitoring programs [*American Textile Manufacturers Institute v. Donovan,* 539]. The D.C. Circuit also cited this rationale in upholding the MRP provisions in the lead

standard [*United Steelworkers of America v. Marshall,* 647 F.2d at 1228].

49. See Hattis, Rothenberg, and Ashford, *OSHA Policy on Medical Surveillance and Removal Provisions* for a discussion of the usefulness of a generic MRP standard.

50. 29 U.S.C. § 669 (a)(5) (1985), emphasis added.

51. Ibid., emphasis added.

52. 15 U.S.C. §§ 2601–2629 (1982). Section 2601(b)(1) states, "It is the policy of the United States that . . . adequate data should be developed with respect to the effect of chemical substances and mixtures on health and the environment and that the development of such data should be the responsibility of those who manufacture and those who process such chemical substances and mixtures."

53. Ibid., §§ 2603, 2604, and 2607 (1982).

54. 53 *Fed. Reg.* 48,830 et seq. (December 2, 1988). Biological monitoring for "reconstructive exposure assessment" is specifically included.

55. 40 C.F.R. § 712 (1988), as amended 42 *Fed. Reg.* 46,281 (November 16, 1988). Chemicals are added to the list from time to time.

56. 15 U.S.C. § 2607(a)(2) (1982).

57. 40 C.F.R. § 712.7 (1988). Further, EPA has defined "known to or reasonably ascertainable by" in the rule in a somewhat restrictive manner. It goes no further than information that "a reasonable person . . . could obtain without unreasonable burden" [40 C.F.R. § 712.3(g) (1988)]. It is not clear that this would support a requirement to perform human monitoring.

58. 40 C.F.R. § 704 (1988), as amended 53 *Fed. Reg.* 51,698 (December 22, 1988).

59. Ibid., § 716, as amended 54 *Fed. Reg.* 8,484 (February 28, 1989). Chemicals are added to the list from time to time.

60. Ibid., § 716.3.

61. 15 U.S.C. § 2607(d)(1)(B)and(C) (1982).

62. 40 C.F.R. § 716.10, 716.20, and 716.25 (1988).

63. 15 U.S.C. § 2607(c) (1982).

64. 40 C.F.R. § 717.3(i) (1988).

65. The rule specifies that the allegations may come from "any person, such as an employee of the firm, individual consumer, a neighbor of the firm's plant, another firm on behalf of its employees or an organization on behalf of its members" [40 C.F.R. § 717.10(c) (1988)]. The language of the act places no restriction on who may report.

66. 15 U.S.C. § 2607(e) (1982).

67. 43 *Fed. Reg.* 11,110–11,112 (March 16, 1978).

68. 48 *Fed. Reg.* 38, 178 (August 22, 1983).

69. The EPA published three volumes of preliminary evaluations of initial section 8(e) notices [*TSCA Chemicals-in-Progress Bulletin* (1983) 4:12].

70. *Cussimanio v. Kansas City S. Ry.,* 5 Kan. App. 2d 379, 383–384, 617 P.2d 107, 112 (1980).

Introduction to Part II

1. R. S. Galen and S. R. Gambino, *Beyond Normality: The Predictive Value and Efficiency of Medical Diagnosis* (New York: John Wiley & Sons, 1975), 115.

2. B. MacMahon and T. F. Pugh, *Epidemiology: Principles and Methods* (Boston: Little, Brown, 1970), 60–61.

3. Ibid.

4. Galen and Gambino, *Beyond Normality,* 115.

5. See McMahon and Pugh, *Epidemiology,* 60–61.

6. Subcommittee on Investigations and Oversight of the Committee on Science and Technology, *Genetic Screening and the Handling of High-Risk Groups in the Workplace,* 97th Cong., 1st Sess. (1981), 126–128 (statement of Dr. Paul Rockey, U.S. Public Health Service, Transcript No. 53).

7. D. K. Parkinson and M. J. Grennan, Jr., "Establishment of Medical Surveillance in Industry: Problems and Procedures," *Journal of Occupational Medicine* (1986) 28(8):774.

8. P. Hughes, "Recent and Potential Advances Applicable to the Protection of Worker's Health—Biological Monitoring I," in *Assessment of Toxic Agents at the Workplace: Roles of Ambient and Biological Monitoring,* A. Berlin, R. E. Yodaiken and B. A. Henman, eds. (Boston: Martinus Nijoff, 1984), 78.

9. See S. Crisp and H. Egan, "Standardisation, Good Laboratory Practice and Quality Control: Exchange of Information and International Cooperation II," in *Assessment of Toxic Agents at the Workplace: Roles of Ambient and Biological Monitoring,* A. Berlin, R. E. Yodaiken, and B. A. Henman, eds. (Boston: Martinus Nijoff, 1984), 555–565; Hulka, "Screening for Cancer," 688.

Chapter 3. Medical Surveillance

1. Parkinson and Grennan, "Problems and Procedures," 772.

2. Ibid.

3. Ibid., 773.

4. Ibid., 776.

5. Ibid. See also discussion on frequency of disease in a tested population in the Introduction to Part II.

6. 43 *Fed. Reg.* 52,965 (November 14, 1978).

7. Halperin, Ratcliffe, Frazier, et al., "Medical Screening in the Workplace," 549.

8. A. McGehee Harvey, J. Bordley III, and J. A. Barondess, *Differential Diagnosis: The Interpretation of Clinical Evidence,* 3rd ed. (Philadelphia: W. B. Saunders, 1979), 11.

9. P. Cutler, *Problem Solving in Clinical Medicine: From Data to Diagnosis,* 2nd ed. (Baltimore: Williams & Wilkins, 1985), 103. See also the general discussion on variability in Chapter 8.

10. Ibid.

11. Ibid., 104.

12. Ibid., 16.

13. E. Brunwald, K. J. Isselbacher, R. G. Petersdorf, J. D. Wilson, J. B. Martin, and A. S. Fauci, eds., *Harrison's Principles of Internal Medicine,* 11th ed. (New York: McGraw-Hill, 1987), A-3.

14. M. J. Coye, J. A. Lowe, and K. T. Maddy, "Biological Monitoring of Agricultural Workers Exposed to Pesticides: I. Cholinesterase Activity Determinations," *Journal of Occupational Medicine* (1986) 28(8):620–621.

15. Cutler, *Problem Solving,* 104.

16. K. M. Bang, S. Tillett, S. K. Hoar, A. Blair, and V. McDougall, "Sensitivity of Fecal Hemoccult Testing and Flexible Sigmoidoscopy for Colorectal Cancer Screening," *Journal of Occupational Medicine* (1986) 28(8):711.

17. Ibid.

18. Ibid., 709.

19. Ibid., 710.

20. 29 C.F.R. § 1910.1025(j)(3)(ii)(D)(1) (1988).

21. J. B. Wallach, *Interpretation of Diagnostic Tests: A Handbook Synopsis of Laboratory Medicine,* 3rd ed. (Boston: Little, Brown, 1978), 40.

22. Cutler, *Problem Solving,* 327.

23. R. S. Fontana, D. R. Sanderson, L. B. Woolner, W. F. Taylor, W. E. Miller, and J. R. Muhm, "Lung Cancer Screening: The Mayo Program," *Journal of Occupational Medicine* (1986) 28(8):746.

24. Ibid. See also Frost, Ball, Levin, et al., "Sputum Cytopathology," 694.

25. Frost, Ball, Levin, et al., "Sputum Cytopathology," 694.

26. Ibid., 693.

27. Ibid., 696 and 699.

28. Ibid., 697.

29. Ibid., 700.

30. Hulka, "Screening for Cancer," 690.

31. K. H. Kilburn, "Medical Screening for Lung Cancer: Perspective and Strategy," *Journal of Occupational Medicine* (1986) 28(8):716.

32. Ibid., 715.

33. See J. K. Frost, W. C. Ball, M. L. Levin, M. S. Tockman, R. R. Baker, D. Carter, J. C. Eggleston, Y. S. Erozan, P. K. Gupta, N. F. Khouri, B. R. Marsh, and F. P. Stitik, "Early Lung Cancer Detection: Results of the Initial (Prevalence) Radiologic and Cytologic Screening in the Johns Hopkins Study," *American Review of Respiratory Diseases* (1984) 130(4):549–554; B. J. Flehinger, M. R. Melamed, M. B. Zaman, R. T. Heelan, W. B. Perchick, and N. Martini, "Early Lung Cancer Detection: Results of the Initial (Prevalence) Radiologic and Cytologic Screening in the Memorial Sloan-Kettering Study," *American Review of Respiratory Diseases* (1984) 130(4):555–560; and R. S. Fontana, D. R. Sanderson, W. F. Taylor, L. B. Woolner, W. E. Miller, J. R. Muhm, and M. A. Uhlenhopp, "Early Lung Cancer Detection: Results of the Initial (Prevalence) Radiologic and Cytologic Screening in the Mayo Clinic Study," *American Review of Respiratory Diseases* (1984) 130(4):561–565.

34. See Flehinger, Melamed, Zaman, et al., "Sloan-Kettering Study," 559; Frost, Ball, Levin, et al., "Johns Hopkins Study," 553.

35. See Fontana, Sanderson, Taylor, et al., "Mayo Clinic Study,"564.

36. Hulka, "Screening for Cancer," 690.

37. Fontana, Sanderson, Taylor, et al., "Mayo Clinic Study," 564.

38. Ibid.

39. See Frost, Ball, Levin, et al., "Johns Hopkins Study," 554; Flehinger, Melamed, Zaman, et al., "Sloan-Kettering Study," 560.

40. See Frost, Ball, Levin, et al., "Sputum Cytopathology," 692.

41. Ibid., 694.

42. Ibid.

43. Ibid.

44. K. Kreiss, "Approaches to Assessing Pulmonary Dysfunction and Susceptibility in Workers," *Journal of Occupational Medicine* (1986) 28(8):664, 668.

45. Ibid., 665.

46. Ibid., 665–667.

47. Ibid., 668.

48. Ibid.

49. Ibid., 664.

50. Ibid., 668.

Chapter 4. Genetic Monitoring

1. See note 40 in Chapter 1.

2. See note 41 in Chapter 1 and accompanying text.

3. *OTA Report,* ix.

4. See A. Bloom, ed., *Guidelines for Studies of Human Populations Exposed to Mutagenic and Reproductive Hazards* (White Plains, N.Y.: March of Dimes Birth Defects Foundation, 1981), 3.

5. There are three main lines of evidence supporting the somatic mutation theory of carcinogenesis. The first is that human cancers generally appear to originate within single cells [A. G. Knudson, "Genetics and Etiology of Human Cancer," *Advances in Human Genetics* (1977) 8:1–66; P. J. Fialkow, "Clonal Origin and Stem Cell Evolution of Human Tumors," in *Genetics of Human Cancer,* J. J. Mulvihill, R. W. Miller, and J. F. Fraumeni, Jr., eds. (New York: Raven, 1977), 439–453]. The second is that some well-characterized deficiencies in DNA repair lead to greatly increased cancer risk [J. E. Cleaver and D. Bootsma, "Xeroderma Pigmentosum: Biochemical and Genetic Characteristics," *Annual Review of Genetics* (1975) 9:19–38]. The most conclusive line of evidence is that the carcinogenic phenotype can be transferred among cells with DNA with "oncogenes" that differ from their normal counterparts in simple ways [J. L. Marx, "Gene Transfer Yields Cancer Clues," *Science* (1982) 215:955; G. M. Cooper, "Cellular Transforming Genes," *Science* (1982) 218:801; J. L. Marx, "The N-myc Oncogene in Neural Tumors," *Science* (1984) 224:1088; T. G. Krontiris, N. A. DiMartino, M. Colb, and D. R. Parkinson, "Unique Allelic Restriction Fragments of the Human Ha-ras Locus in Leukocyte and Tumor DNAs of Cancer Patients," *Nature* (1985) 313:369–374].

6. V. L. Dellarco, K. H. Mavournin, and R. R. Tice, "Aneuploidy and Health Risk Assessment: Current Status and Future Directions," *Environmental Mutagenesis* (1985) 7(3):405–424.

7. R. H. Martin, W. Balkan, K. Burns, and C. C. Lin, "Chromosonal Analysis of Human Spermatozoa: Results from 18 Normal Men," *American Journal of Human Genetics* (1982) 34(3):459–468. The chromosomal analysis of human sperm involves in vitro fertilization of hamster oocytes followed by culturing and chromosomal analysis. It is extremely promising and valuable because previously there has been no way to directly detect genetic damage in germ cells.

8. *OTA Report,* 10.

9. V. F. Garry, J. Hozier, D. Jacos, R. L. Wade, and P. G. Gray, "Ethylene Oxide: Evidence of Human Chromosomal Effects," *Environmental Mutagenesis* (1979) 1(4):375–382; C. Hogstedt, L. Avinger, and A. Gustavsson, "Epidemiologic Support for Ethylene Oxide as a Cancer Causing Agent," *Journal of the American Medical Association* (1986) 255(12):1575–1578.

10. H. Norppa, M. Sorsa, H. Vanio, P. Gröhn, E. Heinonen, L. Holsti, and E. Nordman, "Increased Sister Chromatid Exchange Frequencies in Lymphocytes of Nurses Handling Cytostatic Drugs," *Scandinavian Journal of Work, Environment and Health* (1980) 6(4):299–301; S. Selevan, M. J. Lindbohm, R. Hornung, and K. Hemminki, "A Study of Occupational Exposure to Antineoplastic Drugs and Fetal Loss in Nurses," *New England Journal of Medicine* (1985) 313:1173–1178.

11. See B. J. Dabney, "The Role of Human Genetic Monitoring in the Workplace," *Journal of Occupational Medicine* (1981) 23(9):626, for a discussion of this proposal.

12. See Legator and Ward, "Animal and Human Studies," 182.

13. See note 40 in Chapter 1.

14. S. Wolff, "Chromosome Aberrations, Sister Chromatid Exchanges and the Lesions That Produce Them," in *Sister Chromatid Exchanges,* S. Wolff, ed. (New York: John Wiley & Sons, 1982), 41–57; H. J. Evans, "Molecular Mechanisms in the Induction of Chromosome Aberrations," *Developmental Toxicology and Environmental Science* (1977) 2:57–74.

15. I. Nordenson, G. Beckman, L. Beckman, and S. Nordstrom, "Occupational and Environmental Risk in and around a Smelter in Northern Sweden, II. Chromosomal Aberrations in Workers Exposed to Arsenic," *Hereditas* (1978) 88(1):47–50; V. Srb, E. Kucova and M. Musil, "Testing Genotoxic Activity in the Shops with an Asbestos Risk: II. Cytogenetic Examination of Lymphocytes of Human Peripheral Blood," *Pracovni Lekarstvi* (1985) 37(3):76–80; I. M. Tough and W. M. Court-Brown, "Chromosome Aberrations and Exposure to Ambient Benzene," *Lancet* (1965) 1:684.; L. V. Samosh, "Chromosome Aberrations in Lymphocytes of Persons Working with Polychloropinene under Agriculture Conditions," *Tsitologia Genetika* (1981) 15(1):62–67; F. Sarto, I. Gominato, V. Bianchi, and A. G. Levis, "Increased Incidence of Chromosomal Aberrations and Sister Chromatid Exchanges in Workers Exposed to Chromic Acid (Cr_2O_3) in Electroplating Factories," *Carcinogenesis* (1982) 3(9):1011–1016; M. N. Rabello, W. Becak, W. F. de Almeida, P. Pigati, M. T. Ungaro, T. Murata, and C. A. B. Pereira, "Cytogenetic Study on Individuals Occupationally Exposed to DDT," *Mutation Research* (1975) 28(3):449–454; I. Nordenson, A. Sweins, E. Dahlgren, and L. Beckman, "A Study of Chromosomal Aberrations in Miners Exposed to Diesel Exhausts," *Scandinavian Journal of Work, Environment and Health* (1981) 7(1):14–17; M. Kucerova, V. S. Zhurkov, Z. Polivkova, and J. E. Ivanova, "Mutagenic Affect of Epichlorohydrin, II. Analysis of Chromosomal Aberrations in Lymphocytes of Persons Occupationally Exposed to Epichlorohydrin," *Mutation Research* (1977) 48(3–4):355–360; P. Stolley, K. Soper, S. Galloway, W. Nichols, S. Norman, and S. Wolman, "Sister Chromatid Exchanges in Association with Occupational Exposure to Ethylene Oxide," *Mutation Research* (1984) 129(1):89–102; J. Maki-Paakkanen, M. Sorsa, and H. Vainio, "Chromosome Aberrations and Sister Chromatid Exchanges in Lead-Exposed Workers," *Hereditas* (1981) 94(2):269–275; E. Schmid, M. Bauchinger, and J. Dresp, "Chromosome Analyses of Workers from a Pentachlorophenol Plant," *Mutagens in Our Environment,* M. Sorsa and A. Vainio, eds. (New York: Alan Liss, 1982), 471–477; L. Camurri, S. Codeluppi, C. Pedroni, and L. Scarduelli, "Chromosomal Aberrations and Sister-Chromatid Exchanges in Workers Exposed to Styrene," *Mutation Research* (1983) 119(3):361–369; M. Bauchinger, E. Schmid, J. Dresp, J. Kolin-Gerresheim, R. Hauf, and E. Sulir, "Chromosome Changes in Lymphocytes after Occupational Exposure to Toluene," *Mutation Research* (1982) 102(4):439–445; A. Ducatman, K. Kirschhorn, and I. J. Selikoff, "Vinyl Chloride Exposure and Human Chromosome Aberrations," *Mutation Research* (1975) 31(3):163–168.

16. J. Ashby and C. R. Richardson, "Tabulation and Assessment of 113 Human Surveillance Cytogenetic Studies Conducted between 1965 and 1984," *Mutation Research* (1985) 154(2):111–133.

17. D. C. Lloyd, "An Overview of Radiation Dosimetry by Conventional Cytogenic Methods," in *Biological Dosimetry,* W. G. Eisert and M. L. Mendelsohn, eds. (Berlin: Springer-Verlag, 1984), 3–14.

18. For example, Legator believes that there is in fact a link between chromosomal abnormalities and cancer. The detection of chromosome abnormalities indicates that the chemical is in all likelihood a human carcinogen–mutagen [Legator and Ward, "Animal and Human Studies," 176]. See also Perera, "Potential Usefulness" and "Molecular Cancer Epidemiology"; A. Forni, "Chromosomal Aberrations in Monitoring

Exposure to Mutagens–Carcinogens," in *International Seminar on Methods of Monitoring Human Exposure to Carcinogenic and Mutagenic Agents,* A. Berlin, M. Draper, K. Hemminki, and H. Vainio, eds. (Lyon: IARC Scientific Publications, 1984), 325–337.

19. J. J. Yunis, "The Chromosomal Basis of Human Neoplasia," *Science* (1983) 221:227–235.

20. H. J. Evans, "What Has Been Achieved with Cytogenetic Monitoring?" in *Monitoring of Occupational Genotoxicants,* M. Sorsa and H. Norppa, eds. (New York: Alan Liss, 1986), 3–24.

21. Visualization of SCEs is accomplished by adding the thymidine analogue 5-bromodeoxyuridine (BrdUrd) to cells (such as lymphocytes, after they have been extracted from the blood, placed in culture, and stimulated to divide), which then undergo two mitotic divisions. Chromatids are differentially stained, after two rounds of semiconservative DNA replication and subsequent mitotic arrest, on the basis of the amount of BrdUrd that was incorporated into the chromatids. Thus, unlike CAs, SCEs must be measured in cells that have twice replicated their DNA in tissue culture [P. E. Perry and S. Wolff, "New Giemsa Method for Differential Staining of Sister Chromatids," *Nature* (1974) 261:156–158].

22. S. Wolff, J. Bodycote, and R. B. Painter, "Sister Chromatic Exchanges Induced in Chinese Hamster Cells by UV Irradiation at Different Stages of the Cell Cycle: The Necessity for Cells to Pass through S," *Mutation Research* (1974) 25(1):73–81.

23. See Wolff, "Lesions," 41–57.

24. M. Sorsa, "Monitoring of Sister Chromatid Exchange and Micronuclei as Biological Endpoints," in *International Seminar on Methods of Monitoring Human Exposure to Carcinogenic and Mutagenic Agents,* A. Berlin, M. Draper, K. Hemminki, and H. Vainio, eds. (Lyon: IARC Scientific Publications, 1984), 339–349.

25. T. Watanabe, A. Endo, Y. Kato, S. Shima, T. Watanabe, and M. Ikeda, "Cytogenetics and Cytokinetics of Cultured Lymphocytes from Benzene-Exposed Workers," *International Archives of Occupational and Environmental Health* (1980) 46(1):31–41; F. Funes-Cravioto, C. Zapata-Gayo, D. Kolmodin-Hedman, B. Lambert, J. Lindsten, E. Nordberg, M. Nordenskjold, R. Olin, and A. Sensson, "Chromosome Aberrations and Sister-Chromatid Exchange in Workers in Chemical Laboratories and a Rotoprinting Factory and in Children of Women Laboratory Workers," *Lancet* (1977) 2:322–325; B. Hogstedt, B. Akesson, K. Axell, B. Gullberg, F. Mitelman, R. W. Pero, S. Skerfving, and H. Welinder, "Increased Frequency of Lymphocyte Micronuclei in Workers Producing Reinforced Polyester Resin with Low Exposure to Styrene," *Scandinavian Journal of Work, Environment and Health* (1983) 9(3):241–246; D. Anderson, C. R. Richardson, I. F. H. Purchase, H. J. Evans, and M. L. O'Riordan, "Chromosomal Analyses in Vinyl Chloride Exposed Workers: Comparison of the Standard Technique with the Sister-Chromatid Exchange Technique," *Mutation Research* (1981) 83(1):137–144; R. Tice, B. Lambert, K. Morimoto, and A. Hollaender, "A Review of the International Symposium on Sister Chromatid Exchanges: Twenty-Five Years of Experimental Research," *Environmental Mutagenesis* (1984) 6(5):737–752.

26. S. Wolff, "Problems and Prospects in the Utilization of Cytogenetics to Estimate Exposure at Toxic Chemical Waste Dumps," *Environmental Health Perspectives* (1983) 48:25–27.

27. Bloom, ed., *Mutagenic and Reproductive Hazards,* 5.

28. See Stolley, Soper, Galloway, et al., "Ethylene Oxide," 89–102.

29. See Tice, Lambert, Morimoto, et al., "Twenty-Five Years of Experimental Research," 737–752, emphasis added.

30. H. F. Stich and M. P. Rosin, "Micronuclei in Exfoliated Human Cells as a Tool for

Studies in Cancer Risk and Cancer Intervention," *Cancer Letters* (1984) 22(3):241–253.

31. The National Institute of Environmental Health Sciences views micronuclei as a probable method of choice for measuring exposure in slowly dividing or nondividing cells, such as unstimulated lymphocytes or exfoliated epithelial cells [National Institute of Environmental Health Sciences, "Biochemical and Cellular Markers of Chemical Exposure and Preclinical Indicators of Disease," in *Human Health and the Environment: Some Research Needs*, N.I.H. Publication No. 86-1277 (Washington, D.C.: U.S. Government Printing Office, 1986), 203–267.

32. J. A. Heddle, D. H. Blakey, A. M. V. Duncan, M. T. Goldberg, H. Newmark, M. J. Wargovich, and W. R. Bruce, "Micronuclei and Related Nuclear Anomalies as a Short-Term Assay for Colon Carcinogens," in *Indicators of Genotoxic Exposure*, Banbury Report 13, B. A. Bridges, B. E. Butterworth, and I. B. Weinstein, eds. (New York: Cold Spring Harbor Laboratory, 1982), 367–377.

33. Hogstedt, Akesson, Axell, et al., "Low Exposure to Styrene," 271–276; B. Hogstedt, B. Gullberg, E. Mark-Vendel, F. Mitelman, and S. Skerfving, "Micronuclei and Chromosome Aberrations in Bone Marrow Cells and Lymphocytes of Humans Exposed Mainly to Petroleum Vapors," *Hereditas* (1981) 94(2):179–187.

34. See Ashby and Richardson, "Tabulation and Assessment," 111–133.

35. A. V. Carrano, J. L. Minkler, D. G. Stetka, and D. H. Moore II, "Variation in the Baseline Sister Chromatid Exchange Frequency in Human Lymphocytes," *Environmental Mutagenesis* (1980) 2(3):325–337; Bloom, ed., *Mutagenic and Reproductive Hazards*, 4; *OTA Report*, 70. Fluctuations due to intra- and interindividual variations make cytogenetic monitoring results very difficult to interpret, give them limited utility, and make it particularly difficult to define either a "normal" or "biologically significant" range for testing results.

36. A. V. Carrano and A. P. Natarajan, "Considerations for Population Monitoring Using Cytogenetic Techniques, ICPEMC Pub. No. 14," *Mutation Research* (1988) 204(3):379–406.

37. *OTA Report*, 74.

38. See Forni, "Mutagens–Carcinogens," 325–327.

39. See note 18 in this chapter.

40. Wolff, "Problems and Prospects," 25; S. A. Latt, J. Allen, S. E. Bloom, A. Carrano, E. Falke, D. Kram, E. Schneider, R. Schreck, R. Tice, B. Whitfield, and S. Wolff, "Sister-Chromatid Exchanges: A Report of the *Gene-Tox* Program," *Mutation Research* (1981) 87(1):17–62. A complete, detailed discussion of SCEs is provided.

41. See A. Sharma and G. Talukder, "The Effects of Metals on Chromosomes of Higher Organisms," *Environmental Mutagenesis* (1987) 9(2):191–226.

42. K. Kelsey, D. Christiani, and J. B. Little, "Enhancement of Benzo(a)pyrene Induced Sister Chromatid Exchanges in Lymphocytes from Cigarette Smokers Occupationally Exposed to Asbestos," *Journal of the National Cancer Institute* (1986) 72(2):321–327; W. N. Rom, G. K. Livingston, K. R. Casey, S. D. Wood, M. J. Egger, G. L. Chin, and L. Jerominski, "Sister Chromatid Exchange Frequency in Asbestos Workers," *Journal of the National Cancer Institute* (1983) 70(1):45–48.

43. R. D. Harbison, "Teratogens," in *Casarett and Doull's Toxicology: The Basic Science of Poisons*, 2nd ed., J. Doull, C. Klaassen, and M. Amdur, eds. (New York: Macmillan, 1980), 166.

44. S. A. Latt, R. R. Schrenck, K. S. Loveday, C. P. Dougherty, and C. F. Shuler, "Sister Chromatid Exchanges," *Advances in Human Genetics* (1980) 10:282–283.

45. See Stich and Rosin, "Exfoliated Human Cells," 241–253.

46. Perera, "Molecular Cancer Epidemiology," 887–898.

47 See Forni, "Mutagens–Carcinogens," 325–327.

48. *OTA Report,* 163.

49. Dabney, "Human Genetic Monitoring in the Workplace," 626–631.

50. *OTA Report,* 75.

51. See, for example, S. Green and A. Auletta, "Editorial Introduction to the Reports of 'The Gene-Tox Program,'" *Mutation Research* (1980) 76(2):165–168; M. D. Waters and A. Auletta, "The GENE-TOX Program: Genetic Activity Evaluation," *Journal of Chemical Information and Computer Science* (1981) 21(1):35–38; Bloom, ed., *Mutagenic and Reproductive Hazards,* 123–125.

52. Bloom, ed., *Mutagenic and Reproductive Hazards,* 127.

53. *OTA Report,* 76.

54. For example, the presence of mutagens in the urine may indicate exposure to a mutagenic agent or an agent that forms a mutagenic metabolite, and the excretion of the mutagen may work as a protective process. Conversely, the absence of mutagens in the urine of those exposed may give a false sense of security; the mutagen may not be excreted because it is bound to cellular molecules, possibly posing a hazard [Bloom, ed., *Mutagenic and Reproductive Hazards,* 127].

55. Ibid., 128. According to Dabney, "Further research and comparison with other tests need to be completed before any judgment can be made on the general utility of body fluid analysis" [Dabney, "Human Genetic Monitoring in the Workplace," 627].

56. See Perera, "Significance of DNA and Protein Adducts," 255–269.

57. F. P. Perera and I. B. Weinstein, "Molecular Epidemiology and Carcinogen–DNA Adduct Detection: New Approaches to Studies of Human Cancer Causation," *Journal of Chronic Diseases* (1982) 35(7):581–600; D. B. Hattis, "The Promise of Molecular Epidemiology for Quantitative Risk Assessment," *Risk Analysis* (1986) 6(2):181–193.

58. Perera, "Molecular Cancer Epidemiology," 890.

59. C. J. Calleman, L. Ehrenberg, B. Jansson, S. Osterman-Golkar, D. Segerback, K. Svensson, and C. A. Wachtmeister, "Monitoring and Risk Assessment by Means of Alkyl Groups in Hemoglobin in Persons Occupationally Exposed to Ethylene Oxide," *Journal of Environmental Pathology and Toxicology* (1978) 2(2):427–442; D. H. Phillips, K. Hemminki, A. Alhonen, A. Hewer, and P. L. Grover, "Monitoring Occupational Exposure to Carcinogens: Detection by ^{32}P-Postlabelling of Aromatic DNA Adducts in White Blood Cells from Iron Foundry Workers," *Mutation Research* (1988) 204(3):531–541; F. P. Perera, K. Hemminki, T. L. Young, D. Brenner, G. Kelly, and R. M. Santella, "Detection of Polycyclic Aromatic Hydrocarbon–DNA Adducts in White Blood Cells of Foundry Workers," *Cancer Research* (1988) 48(8):2288–2291; see also Perera, "Molecular Cancer Epidemiology," 890.

60. Perera is optimistic that her line of research will eventually have predictive value for cancer on a group basis [Perera, "Potential Usefulness," 141–145].

61. D. Hattis, L. Erdreich, and T. DiMauro, *Human Variability in Parameters That Are Potentially Related to Susceptibility to Carcinogenesis—I. Preliminary Observations,* CTPID 86-4 (Massachusetts Institute of Technology, Center for Technology, Policy and Industrial Development, 1986); H. L. Gurtoo, C. J. Williams, K. Gottlieb, A. I. Mulhern, L. Caballes, J. B. Vaught, A. J. Marinello, and S. K. Bansal, "Population Distribution of Placental Benzo(a)pyrene Metabolism in Smokers," *International Journal of Cancer* (1983) 31(1):29–37; C. C. Harris, H. Autrup, G. D. Stoner, B. F. Trump, E. Hillman, P. W. Schafer, and A. M. Jeffrey, "Metabolism of Benzo(a)pyrene, N-nitrosodimethylamine, and N-nitrosopyrrolidine and Identification of the Major Carcinogen–DNA Adducts Formed in Cultured Human Esophagus," *Cancer Research* (1979) 39(11):4401–4406.

62. R. J. Albertini, L. M. Sullivan, J. K. Berman, C. J. Greene, J. A. Stewart, J. M. Silveira, and J. P. O'Neill, "Mutagenicity Monitoring in Humans by Autoradiographic Assay for Mutant T Lymphocytes," *Mutation Research* (1988) 204(3):481–492; J. Cole, M. H. L. Green, S. E. James, L. Henderson, and H. Cole, "A Further Assessment of Factors Influencing Measurements of Thioguanine-Resistant Mutant Frequency in Circulating T-Lymphocytes," *Mutation Research* (1988) 204(3):493–507.

63. Albertini, Sullivan, Berman, et al., "Mutagenicity Monitoring," 481–492.

64. R. G. Langlois, W. L. Bigbee, S. Kyoizumi, N. Nakamura, M. A. Bean, M. Akiyama, and R. H. Jensen, "Evidence for Increased Somatic Cell Mutations at the Glycophorin A Locus in Atomic Bomb Survivors," *Science* (1987) 236:445–448.

65. Dabney, "Human Genetic Monitoring in the Workplace," 627.

66. *OTA Report,* 75.

67. Bloom, ed., *Mutagenic and Reproductive Hazards,* 118, emphasis added.

Chapter 5. Biological Monitoring

1. Zielhuis and Henderson, "Definitions," 251.

2. Ibid.

3. Committee on Biological Markers of the National Research Council, "Biological Markers in Environmental Health Research," 4. The "biologically effective dose" is defined by the committee as the amount of material interacting with critical subcellular, cellular, and tissue targets or with an established surrogate. See also D. Hattis, "The Use of Biological Markers in Risk Assessment," *Statistical Science* (1988) 3(3):358–366.

4. Zielhuis and Henderson, "Definitions," 250.

5. Berlin, Yodaiken, and Henman, eds. *Assessment of Toxic Agents,* 201. See also the discussion of interindividual variability in Chapter 8.

6. Lauwerys, *Industrial Chemical Exposure,* 1.

7. Ibid., 4.

8. A. C. Monster, "Biological Monitoring of Chlorinated Hydrocarbon Solvents," *Journal of Occupational Medicine* (1986) 28(8):585.

9. Ibid.

10. Lauwerys, *Industrial Chemical Exposure,* 5.

11. P. Schulte, W. Halperin, M. Herrick, and B. Connally, "The Current Focus of Biological Monitoring," in *Occupational and Environmental Chemical Hazards: Cellular and Biochemical Indices for Monitoring Toxicity,* V. Foa, E. A. Emmett, M. Maroni, and A. Colombi, eds. (Chichester: Ellis Horwood, 1987), 54. Schulte, Halperin, Herrick, et al. reviewed 3,738 articles in nine environmental or occupational health journals for the period 1981–1985. Of those articles, 585 studies (15.6%) involved biological monitoring: 69% of those biological monitoring studies looked to measure the presence of a toxin; 19% of the biological monitoring studies used metabolites as the parameter of interest.

12. Ibid., 59.

13. G. Atherley, "Biomedical Surveillance" (editorial), *American Journal of Industrial Medicine* (1985) 7(4):270.

14. Berlin, Yodaiken, and Henman, eds., *Assessment of Toxic Agents,* XXV.

15. R. Zielhuis, "Biological Monitoring," *Scandinavian Journal of Work, Environment and Health* (1978) 4(1):13.

16. E. Ward, D. Clapp, W. Tolos, and D. Groth, "Efficacy of Urinary Monitoring for

4,4'-Methylenebis (2-Chloroaniline)," *Journal of Occupational Medicine* (1986) 28(8):640.

17. Ibid.

18. Z. Bardodej, "Biological Monitoring of Exposure to Chemical Pollutants, Exposure Tests, Biological Limits and Methods of Analysis: A Review," *Developments in Toxicology and Environmental Science* (1980) 8:335, 338.

19. Atherley, "Biomedical Surveillance," 270.

20. Ibid.

21. P. Hughes, "Recent and Potential Advances Applicable to the Protection of Workers' Health—Biological Monitoring I," in *Assessment of Toxic Agents at the Workplace: Roles of Ambient and Biological Monitoring,* A. Berlin, R. E. Yodaiken, and B. A. Henman, eds. (Boston: Martinus Nijoff, 1984), 79–80.

22. See, for example, Monster, "Chlorinated Hydrocarbon Solvents," 586 [Urinary excretion of metabolites for monochloroethylene (vinyl chloride) is promising, but more research is needed]; C. A. Franklin, N. I. Muir, and R. P. Moody, "The Use of Biological Monitoring in the Estimation of Exposure during the Application of Pesticides," *Toxicology Letters* (1986) 33(1–3):127–136 [More information is needed on species and site variations in dermal absorption before exposure estimates can confidently be corrected to estimate the absorbed dose of pesticides]; M. J. Coye, J. A. Lowe, and K. J. Maddy, "Biological Monitoring of Agricultural Workers Exposed to Pesticides: II. Monitoring of Intact Pesticides and Their Metabolites," *Journal of Occupational Medicine* (1986) 28(8):634 [Few methods have been developed to measure chlorinated hydrocarbons in urine. Research is urgently needed for biological indices associated with pesticide exposures, particularly for neurological, carcinogenic, and reproductive effects]; P. O. Droz and M. P. Guillemin, "Occupational Exposure Monitoring Using Breath Analysis," *Journal of Occupational Health* (1986) 28(8):595 [Knowledge is needed on intraindividual and interindividual variability and toxicokinetics before data relating to breath analysis can be properly interpreted]; Ward, Clapp, Tolos, et al., "Urinary Monitoring," 639 [Information necessary to correlate dose levels of 2-chloroaniline to cancer risk in humans is not available, and there are no good epidemiologic studies from which to derive a dose–response curve]; and Zielhuis and Henderson, "Definitions," 251 [In general, reliable risk estimations for known amounts of carcinogens in the target tissues are still not possible].

23. See Schulte, Halperin, Herrick, et al., "Current Focus," 50–66.

24. Ibid., 56. Schulte, Halperin, Herrick, et al. noted, for example, that most studies on lead address the relationship between lead in the air and the concentration of lead in the blood. There is a continuing need, however, for an analysis of lead's effects on sperm.

25. Hughes, "Recent and Potential Advances," 76.

26. Schulte, Halperin, Herrick, et al., "Current Focus," 56.

27. V. Foa and L. Alessio, "Biological Monitoring," in *Encyclopaedia of Occupational Health and Safety,* Vol. 1, 3rd ed., L. Parmeggiani, tech. ed. (Geneva: International Labour Office, 1983), 274.

28. Coye, Lowe, and Maddy, "Intact Pesticides," 629.

29. Ibid.

30. Lauwerys, *Industrial Chemical Exposure,* 5.

31. L. K. Lowry, "Biological Exposure Index as a Complement to the TLV," *Journal of Occupational Medicine* (1986) 28(8):578.

32. R. S. Waritz, "Biological Indicators of Chemical Dosage and Burden," in *Patty's Industrial Hygiene and Toxicology,* Vol. 3, 3rd ed., L. J. Cralley and L. V. Cralley, eds. (New York: John Wiley & Sons, 1978), 257, 263, 265. See also the discussion on variability in Chapter 8.

33. 43 *Fed. Reg.* 53,001 (November 14, 1978).

34. 43 *Fed. Reg.* 53,001–53,002 (November 14, 1978).

35. 29 C.F.R. § 1910.1025(j)(4)(ii) (1988).

36. M. Ogata, Y. Takatsuka, and K. Tomokuni, "Excretion of Organic Chlorine Compounds in the Urine of Persons Exposed to Vapours of Trichloroethylene and Tetrachloroethylene," *British Journal of Industrial Medicine* (1971) 28(4):390.

37. Monster, "Chlorinated Hydrocarbon Solvents," 588. See also A. C. Monster and R. L. Zielhuis, "Chlorinated Hydrocarbon Solvents," in *Human Biological Monitoring of Industrial Chemical Series,* EUR 8476 EN, L. Alessio, A. Berlin, R. Roi, and M. Boni, eds. (Lumexbourg: Commission of the European Communities, 1983), 45.

38. Lauwerys, *Industrial Chemical Exposure,* 5.

39. R. Baselt, *Biological Monitoring Methods for Industrial Chemicals* (Littleton, Mass.: PSG Publishing, 1980), 3.

40. Ibid.

41. Committee on Biological Markers of the National Research Council, "Biological Markers in Environmental Health Research," 5.

42. Approximately 30% of the biological monitoring studies published during a 5-year period involved the use of urine specimens [Schulte, Halperin, Herrick,. et al., "Current Focus," 58].

43. Waritz, "Chemical Dosage," 294–295. It is also customary laboratory practice in the United States to correct urine samples to a specific gravity of 1.024 for comparability. Specific gravity is defined as "the weight of a substance compared with that of an equal volume of another substance taken as a standard" [*Dorland's Illustrated Medical Dictionary,* 27th ed. (Philadelphia: W. B. Saunders, 1988), 718; H. B. Elkins, L. D. Pagnotto, and H. L. Smith, "Concentration Adjustments in Urinalysis," *American Industrial Hygiene Association Journal* (1974) 35(9):559, 565]. Some investigators have used values of 1.016 and 1.018 [Baselt, *Monitoring Methods,* 2].

44. Franklin, Muir, and Moody, "Estimation of Exposure during the Application of Pesticides," 10.

45. Foa and Alessio, "Biological Monitoring," 274.

46. Ibid.

47. Ward, Clapp, Tolos, et al., "Urinary Monitoring," 639.

48. Ibid.

49. Ibid., 638.

50. Ibid.

51. 29 C.F.R. § 1910.1028 (1988).

52. Ibid., § 1910.1028(i)(4)(i).

53. Ibid., § 1910.1028(i)(4)(ii–iii).

54. National Institute for Occupational Safety and Health, U.S. Department of Health, Education, and Welfare, *Criteria for A Recommended Standard . . . Occupational Exposure to Inorganic Fluorides,* Pub. No. 76-103, (Washington, D.C.: U.S. Government Printing Office, 1975), 3.

55. If the preshift sample has a fluoride level of 4.0 mg/l or the postshift sample has a level of 7.0 mg/l, "steps shall be taken to evaluate *dietary sources,* personal hygiene, basic work practices, and environmental controls" [Ibid., emphasis added].

56. National Institute for Occupational Safety and Health, *NIOSH/OSHA Guidelines,* 19.

57. H. J. Docter and R. L. Zielhuis, "Phenol as a Measure of Benzene Exposure," *Annals of Occupational Hygiene* (1967) 10(4):318, 323.

58. G. J. Roush and M. G. Ott, "A Study of Benzene Exposure Versus Urinary Phenol Levels," *American Industrial Hygiene Association Journal* (1977) 38(2):67, 74.

59. 29 C.F.R. § 1910.1028(c) (1988).

60. W. A. Fishbeck, R. R. Langner, and R. J. Kociba, "Elevated Urinary Phenol Levels Not Related to Benzene Exposure," *American Industrial Hygiene Association Journal* (1975) 36(11):820, 824. The results of the Fishbeck, Langner, and Kociba study must be interpreted and generalized with caution, because only one worker who used over-the-counter medicines was sampled. Increased amounts of urinary phenol are found after taking drugs containing phenolic groups. See Foa and Alessio, "Biological Monitoring," 273.

61. Waritz, "Chemical Dosage," 286–287; H. Ohtsuji and M. Ikeda, "Quantitative Relationship between Atmospheric Phenol Vapour and Phenol in the Urine of Workers in Bakelite Factories," *British Journal of Industrial Medicine* (1972) 29(1):70. Results of the Ohtsuji and Ikeda study are necessarily limited by its small sample size of seven.

62. Berlin, Yodaiken, and Henman, eds., *Assessment of Toxic Agents,* XVII.

63. Up to now, urine has been the specimen of choice in the routine monitoring of styrene, and there is a relatively good correlation between the concentration of styrene in the ambient air and the amount of urinary metabolites [K. Engstrom, "Styrene," in *Biological Monitoring and Surveillance of Workers Exposed to Chemicals,* A. Aitio, V. Riihimaki, and H. Vainio, eds. (Washington, D.C.: Hemisphere, 1984), 101–102.

64. National Institute of Occupational Safety and Health, U.S. Department of Health, Education, and Welfare, *Occupational Diseases: A Guide to Their Recognition,* Pub. No. 77-181, M. M. Key, A. F. Henschel, J. Butler, R. N. Ligo, and I. R. Tabershaw, eds. (Washington, D.C.: U.S. Government Printing Office, 1977), 347. See also L. Alessio, P. Odone, G. Bertelli, and V. Foa, "Cadmium," in *Human Biological Monitoring of Industrial Chemicals Series,* EUR 8476 EN, L. Alessio, A. Berlin, R. Roi, and M. Boni, eds. (Luxembourg: Commission of the European Communities, 1983), 25–44.

65. R. Lauwerys, "Current Use of Ambient and Biological Monitoring: Reference Workplace Hazards. Inorganic Toxic Agents—Cadmium I," in *Assessment of Toxic Agents at the Workplace: Roles of Ambient and Biological Monitoring,* A. Berlin, R. E. Yodaiken, and B. A. Henman, eds. (Boston: Martinus Nijoff, 1984), 114.

66. Berlin, Yodaiken, and Henman, eds., *Assessment of Toxic Agents,* XVII.

67. H. M. Perry and E. F. Perry, "Current Use of Ambient and Biological Monitoring: Reference Workplace Hazards. Inorganic Toxic Agents—Cadmium II," in *Assessment of Toxic Agents at the Workplace: Roles of Ambient and Biological Monitoring,* A. Berlin, R. E. Yodaiken, and B. A. Henman, eds. (Boston: Martinus Nijoff, 1984), 137.

68. Ward, Clapp, Tolos, et al., "Urinary Monitoring," 640.

69. Ibid., 641.

70. P. Bloch and I. M. Shapiro, "An X-Ray Fluorescence Technique to Measure In Situ the Heavy Metal Burdens of Persons Exposed to These Elements in the Workplace," *Journal of Occupational Medicine* (1986) 28(8):610.

71. Ibid.

72. T. Pierce, "Immunoassay as a Screening Tool for Industrial Toxicants," *Journal of Occupational Medicine* (1986) 28(8):589–591.

73. R. D. Soule, "Industrial Hygiene Sampling and Analysis," in *Patty's Industrial Hygiene and Toxicology,* Vol. 1, 3rd ed., G. Clayton and F. Clayton, eds. (New York: John Wiley & Sons, 1978), 707, 765.

74. Schulte, Halperin, Herrick, et al., "Current Focus," 58.

75. Soule, "Sampling Analysis," 765–767; see also Monster and Zielhuis, "Chlorinated Hydrocarbon Solvents," 45.

76. Droz and Guillemin, "Breath Analysis," 593.

77. Soule, "Sampling Analysis," 765.

78. Waritz, "Chemical Dosage," 299.

79. Ibid., 295.

80. Ibid.

81. Monster, "Chlorinated Hydrocarbon Solvents," 585.

82. Ibid., 586.

83. Ibid.

84. Ibid.

85. Ibid.

86. Droz and Guillemin, "Breath Analysis," 593 (Factors 1–4).

87. Waritz, "Chemical Dosage," 295–296 (Factors 5–12).

88. Baselt, *Monitoring Methods,* 2.

89. R. D. Stewart, C. L. Hake, and J. E. Peterson, "Use of Breath Analysis to Monitor Trichloroethylene Exposures," *Archives of Environmental Health* (1974) 29(1):6.

90. Waritz, "Chemical Dosage," 302.

91. Gompertz, "Solvents," 408.

92. Waritz, "Chemical Dosage," 296.

93. Ibid., 297.

94. Droz and Guillemin, "Breath Analysis," 601.

95. Ibid.

96. Ibid.

97. Monster, "Chlorinated Hydrocarbon Solvents," 601.

98. L. B. Lave and E. Callison, "Multidisciplinary Approach to Prevention and Health Protection by Monitoring: Role of Individual Disciplines. The Economist: Economic Analysis of Prevention and Protection I," in *Assessment of Toxic Agents at the Workplace: Roles of Ambient and Biological Monitoring,* A. Berlin, R. E. Yodaiken and B. A. Henman, eds. (Boston: Martinus Nijoff, 1984), 358.

99. Schulte, Halperin, Herrick, et al., "Current Focus," 57.

100. Baselt, *Monitoring Methods,* 2.

101. R. M. Griffin, "Biological Monitoring for Heavy Metals: Practical Concerns," *Journal of Occupational Medicine* (1986) 28(8):615–616.

102. Like the lead standard, the benzene standard contains a provision for medical removal protection (MRP) based on certain monitoring results [29 C.F.R. § 1910.1028(i)(8)and(9) (1988)]. The two standards differ, however, as to the trigger for medical removal. A worker exposed to lead can receive MRP benefits on the basis of *biological monitoring results* (i.e., *uptake),* whereas a worker exposed to benzene triggers MRP benefits on the basis of *medical surveillance results* (i.e., a nonspecific *effect* showing that exposure has occurred). In the case of benzene, MRP is instituted when medical surveillance test results indicate abnormal findings in serum blood counts.

103. 29 C.F.R. § 1910.1025(j)(2)(i) (1988).

104. See National Institute for Occupational Safety and Health, *NIOSH/OSHA Guidelines.*

105. R. R. Lauwerys, "Cadmium," in *Biological Monitoring and Surveillance of Workers Exposed to Chemicals,* A. Aitio, V. Riihimaki, and H. Vainio, eds. (Washington, D.C.: Hemisphere, 1984), 44.

106. Perry and Perry, "Cadmium II," 137.

107. Berlin, Yodaiken, and Henman, eds. *Assessment of Toxic Agents,* XVI. See also Alessio, Berlin, Roi, et al., eds., *Human Biological Monitoring of Industrial Chemicals Series.*

108. Committee on Science, Engineering and Public Policy, *Report of the Research Briefing Panel on Human Health Effects of Hazardous Chemical Exposures* (Washington, D.C.: National Academy of Sciences, 1983), 7. The committee believes that the "development and validation of techniques of high sensitivity and specificity [see the Introduction to Part II] . . . would be powerful tools for direct evaluation of human

exposure to environmental chemicals and its impact on human health." The committee cited the lack of available information to measure or verify actual human exposure as one rationale for the recommended research. According to the committee, "Specific *biologic markers* of human exposure (as an adjunct to *environmental monitoring*) . . . offer a great opportunity to improve the ability to assess the effects of chemicals" (emphasis added).

109. Committee on Science, Engineering and Public Policy, *Report on Human Health Effects of Hazardous Chemical Exposures,* 7.

110. See Committee on Biological Markers of the National Research Council, "Biological Markers in Environmental Health Research," 3–9.

111. Ibid.

112. See Berlin, Yodaiken, and Henman, eds., *Assessment of Toxic Agents.*

113. The series is entitled "Industrial Health and Safety" and includes the following monographs: *Human Biological Monitoring of Industrial Chemicals,* EUR 8476 EN, L. Alessio, A. Berlin, R. Roi, and M. Boni, eds. (Luxembourg: Commission of the European Communities, 1983) (includes R. Lauwerys, "Benzene"; L. Alessio, P. Odone, G. Bertelli, and V. Foa, "Cadmium"; A. C. Monster and R. L. Zielhuis, "Chlorinated Hydrocarbon Solvents"; L. Alessio and V. Foa, "Lead"; H. Valentin and R. Schiele, "Manganese"; H. Valentin and K. H. Schaller, "Titanium"; and R. Lauwerys, "Toluene"); *Biological Indicators for the Assessment of Human Exposure to Industrial Chemicals,* EUR 10704 EN, L. Alessio, A. Berlin, M. Boni, and R. Roi, eds. (Luxembourg: Commission of the European Communities, 1986) (includes L. Alessio, A. Dell'Orto, and A. Forni, "Alkyl Lead Compounds"; R. Lauwerys, "Diethylformamide"; V. Foa and G. Bertelli, "Mercury"; and M. Maroni, "Organophosphorus Pesticides"); and *Biological Indicators for the Assessment of Human Exposure to Industrial Chemicals,* EUR 11135 EN, L. Alessio, A. Berlin, M. Boni, and R. Roi, eds. (Luxembourg: Commission of the European Communities, 1987) (includes N. J. van Sittert and W. F. Tordoir, "Aldrin and Dieldrin"; V. Foa, A. Colombi, M. Maroni, and M. Buratti, "Arsenic"; A. Ferioli, R. Roi, and L. Alessio, "Cobalt"; N. J. van Sittert and W. F. Tordoir, "Endrin"; and K. H. Schaller and G. Triebig, "Vanadium").

114. H. B. Elkins, L. D. Pagnatto, and H. L. Smith, "Excretory and Biologic Threshold Limits," *American Industrial Hygiene Association Journal* (1967) 28(4):305, 307.

115. Zielhuis, "Biological Monitoring," 13.

116. American Conference of Governmental Industrial Hygienists, *TLVs: Threshold Limit Values and Biological Exposure Indices for 1987–1988* (Cincinnati, Ohio: American Conference of Governmental Industrial Hygienists, 1987), 53.

117. L. K. Lowry, "Biological Limit Values," in *Methods for Biological Monitoring,* T. J. Kneip and J. V. Crable, eds. (Washington, D.C.: American Public Health Association, 1988), 109, citing R. R. Lauwerys and A. Bernard, "Biological Monitoring of Toxic Chemicals: Present Position and Perspectives of Development" (in French), *Scandinavian Journal of Work, Environment and Health* (1985) 11(3):155–164.

118. American Conference of Governmental Industrial Hygienists, *Threshold Limit Values,* 53. For an excellent review of the history of the development of BEIs, see Lowry, "Biological Limit Values." See also the official ACGIH version of the history in V. Thomas, L. K. Lowry, J. Rosenberg, A. Thomas, and M. Zavon, "Development of Biological Exposure Indices (BEIs)," *Annals of the American Conference on Industrial Hygiene* (1985) 12:19–25.

119. Elkins, Pagnatto, and Smith, "Excretory and Biologic Threshold Limits," 306–307.

120. American Conference of Governmental Industrial Hygienists, *Threshold Limit Values,* 53.

121. Ibid., 54.

122. Zielhuis, "Biological Monitoring," 13.

123. Otherwise, they reported, "it would be highly detrimental to workers' faith in occupational health and safety programs designed to protect worker health, if [they] varied with place of employment or when crossing national boundaries" [Berlin, Yodaiken, and Henman, eds., *Assessment of Toxic Agents,* XVIII–XIX]. "Where the threshold limit values in air are well documented and the absorption balance, biotransformation pathways and elimination kinetics of [the] pollutant and its metabolic products are known, then the biological limit can be derived from the experimentally established relationship between pollutant concentrations in air and in biological material" [Bardodej, "Biological Monitoring of Exposure to Chemical Pollutants," 338].

124. Zielhuis, "Biological Monitoring," 5–6. The seven European governments that provided positive responses were Denmark, France, the Federal Republic of Germany, Great Britain, Ireland, Italy, and the Netherlands.

125. See note 113 in this chapter.

126. World Health Organization, *Recommended Health-Based Limits in Occupational Exposure to Heavy Metals,* Technical Report Series 647 (Geneva: World Health Organization, 1980), World Health Organization, *Recommended Health-Based Limits in Occupational Exposure to Selected Organic Solvents,* Technical Report Series 664 (Geneva: World Health Organization, 1981), and World Health Organization, *Recommended Health-Based Limits in Occupational Exposure to Pesticides,* Technical Report Series 677 (Geneva: World Health Organization, 1982), all cited in Lowry, "Biological Limit Values."

127. American Conference of Governmental Industrial Hygienists, *Threshold Limit Values,* 58–60.

128. See Lowry, "Biological Limit Values," 113–114, for a listing and explanation of the BEIs.

129. Ibid., 113.

130. American Conference of Governmental Industrial Hygienists, *Threshold Limit Values,* 61–63.

131. E. J. Calabrese, *Methodological Approaches to Deriving Environmental and Occupational Health Standards* (New York: John Wiley & Sons, 1978), 243.

132. Ibid.

133. Waritz, "Chemical Dosage," 287.

134. Ibid.

135. Lauwerys, *Industrial Chemical Exposure,* 4.

136. Elkins, Pagnatto, and Smith, "Excretory and Biological Threshold Limits," 307–309.

137. American Conference of Governmental Industrial Hygienists, *Threshold Limit Values,* 54. See also the discussion on variability in Chapter 8.

138. Ibid., 54.

139. Ibid., 53.

140. 29 C.F.R. § 1910.1025(k)(1)(i)(D) (1988).

141. National Institute for Occupational Safety and Health, *Criteria for Fluorides,* 3.

142. Lowry, "Biological Limit Values," 118.

Chapter 6. Genetic and Other Sensitivity Screening

1. See J. Himmelstein and G. Pransky, eds., "Worker Fitness and Risk Evaluations," *Occupational Medicine: State of the Art Reviews* (1988) 3(2).

2. P. A. Schulte and W. E. Halperin, "Genetic Screening and Monitoring for Workers," in *Recent Advances In Occupational Health*, J. M. Harrington, ed. (London: Churchill Livingstone, 1987), 135–154.

3. *OTA Report*, 89–105.

4. See Schulte and Halperin, "Genetic Screening and Monitoring Workers," 135–154.

5. E. Beutler, *Hemolytic Anemias in Disorders of Red Cell Metabolism* (New York: Plenum, 1978), as cited in Schulte and Halperin, "Genetic Screening and Monitoring Workers," 135.

6. See P. Larizza, P. Brunetti, and F. Grignani, "Anemie Emoltiche Enzimopeniche," *Hematologica* (1960) 45(1):1–90, 129–212; L. S. Djerassi and L. Vitany, "Haemolytic Episode in G6PD Deficient Workers Exposed to TNT," *British Journal of Industrial Medicine* (1975) 32(1):54–58, as cited in Schulte and Halperin, "Genetic Screening and Monitoring Workers," 135–154.

7. Sickle cell anemia is caused by the substitution of a single amino acid in the oxygen-carrying protein hemoglobin. Both copies of the hemoglobin gene must be affected in order to produce clinical disease. A much larger number of people who carry one copy of the altered gene ("sickle cell trait") are not obviously affected. Whether these people are at any increased risk when oxygen concentrations are low (as in unpressurized air planes) is not clear. According to Schulte and Halperin, "The fear of sickling in unpressurized aeroplanes led the U.S. Air Force to screen pilot candidates. Recently the policy of exclusion of such candidates was abandoned for lack of evidence that applicants with sickle cell trait demonstrated evidence of sickling when exposed to controlled hypoxic conditions in air chambers during training (Personal communication, Dr. Hugh Smith, U.S. Air Force)" [Schulte and Halperin, "Genetic Screen-Monitoring Workers," 137]. Thalassemia is a genetically determined reduction in the rate of synthesis of hemoglobin.

8. W. Kalow, H. W. Goedde, and D. P. Agarwal, eds., *Ethnic Differences in Reactions to Drugs and Xenobiotics* (New York: Liss, 1986).

9. A. Janoff, "Biochemical Links between Cigarette Smoking and Pulmonary Emphysema," *Journal of Applied Physiology: Respiratory, Environmental and Exercise Physiology* (1983) 55(2):285–294.

10. Ibid. See also T. D. Tetley, S. F. Smith, G. H. Burton, A. J. Winning, N. T. Cook, and A. Guz, "Effects of Cigarette Smoking and Drugs on Respiratory Tract Proteases and Antiproteases," *European Journal of Respiratory Disease* (1987) 153 Suppl. 71:93–102.

11. Schulte and Halperin, "Genetic Screening and Monitoring Workers," 138.

12. Ibid.

13. M. Lappe, "Ethical Issues in Genetic Screening for Susceptibility to Chronic Lung Disease," *Journal of Occupational Medicine* (1988) 30(6):493–501.

14. Ibid.

15. D. B. Clayson and R. C. Garner, "Carcinogenic Aromatic Amines and Related Compounds," in *Chemical Carcinogens*, ACS Monograph 173, C. E. Searle, ed. (Washington, D.C.: American Chemical Society, 1976), 366–461; R. D. Combes and R. B. Haveland-Smith, "A Review of the Genotoxicity of Food, Drug and Cosmetic Colours and Other Azo, Triphenylmethane and Xanthene Dyes," *Mutation Research* (1982) 98(2):101–248.

16. G. M. Lower, Jr., "Molecular Epidemiology of Arylamine-Induced Urinary Bladder Cancer: Some Theoretical Considerations," *Federation Proceedings* (1983) 42(14):3094–3097.

17. G. M. Lower, Jr., and G. T. Bryan, "Enzymic Deacetylation of Carcinogenic Arylacetamides by Tissue Microsomes of the Dog and Other Species," *Journal of Toxicology and Environmental Health* (1976) 1(3):421–432.

18. R. A. Cartwright, R. W. Glashan, H. J. Rogers, R. A. Ahmad, D. B. Hall, E. Higgins, and M. A. Kahn, "The Role of N-acytyltransferase Phenotypes in Bladder Carcinogenesis: A Pharmaco-Genetic Epidemiological Approach to Bladder Cancer," *Lancet* (1982) 2:842–846.

19. D. Hattis, S. Bird, and L. Erdreich, *Human Variability in Susceptibility to Anticholinesterase Agents*, CTPID 87-4 (Massachusetts Institute of Technology, Center for Technology, Policy and Industrial Development, 1987).

20. H. Eiberg and J. Mohr, "Genetics of Paroxonase," *Annals of Human Genetics* (1981) 45(4):323–330.

21. *OTA Report,* 98–99.

22. *Genetic Screening of Workers, Hearings before the Subcommittee on Investigations and Oversight of the House Committee on Science and Technology,* 97th Cong., 2nd Sess., 21 (1982) (statement of Geoffrey M. Karney, Project Director, Biological Applications Program, OTA, discussing traits for G6PD, sickle cell, and alpha and beta thalassemias).

23. This statement is supported by the fact that the DuPont Corporation, which had conducted G6PD testing at its Deepwater, N.J. plant until mid-1980, discontinued giving the tests to both black workers and white workers of Mediterranean ancestry. The company determined that the test did not have good predictive capability and was not helpful "in [its] attempt to place people in jobs where there would be no unusual health risk" [G. Hess, "Is Genetic Screening a Chemical Industry Ploy?" *Chemical Marketing Reporter* (1981) 220(24):42; see also R. Severo, "Screening of Blacks by Dupont Sharpens Debate on Gene Tests," *New York Times,* February 4, 1980, Sec. 1, 1].

24. R. Severo, "59 Top U.S. Companies Plan Genetic Screening," A12; *OTA Report,* 9. Proponents of genetic screening believe that employees with particular genetic traits may be more "susceptible" to certain illnesses than employees without the trait in industries where both groups are exposed to the same substance. For example, as discussed earlier in the text, a deficiency of the red blood cell component G6PD is believed by some to cause affected individuals to become anemic when exposed to certain substances, such as oxidizing agents [see note 11 in Chap. 8]. By preventing workers with certain genetic traits from performing jobs in which exposure to particular substances may occur, advocates believe that such screening serves a function in reducing the incidence of occupational disease and acts as a means of protecting employees, particularly the "hypersusceptibles," from workplace hazards, because it is not economically feasible to provide an environment that is risk free for all workers.

The critics' arguments against the use of genetic screening include scientific uncertainty, its use as a tool for discriminatory practices, and its use as an alternative to cleaning up the workplace. As far as the scientific community is concerned, "there appears to be very little support at present for biochemical genetic screening. . . . The tests are regarded as arbitrary and, although valid, not very predictive" [Holden, "Looking at Genes in the Workplace," 336. See note 23 in this chapter and accompanying text].

25. The information supplied to OTA that related to industry plans to conduct genetic screening was disclosed at a hearing before Congress on June 22, 1982 [*Genetic Screening of Workers, Hearings before the Subcommittee on Investigations and Over-*

sight of the House Committee on Science and Technology, 7–38]. Previously, on October 14 and 15, 1981, this same subcommittee conducted hearings on screening research regarding human variation and the application of that research to occupational settings [*Genetic Screening and the Handling of High-Risk Groups in the Workplace, Hearings Before the Subcommittee on Investigations and Oversight of the House Committee on Science and Technology,* 97th Cong., 1st Sess. (1981)].

26. E. J. Calabrese, *Predicting Susceptibility to Occupational Diseases via Genetic Markers* (report submitted to the Office of Technology Assessment, March 1982), 2.

27. E. J. Calabrese, *Nutrition and Environment Health: The Influence of Nutritional Status on Pollutant Toxicity and Carcinogenicity,* Vol. 1 (New York: John Wiley & Sons, 1980), 379.

28. Calabrese, "Predicting Susceptibility," 79; see also notes 6 and 7 in this chapter.

29. Regarding the general application of genetic screening, OTA concluded, "Biological foundations of the concept of genetic screening to identify predispositions to occupational diseases are sound" [*OTA Report,* 99]. OTA further stated, however, that the predictive value of the test is low in the general population so epidemiological studies using genetic screening tests could be "seriously flawed" [*OTA Report,* 11]. On the basis of these conclusions, OTA indicated that more research on tests identifying traits in the general population and more epidemiological studies need to be conducted. This recommendation is consistent with OTA's conclusion on the overall state of the art that, presently, "none of the current genetic tests evaluated by OTA meets established scientific criteria for routine use in an occupational setting" [*OTA Report,* 9].

30. See discussion in N. A. Ashford, *Crisis in the Workplace: Occupational Disease and Injury* (Cambridge, Mass.: MIT Press, 1976), 118. See also H. E. Stokinger and L. D. Scheel, "Hypersusceptibility and Genetic Problems in Occupational Medicine—A Consensus Report," *Journal of Occupational Medicine* (1973) 15(7):564, 572–573.

31. Ashford, *Crisis in the Workplace,* 118.

32. "A Test for Cancer-Prone People," *Chemical Week,* August 18, 1982, 23. The recipient of the contract stated that the test could be used in industries where "workers are exposed to radiation or carcinogenic chemicals, allowing employers to *screen out workers with a high susceptibility to cancer*—perhaps 2–3% of the population" ["A Test for Cancer-Prone People," 23, emphasis added]. The test could be as "simple as 'detecting VD'" and would be marketed as a "simple kit" ["A Test for Cancer-Prone People," 23]. It is possible that industries that use carcinogens in the workplace would use the screening technique.

33. *OTA Report,* 9, 89, 100.

34. Regarding screening as a general practice for sickle cell trait, Marc Rothstein, professor of law at West Virginia University, stated, "Because certain biochemical genetic tests have a marked impact along racial lines, any differentiation based on such a test would establish a prima facie case of discrimination" [Severo, "59 Top U.S. Companies Plan Genetic Screening," A12; see also Rothstein, "Employee Selection Based on Susceptibility," 1389–1391].

35. See note 4 in Chapter 8 and accompanying text.

36. P. DeSilva, "TLVs to Protect 'Nearly All Workers,'" *Applied Industrial Hygiene* (1986) 1(1):49–53.

37. H. Nordman, "Atopy and Work," *Scandinavian Journal of Work, Environment and Health* (1984) 10(6):481–485.

38. M. R. Cullen, "The Worker with Multiple Chemical Sensitivities: An Overview," *Occupational Medicine: State of the Art Reviews* (1987) 2(4):655–661.

39. I. R. Bell, *Clinical Ecology* (Bolinas, Calif.: Common Knowledge Press, 1982); N. A. Ashford and C. S. Miller, *Chemical Exposures: Low Levels and High Stakes* (New York: Van Nostrand, Reinhold, 1990).

40. I. I. Lutsky, J. H. Kalbfleisch, and J. N. Fink, "Occupational Allergy to Laboratory Animals: Employer Practices," *Journal of Occupational Medicine* (1983) 25(5):372–376.

41. D. M. Roberts, "The Incidence of Atopy in a Working Population," *Journal of the Society of Occupational Medicine* (1987) 37(4):106–110.

42. C. A. Newill, R. Evans III, and M. J. Khoury, "Preemployment Screening for Allergy to Laboratory Animals: Epidemiologic Evaluation of Its Potential Usefulness," *Journal of Occupational Medicine* (1986) 28(11):1158–1164.

43. T. H. Lam and K. P. Yau, "Medical Examination and Surveillance of Compressed Air Workers in Hong Kong," *Journal of the Society of Occupational Medicine* (1988) 38(1–2):9–12.

44. Note, however, the recent marked interest in non-IgE–mediated chemical sensitivity, N. A. Ashford and C. S. Miller, *Chemical Exposures,* cited in note 39 of this chapter.

Chapter 7. The Frequency and Timing of Examinations

1. National Institute for Occupational Safety and Health, *NIOSH/OSHA Guidelines.*

2. Ogata, Takatsuka, and Tomokuni, "Excretion of Organic Chlorine Compounds," 390.

3. H. Frumkin and B. S. Levy, "Carcinogens," in *Occupational Health: Recognizing and Preventing Work-Related Disease,* B. S. Levy and D. H. Wegman, eds. (Boston: Little, Brown, 1983), 164.

4. 51 *Fed. Reg.* 22,702 (June 20, 1986).

5. 29 C.F.R. § 1910.1001(l)(3)(ii), Table 2 (1988).

6. J. Ratcliffe, *The Usefulness of Medical Screening Examinations in the Prevention of Occupational Diseases* (1982), 2 (unpublished paper prepared for the National Institute for Occupational Safety and Health).

7. U.S. Department of Labor, *An Interim Report for Congress on Occupational Diseases* (Washington, D.C.: U.S. Government Printing Office, 1980), 120.

8. Occupational Medical Practice Committee of the American Occupational Medical Association, "Scope of Occupational Health Programs and Occupational Medical Practice, Committee Report," *Journal of Occupational Medicine* (1979) 21(7):497, 498–499.

9. National Institute for Occupational Safety and Health, Centers for Disease Control, *SENSOR: Sentinel Event Notification System for Occupational Risks—A Proposal* (Atlanta, Ga.: U.S. Department of Health and Human Services, 1987), 4.

10. 29 CFR §§ 1910.1001(g)(3)(iv), .1017(k)(5), .1043(f)(2)(iv), .1025(k), .1047(i)-(4)(B), and .1028 (1988). The guidance in the asbestos standard addresses options given an employee if an examining physician determines, on the basis of medical examination results, that the employee will not be able to perform his or her job in a normal manner if wearing a respirator. The action taken may or may not be based on abnormal human monitoring results alone. For example, § 1910.1001(l)(7)(i)(B) states that action may be taken on the basis of the physician's "recommended limitations on the employee."

11. 29 C.F.R. § 1910.1025(j)(2)(ii) (1988).

12. Ibid., § 1910.1028(i)(5)and(4)(iii).

13. Ibid., § 1910.1047(i)(4)(B) and (i)(ii)(2)(F) for ethylene oxide; .1043(h)(5)(i)(C) (emphasis added) for cotton dust; and .1001(l)(7)(i)(B) for asbestos (1988). It is interesting to note that the proposed ethylene oxide rule was even more specific, requiring the

physician to include "any recommended limitations on the employee's *exposure*" [48 *Fed. Reg.* 17,312 (April 21, 1983, emphasis added].

14. 29 C.F.R. § 1910.1001(g)(3)(iv) for asbestos; .1017(k)(5) for vinyl chloride; .1043(f)(2)(iv) for cotton dust; .1025(k) for lead; and .1028(i)(8)and(9) for benzene (1988). The vinyl chloride standard [.1017(k)(5)] requires removal if the physician determines that an employee's health would be "materially impaired" by continued exposure. The asbestos [.1001(g)(3)] and cotton dust [.1043(f)(2)(iv)] standards, however, provide the opportunity for removal on the basis of the employee's inability to wear a respirator.

The distinction between medical removal and MRP is an important one [see discussion in text accompanying notes 45–49 in Chapter 2]. Note that MRP for the lead [.1025(k)] and benzene [.1028(i)(8)and(9)] standards is specifically provided for and is triggered by results from medical surveillance for benzene or biological monitoring tests for lead.

15. 43 *Fed. Reg.* 52,972 (November 14, 1978), emphasis added. Note that the medical surveillance provisions of the lead standard include biological monitoring.

16. Ibid., 52,976.

17. 29 C.F.R. § 1910.1025, App. B, Sec. IX (1988).

18. Ibid., § 1910.20(c)(6)(i).

19. Ibid.

20. *Genetic Screening and the Handling of High-Risk Groups in the Workplace,* 12 (statement of Everett Dixon, M.D.).

21. R. H. Goldman, "General Occupational Health History and Examination," *Journal of Occupational Medicine* (1986) 28(10):968. See also Cutler, *Problem Solving,* 327–328.

22. Goldman, "Occupational Health History," 968 (Items 1–4).

23. B. S. Levy and D. H. Wegman, "Recognizing Occupational Disease," in *Occupational Health: Recognizing and Preventing Work-Related Diseases,* B. S. Levy and D. H. Wegman, eds. (Boston: Little, Brown, 1983), 30–34 (Items 5–7).

24. Ibid., 29.

25. Parkinson and Grennan, "Problems and Procedures," 773.

26. J. M. Ratcliffe, W. E. Halperin, T. M. Frazier, D. S. Sundin, L. Delaney, and R. W. Hornung, "The Prevalence of Screening in Industry: Report from the National Institute for Occupational Safety and Health National Occupational Hazard Survey," *Journal of Occupational Medicine* (1986) 28(10):907, citing preliminary data from the NIOSH National Occupational Exposure Survey 1981–1983.

27. *Genetic Screening and the Handling of High-Risk Groups in the Workplace,* 12. See also Goldman, "Occupational Health History," 967.

28. Goldman, "Occupational Health History," 967.

29. Occupational Medical Practice Committee, "Scope of Occupational Health," 498.

30. Goldman, "Occupational Health History," 968.

31. Ibid.

32. Ibid.

33. J. Spencer Felton, "The Industrial Medical Department," in *Environmental and Occupational Medicine,* W. N. Rom, ed. (Boston: Little, Brown, 1983), 945.

34. R. Severo, "Screening of Blacks by Dupont," *New York Times,* 1.

35. C. F. Reinhardt, "Chemical Hypersusceptibility," *Journal of Occupational Medicine* (1978), 20(5):320.

36. M. Lavine, "Industrial Screening Programs for Workers," *Environment* (1982) 24(5):26–28.

37. Severo, "Screening of Blacks by Dupont," *New York Times,* 13.

38. Ibid.

39. The OSHA standards all require periodic examinations, usually annually or semiannually. The *NIOSH/OSHA Occupational Health Guidelines* recommends periodic testing, with the timing determined on a chemical-by-chemical basis.

40. This is a 23% increase over the percentage of workers periodically tested during 1972–1974 [Ratcliffe, Halperin, Frazier, et al., "The Prevalence of Screening in Industry," 907].

41. Goldman, "Occupational Health History," 971.

42. Schilling, "Role of Medical Examination in Protecting Worker Health," 555. There are three categories of threshold limit values as described by the American Conference of Governmental Industrial Hygienists:

1. TLV time-weighted average (TWA)—the TWA concentration for a normal 8-hour workday and a 40-hour workweek, to which nearly all workers may be repeatedly exposed, day after day, without adverse effect.
2. TLV short-term exposure limit (STEL)—the concentration to which workers can be exposed continuously for a short period of time without suffering certain effects, such as irritation or chronic or irreversible tissue damage. The STEL is recommended only where toxic effects have been reported from high short-term exposures in either humans or animals.
3. TLV ceiling—the concentration that should not be exceeded during any part of the working exposure. [American Conference of Governmental Industrial Hygienists, *Threshold Limit Values,* 4]

43. Goldman, "Occupational Health History," 972.

44. See Occupational Medical Practice Committee, "Scope of Occupational Health," 498.

45. *Genetic Screening and the Handling of High-Risk Groups in the Workplace,* 12.

46. National Institute for Occupational Safety and Health, *Occupational Diseases,* 437.

47. 40 *Fed. Reg.* 54,520–54,521 (November 24, 1975).

48. R. P. Beliles, "OSHA Occupational Health Standards and the Sensitive Worker," *Annals of the American Conference of Governmental Industrial Hygienists* (1982) 3:71, 75.

49. 40 *Fed. Reg.* 54,530 (November 24, 1975).

50. National Institute for Occupational Safety and Health, *Occupational Diseases,* 437.

51. Canadian Task Force on the Periodic Health Examination, "The Periodic Health Examination," *Canadian Medical Association Journal* (1979) 121(9):1193.

52. Goldman, "Occupational Health History," 973.

53. BioTechnology, Inc., *OSHA Medical Surveillance Requirements and NIOSH Recommendations for Employees Exposed to Toxic Substances and Other Work Hazards* (Falls Church, Va.: Biotechnology, Inc., 1980) (report prepared under contract no. NASW 3510 for the National Aeronautics and Space Administration Occupational Health Office).

54. 29 C.F.R. § 1910.1025(k)(1)(iii)(A)(1)–(3) (1988).

55. Ibid., § 1910.1025(k)(1)(iii)(A)(4).

56. Occupational Medical Practice Committee, "Scope of Occupational Health," 498.

57. Subpart 3 of the medical surveillance provisions of the vinyl chloride standard states, "Each employee exposed to an emergency shall be afforded appropriate medical

surveillance" [29 C.F.R. § 1910.1017(k)(3) (1988)]. An "emergency" in the vinyl chloride standard is defined as "any occurrence such as, but not limited to, equipment failure, or operation of a relief device which is likely to, or does, result in massive release of vinyl chloride" [29 C.F.R. § 1910.1017(b)(5)].

Subpart 6 of the medical surveillance provisions of the 1, 2-dibromo-3-chloropropane (DBCP) standard states, "If the employee is exposed to DBCP in an emergency situation, the employer shall provide the employee with a sperm count test as soon as practicable. . . . The employer shall provide these same tests three months later" [29 C.F.R. § 1910.1044(m)(6)]. The "emergency situation" provision also contains specific requirements for those workers who have had a vasectomy or are unable to produce a sperm specimen. An "emergency" in the DBCP standard is defined as "any occurrence such as, but not limited to, equipment failure, rupture of containers, or failure of control equipment which may, or does, result in an unexpected release of DBCP" [29 C.F.R. § 1910.1044(b)].

The ethylene oxide standard states that the employer is to make medical examinations and consultations available to employees as deemed medically appropriate for exposures during an emergency [29 C.F.R. § 1910.1047(i)(ii)(2)(i)(D)]. The definition of "emergency" in this standard [29 C.F.R. § 1910.1047(b)] parallels that of the DBCP standard.

The benzene standard states that in addition to the medical surveillance provisions required under the standard, the employer is to provide urinary phenol testing if an employee is exposed to benzene in an emergency situation [29 C.F.R. § 1910.1028(i)(4)]. If the results of the urinary phenol test are equal to or greater than 75 mg of phenol per liter of urine, then additional blood testing is required for 3 months following the emergency exposure. The definition of "emergency" in this standard [29 C.F.R. § 1910.1028(b)] parallels that of DBCP.

The formaldehyde standard states that the employer is to make medical examinations available as soon as possible to all employees who have been exposed to formaldehyde in an emergency situation [29 C.F.R. § 1910.1048(l)(5)]. The examination includes a medical and work history; any evidence of eye, nose, or throat irritation; and any other examinations deemed appropriate by the examining physician. The definition of "emergency" in this standard [29 C.F.R. § 1910.1048(b)] is "any occurrence, such as but not limited to equipment failure, rupture of containers, or failure of central equipment that results in an uncontrolled release of a significant amount of formaldehyde."

58. Occupational Medical Practice Committee, "Scope of Occupational Health," 498.

59. 29 C.F.R. §§ 1910.1018(n)(3)(iii), 1910.1029(j)(3)(iv), and 1910.1045(n)(3)(ii) (1988).

60. Ibid., § 1910.1001(l)(4).

61. Ibid, § 1910.1047(i)(ii)(2)(i)(C).

62. National Institute of Occupational Safety and Health, *Criteria for a Recommended Standard . . . Occupational Exposure During the Manufacture and Formulation of Pesticides,* Pub. No. 78-174 (Washington, D. C.: U. S. Government Printing Office, 1978), 10.

63. National Institute of Occupational Safety and Health, *Criteria for a Recommended Standard . . . Occupational Exposures in Coal Gasification Plants,* Pub. No. 78-191, (Washington, D.C.: U.S. Government Printing Office, 1978), 8.

64. Note, however, that workers who sue their employers (usually as manufacturers) for harm caused by exposure to toxic substances ask for, and sometimes get, remuneration for medical monitoring. Note also that proposed legislation in 1987, the High Risk Occupational Disease Notification and Prevention Act of 1987, S79, required notice to retired workers of results of studies conducted by government.

Chapter 8. Human Variability and High-Risk Groups

1. Human monitoring can yield information important for standard setting to ensure that permissible exposure limits protect all workers, or it can be used to encourage the removal of workers from a harmful environment. Section 20(a)(5) of the Occupational Safety and Health Act authorizes the Secretary of Health and Human Services to "establish . . . programs of medical examinations and tests as may be necessary for determining the incidence of occupational illnesses and the *susceptibility* of employees to such illnesses" [29 U.S.C. § 669(a)(5) (1985), emphasis added]. See also R. Friedman, *Sensitive Populations and Environmental Standards.*

2. D. Hattis, L. Erdreich, and M. Ballew, "Human Variability in Susceptibility to Toxic Chemicals: A Preliminary Analysis of Pharmacokinetic Data from Normal Volunteers," *Risk Analysis* (1987) 7(4):415–426.

3. See note 37 in Chapter 9.

4. Calabrese defines high-risk workers as "those individuals who experience toxic and/or carcinogenic effects significantly before the general population as a result of one or more biologic factors, including developmental influences [e.g., pregnancy and aging], genetic factors, nutritional inadequacies, disease conditions, and behavioral or life style characteristics" [Calabrese, *Methodological Approaches,* 47]. Others caution of the need to distinguish between *hypersusceptibility* and a narrower and more specialized use of the term *hypersensitivity* in the field of immunology. According to them, the term *hypersusceptibility* indicates

> an unusually high response to some dose of a substance. This term requires careful interpretation, however, because it is used in several different ways. It may refer to a genetic predisposition to a toxic effect; it may indicate a statistically defined deviation from the mean [average]; it may reflect an observer's subjective impression; or it may be used, incorrectly, as a synonym for hypersensitivity [which] is one form of hypersusceptibility, characterized by an acquired, immunologically mediated sensitization to a substance. [H. Frumkin, "Toxins and Their Effects," in *Occupational Health: Recognizing and Preventing Work-Related Disease,* B. S. Levy and D. H. Wegman, eds. (Boston: Little, Brown, 1983), 134–135.]

Using this definition, workers at high risk may be considered to be hypersusceptible but not necessarily hypersensitive. To avoid confusion, we refrain from using the term *hypersusceptible,* in favor of using the term *high-risk.*

5. For a discussion of hypersensitivity, see Frumkin, "Toxins and Their Effects," 134–135. See also note 4 in this chapter.

6. E. Zuskin and F. Valic, "Change in the Respiratory Response to Coarse Cotton Dust over a Ten-Year Period," *American Review of Respiratory Diseases* (1975) 112(3):417–421.

7. In a recent study of healthy nonsmokers, the annual rate of decline in FEV_1 inferred from cross-sectional studies was observed to be about 21 ml per year in women and 22 to 28 ml per year in men. Longitudinal studies of the same people suggested somewhat smaller age-related declines overall, but with a considerable dependence on age (older people suffering a greater loss in FEV_1 per year) [B. Burrows, M. D. Lebowitz, A. E. Camilli, and R. J. Knudson, "Longitudinal Changes in Forced Expiratory Volume in One Second in Adults. Methodologic Considerations and Findings in Healthy Nonsmokers," *American Review of Respiratory Diseases* (1986) 133(6):974–980]. Other recent data including both smokers and nonsmokers suggest age-related declines of 28 to 35 ml per year in FEV_1 prior to age 50 in women and men, respectively, and an additional long-term decline of 4.4 to 7.4 ml per lifetime pack-years of cigarette smoking (again, in women and men, respectively) [D. W. Dockery, F. E. Speizer, B. G.

Ferris Jr., J. H. Ware, T. A. Louis, and A. Spiro III, "Cumulative and Reversible Effects of Lifetime Smoking on Simple Tests of Lung Function in Adults," *American Review of Respiratory Diseases* (1988) 137(2):286–292]. Other similar data also find 11- to 35-ml per year declines in various subgroups of a random population sample in the Netherlands [R. Rijcken, J. P. Schouten, S. T. Weiss, F. E. Speizer, and R. van der Lende, "The Association of Airways Responsiveness to Respiratory Symptom Prevalence and to Pulmonary Function in a Random Population Sample," *Bulletin of Europeen de Physiopathologie Respiratoire* (1987) 23(4):391–394].

8. Pharmacokinetic parameters in normal healthy adults are analyzed in D. Hattis, L. Erdreich, and M. Ballew, *Human Variability in Susceptibility to Toxic Chemicals—I. A Preliminary Analysis of Pharmacokinetic Data from Normal Volunteers*, CTPID 86-1 (Massachusetts Institute of Technology, Center for Technology, Policy and Industrial Development, 1986); see also a shorter but more accessible version of the same report: Hattis, Erdreich, and Ballew, "Human Variability in Susceptibility." Parameters related to carcinogenic response are assessed in D. Hattis, L. Erdreich, and T. DiMauro, *Human Variability in Parameters That Are Potentially Related to Susceptibility to Carcinogenesis—I. Preliminary Observations*, CTPID 86-4 (Massachusetts Institute of Technology, Center for Technology, Policy and Industrial Development, 1986). Finally, parameters related to exposure, pharmacokinetics, and response to anticholinesterase agents (mostly organophosphate and carbamate insecticides) are assessed in D. Hattis, S. Bird, and L. Erdreich, *Human Variability in Susceptibility to Anticholinesterase Agents*, CTPID 87-4 (Massachusetts Institute of Technology, Center for Technology, Policy and Industrial Development, 1987).

9. J. Doull, "Factors Influencing Toxicology" in *Casarett and Doull's Toxicology: The Basic Science of Poisons,* 2nd ed., J. Doull, C. Klaassen, and M. Amdur, eds. (New York: Macmillan, 1980), 70. In the review of studies related to solvent exposure, one researcher accounts for variability in uptake by noting, "Experimental studies have shown that uptake of any solvent depends on pulmonary ventilation . . . [the solvent's] solubility in blood and tissues and the relative size of adipose tissue [deposits]" [Gompertz, "Solvents," 407].

10. Calabrese, *Methodological Approaches,* 243.

11. See G. Omenn, "Predictive Identification of Hypersusceptible Individuals," *Journal of Occupational Medicine* (1982) 24(5):369–374. For example, individuals with glucose-6-phosphate dehydrogenase deficiency are considered to be more susceptible (i.e., sensitive) to chemicals such as aniline, methylene blue, and naphthalene and to certain drugs like aspirin [J. J. Jandl, "Hematologic Disorders," in *Occupational Health: Recognizing and Preventing Work-Related Disease,* B. S. Levy and D. H. Wegman, eds. (Boston: Little, Brown, 1983), 359]. When such individuals are exposed to these agents, their red blood cells have a decreased capacity to carry oxygen. Also, serum $alpha_1$-antitrypsin deficiency has been linked to emphysema [G. Omenn and A. Motulsky, "'Eco-genetics': Genetic Variation and Susceptibility to Environmental Agents," in *Genetic Issues in Public Health and Medicine,* B. Cohen, A. Lilienfeld, and P. Huang, eds. (Springfield, Ill.: C. C. Thomas, 1978), 89]. See also E. Calabrese, *Pollutants and High-Risk Groups: The Biological Basis of Increased Human Susceptibility to Environmental and Occupational Pollutants* (New York: John Wiley & Sons, 1978), 55.

12. A. Motulsky, "Ecogenetics: Genetic Variation in Susceptibility to Environmental Agents," in *Human Genetics, Proceedings of the Fifth International Congress of Human Genetics,* S. Armendares and R. Lisker, eds. (Amsterdam: Excerpta Medica, 1977), 375–385.

13. Doull, "Factors Influencing Toxicology," 76. One researcher found that genetic factors are predominantly responsible for large interindividual variations in drug

disposition in twin (fraternal and identical) studies. See E. S. Vesell, "Genetic and Environmental Factors Affecting Drug Disposition in Man," *Clinical Pharmacology and Therapeutics* (1977) 22(5, Part 2):659–679.

14. Vesell, "Genetic and Environmental Factors," 659.

15. Gompertz, "Solvents," 409.

16. Calabrese, *Methodological Approaches,* 54.

17. Stokinger and Scheel, "Hypersusceptibility and Genetic Problems in Occupational Medicine," 572–573.

18. See *OTA Report.*

19. Calabrese, *Methodological Approaches,* 54.

20. Section 20(a)(7) of the Occupational Safety and Health Act directs the Secretary of Health and Human Services to "conduct and publish industry-wide studies of the effect of chronic or low level exposure to industrial materials, processes, and stresses on the potential for illness, disease, or loss of functional capacity in *aging adults*" [29 U.S.C. § 669(a)(7) (1985), emphasis added]. The very young and the very old have enhanced susceptibility to respiratory infections [Calabrese, *Methodological Approaches,* 47]. Infants and children show differential absorption of pollutants such as barium, lead, and radium as a function of age [Calabrese, *Pollutants and High-Risk Groups,* 187; see also A. Redolfi, E. Borgogelli, and E. Lodola, "Blood Level of Cimetidine in Relations to Age," *European Journal of Clinical Pharmacology* (1979) 15(4):257–261].

21. Doull, "Factors Influencing Toxicology," 78.

22. Vesell, "Genetic and Environmental Factors," 644.

23. Waritz, "Chemical Dosage," 280.

24. R. W. Tuthill and E. J. Calabrese, "Age as a Function in the Development of Sodium-Related Hypertension," *Environmental Health Perspectives* (1979) 29:35–43.

25. Calabrese, *Pollutants and High-Risk Groups,* 187.

26. Ibid., R. Doll, "An Epidemiological Perspective of the Biology of Cancer," *Cancer Research* (1978) 38(11, Part 1):3573. To date, "one can state that susceptibility to chemical carcinogenesis is associated with relative dysfunctions of the immune system and that age is important because it affects immune function" [M. Bennett, "Effect of Age on Immune Function in Terms of Chemically Induced Cancers," *Environmental Health Perspectives* (1979) 29:17, 20.

27. Waritz, "Chemical Dosage," 298.

28. Doull, "Factors Influencing Toxicology," 77. Animal studies show differences in toxicity based on sex. For example, aspirin and nicotine have been found to be more toxic to female than male rats, and epinephrine and digoxin have been found to be more toxic to male rats and dogs, respectively. There is also inconclusive evidence that benzene is more toxic to women than to men [B. D. Goldstein, "Current Use of Ambient and Biological Monitoring: Reference Workplace Hazards. Organic Toxic Agents—Benzene I," in *Assessment of Toxic Agents at the Workplace: Roles of Ambient and Biological Monitoring,* A. Berlin, R. E. Yodaiken, and B. A. Henman, eds. (Boston: Martinus Nijoff, 1984), 162.

29. Vesell, "Genetic and Environmental Factors," 659.

30. Calabrese, *Methodological Approaches,* 55.

31. Doull, "Factors Influencing Toxicology," 76.

32. Waritz, "Chemical Dosage," 267.

33. Nitrous oxide—D. B. Menzel, "Nutritional Needs in Environmental Intoxication: Vitamin E and Air Pollution, an Example," *Environmental Health Perspectives* (1979) 29:105, 111; lead—Calabrese, *Nutrition and Environmental Health,* 575.

34. Calabrese, *Nutrition and Environmental Health,* 574.

35. Calabrese, *Methodological Approaches,* 51.

36. Ibid., 52.

37. Calabrese, *Nutrition and Environmental Health,* 221.

38. Ibid., 215.

39. Ibid.

40. Calabrese, *Pollutants and High-Risk Groups,* 193.

41. H. Frumkin and B. S. Levy, "Carcinogens," in *Occupational Health: Recognizing and Preventing Work-Related Disease,* B. S. Levy and D. H. Wegman, eds. (Boston: Little, Brown, 1983), 157.

42. Ibid.

43. J. H. Holbrook, "Cigarette Smoking," in *Environmental and Occupational Medicine,* W. N. Rom, ed. (Boston: Little, Brown, 1983), 793. The cilia, which are instrumental in clearing the lungs, may become paralyzed by cigarette smoke [Holbrook, "Cigarette Smoking," 787–788].

44. Ibid., 792–793.

45. Doull, "Factors Influencing Toxicology," 82.

46. E. M. Swartz, "Litigating Household Caustics Injuries," *Case & Comment* (1983) 88(2):3.

47. Sensitization is an immunologically mediated response that requires prior exposure or preconditioning. For example, the use of certain soaps or cosmetics may sensitize an employee to workplace agents that contact the skin, causing or exacerbating a dermatitis.

48. M. Steinberg, "ACGIH TLV's and the Sensitive Worker," *Annals of the American Conference of Governmental Industrial Hygienists* (1982) 3:77.

49. R. Goble, D. Hattis, M. Ballew, and D. Thurston, *Implementation of the Occupational Lead Exposure Standard,* CPA-83-11 (Massachusetts Institute of Technology, Center for Policy Alternatives, 1983).

50. Doull, "Factors Influencing Toxicology," 78.

51. Ibid., 79.

52. Gompertz, "Solvents," 407.

53. S. Lagakos, B. Wessen, and M. Zelen, *Synopsis: The Woburn Health Study, An Analysis of Reproductive and Childhood Disorders and Their Relation to Environmental Contamination* (January 1984) (a study prepared by the Harvard School of Public Health).

54. Holbrook, "Cigarette Smoking," 794.

55. J. Spengler and S. Colome, "The In's and Out's of Air Pollution," *Technology Review* (1982) 85(6):32–38.

56. For example, "nitrogen dioxide within homes increases respiratory infections and decreases lung function in children" [Spengler and Colome, "The In's and Out's," 37].

57. Doull, "Factors Influencing Toxicology," 79.

58. Vesell, "Genetic and Environmental Factors," 660.

59. Calabrese, *Pollutants and High-Risk Groups,* 192.

60. Ibid., 193.

Chapter 9. Consequences to the Worker of Medical Removal

1. 43 *Fed. Reg.* 52,976 (November 14, 1978).

2. Ibid., 52,976, emphasis added. Note that the medical surveillance provisions of the lead standard include biological monitoring.

3. 29 C.F.R. § 1910.1025, App. B, Sec. IX (1988).

4. Ibid., § 1910.1017(k)(5).

5. Ibid., § 1910.1025(k).

6. Ibid., § 1910.1025(j)(2)(iv).

7. 43 *Fed. Reg.* 52,975 (November 14, 1978).

8. 29 C.F.R. § 1910.1025(k)(2)(ii) (1988).

9. Ibid.

10. The agency stated, "Convincing evidence presented during the lead proceedings established that many workers will either refuse or resist meaningful participation in medical surveillance unless economic protection is provided. . . . MRP was included in the final standard as a means of maximizing meaningful participation in medical surveillance provided to lead-exposed workers" [43 *Fed. Reg.* 52,973 (November 14, 1978)].

11. 29 C.F.R. § 1910.1028(i)(8)(i) (1988).

12. Ibid., § 1910.1028(i)(8)(ii).

13. Ibid., § 1910.1028(i)(8)(iii).

14. Ibid., § 1910.1028(i)(8)(iv)and(v).

15. Ibid., § 1910.1028(i)(8)(iv).

16. Ibid.

17. Ibid., § 1910.1028(i)(8)(v).

18. Ibid., § 1910.1028(i)(9)(i).

19. Ibid., § 1910.1028(i)(9)(ii). OSHA believes these rights and benefits are essential "so that the employees are not prevented from participation in the medical examinations by fear of immediately losing their jobs upon the findings of abnormal hematological findings" [52 *Fed. Reg.* 34,559 (September 11, 1987)].

20. 29 C.F.R. § 1910.1028(i)(9) (iii) (1988). OSHA included this provision in order to avoid a "windfall" from MRP to employees who receive compensation or salary during the removal period [52 *Fed. Reg.* 34,559 (September 11, 1987)]. The lead standard contains a parallel provision [29 C.F.R. § 1910.1025(k)(2)(v) (1988)].

21. 29 C.F.R. § 1910.1001(g)(3)(iv) (1988).

22. 43 *Fed. Reg.* 52,976 (November 14, 1978).

23. 29 C.F.R. § 1910.1025(k)(1)(ii)(C) (1988).

24. Ibid., § 1910.1025(k)(2)(vi)(C).

25. 52 *Fed. Reg.* 34,557 (September 11, 1988).

26. Ethylene oxide–29 C.F.R. § 1910.1047(i)(4)(B) (1988). It is interesting to note that the final rule is less specific than the proposed rule, which required the physician to include "any recommended limitations on the employee's *exposure*" [48 *Fed. Reg.* 17,312 (April 21, 1983), emphasis added]. Cotton dust—29 C.F.R. § 1910.1043(h)(5)(i)(C). Asbestos–29 C.F.R. § 1910.1001(l)(7)(i)(B).

27. 29 C.F.R. § 1910.1043(h)(5)(i)(C) (1988), emphasis added.

28. Ibid., § 1910.1001(g)(3)(iv), emphasis added.

29. Ibid., § 1910.1043(f)(2)(iv), emphasis added.

30. 43 *Fed. Reg.* 52,972 (November 14, 1978).

31. 52 *Fed. Reg.* 34,556 (September 11, 1987).

32. 29 C.F.R. §§ 1910.1001(l)(2)(ii) and 1910.1043(h)(2)(i)–(iv) (1988).

33. See 53 *Fed. Reg.* 37,595 and 37,591 (September 27, 1988).

34. The Threshold Limit Values Committee of the American Conference of Governmental Industrial Hygienists advocates removing the sensitive worker, rather than attempting to set a safe level for exposure [See Steinberg, "ACGIH TLV's and the Sensitive Worker"]. For a discussion of OSHA's position on protecting sensitive workers, see Beliles, "OSHA Occupational Health Standards and the Sensitive Worker."

35. Coal miners used to take caged canaries into the mines with them and use them as "monitors." When methane concentrations reached a certain level, the canaries would die, signaling the workers that methane was climbing to unhealthy levels.

36. "Banning Workers to Protect Them," *New York Times,* March 22, 1980, 20.

37. A dose–response relationship reflects the fraction of an exposed population adversely affected as a function of dose. It is, of course, dependent on what is defined as an "effect" or "response." In contrast, a dose–effect relationship is expressed as the fractionary loss of a vital function or organ either for a population average or for an individual (e.g., fraction of liver destroyed as a function of alcohol intake). For a complete discussion of dose–response relationships, see C. D. Klaassen and J. Doull, "Evaluation of Safety: Toxicologic Evaluation," in *Casarett and Doull's Toxicology: The Basic Science of Poisons,* 2nd ed., J. Doull, C. Klaassen, and M. Amdur, eds. (New York: Macmillan, 1980), 17–22.

38. D. Hattis, N. A. Ashford, E. Zolt, J. I. Katz, and G. R. Heaton, *Economic/Social Impact of Occupational Noise Exposure Regulations,* EPA 550/9-77-532 (September 1976) (testimony presented at the OSHA Hearings on the Economic Impact of Occupational Noise Exposure).

39. D. Hattis, "From Presence to Health Impact: Models for Relating Presence to Exposure to Damage," in *Analyzing the Benefits of Health, Safety, and Environmental Regulations,* CPA-82-16 (September 1982) (report submitted to the Environmental Protection Agency by the Massachusetts Institute of Technology, Center for Policy Alternatives).

40. National Institute for Occupational Safety and Health, *Criteria for a Recommended Standard—Hydrogen Cyanide and Cyanide Salts* (Washington, D.C.: Department of Health, Education and Welfare, 1977), 77–108.

41. N. A. Ashford, R. D. Gecht, D. Hattis, and J. I. Katz, *The Effects of OSHA Medical Removal Protection on Labor Costs of Selected Lead Industries,* CPA-77-11 (December 1, 1977) (report submitted to U.S. Department of Labor by the Massachusetts Institute of Technology, Center for Policy Alternatives).

42. See note 5 in Chapter 4.

43. This is one possible interpretation of the results in the National Center for Toxicological Research's "EDO1" study of low-dose carcinogenesis with acetylaminofluorine. In that experiment, whereas liver cancer incidence showed a simple linear no-threshold relationship to dose, the bladder cancer dose–response relationship in the same animals was more suggestive of a process dependent in part on the proliferative response of cells lining the bladder to a direct toxic action of the chemical. Formaldehyde appears to pose a similar case [see D. Hattis, C. Mitchell, J. McCleary-Jones, N. Gorelick, and N. A. Ashford, *Control of Occupational Exposures to Formaldehyde: A Case Study of Methodology for Assessing the Health and Economic Impacts of OSHA Health Standards,* CPA-81-77 (April 1981) (report submitted to the U.S. Department of Labor by the Massachusetts Institute of Technology, Center for Policy Alternatives).

44. See note 137 in Chapter 11.

45. Exposure of males to mutagens is thought to generally pose greater risks than exposure of females because male reproductive cells divide continuously throughout life, whereas female reproductive cells do not usually divide after birth until fertilization. In epidemiological studies of mutation rates for point mutations, mutagenic risks generally show a positive correlation with paternal age (after correction for maternal age) but no similar correlation with maternal age (after correction for paternal age).

46. For prevention of mutagenesis in males, reduction of the body burden of the substance of concern to the desired protective level should occur some months before

conception to allow sensitive postspermatagonial stages in the development of sperm to be purged from the system. Return to the previous job can be permitted safely after conception is confirmed, provided that precautions are taken against the transport of the hazardous substance home on the worker's clothing. For prevention of teratogenesis in pregnant women, reduction of the substance of concern to the desired protective level should occur prior to conception. Return to the previous job should wait in most cases until the completion of the pregnancy or the completion of lactation, depending on an assessment as to whether the substance poses hazards to the child by way of the mother's milk.

47. E. P. Shoub, personal communication, 1979.

Chapter 10. Limitations on the Authority to Require Human Monitoring

1. Although the Occupational Safety and Health Act grants the authority to OSHA and NIOSH to require the employer to perform certain actions, it grants OSHA and NIOSH no similar authority with regard to employees.

2. Section 20(a)(5) of the OSHAct provides, "Nothing in this or any other provision of this Act shall be deemed to authorize or require medical examination, immunization, or treatment for those who object thereto on religious grounds, except where such is necessary for the protection of the health or safety of others" [29 U.S.C. § 669(a)(5) (1985)]. The balance struck here—protection of the rights of the individual except if they are outweighed by the health needs of others—may well be appropriate in attempts to reconcile the purpose of the act with rights of individual privacy.

3. Monitoring done by a private employer, if mandated or expressly authorized by a government agency, is considered "state action" for constitutional purposes. Accordingly, constitutional protections apply. See *Secretary of Transportation v. Railway Labor Executives Association,* 13 O.S.H. Cas. (BNA) 2065, 2068 (U.S. Supreme Court, 1989) (discussed later in this section) and the cases cited therein.

4. See, for example, *Secretary of Transportation v. Railway Labor Executives Association* and *Terry v. Ohio,* 392 U.S. 1 (1968).

5. See, for example, *Roe v. Wade,* 410 U.S. 113 (1973) and *Griswold v. Connecticut,* 381 U.S. 479 (1965). As this book goes to press, the continued viability of *Roe v. Wade* is open to question. The existence of a general Constitutional right to personal privacy as expressed in *Griswold v. Connecticut,* however, appears secure.

6. See, for example, *Secretary of Transportation v. Railway Labor Executives Association* and the cases cited therein.

7. See, for example, *Griswold v. Connecticut.*

8. In *Secretary of Transportation v. Railway Labor Executives Association,* the Supreme Court implied that regulations requiring blood, breath, and urine testing could not be considered "reasonably related to the Government objectives that support them" and that they thus would not be permissible under the Fourth Amendment, if the tests were not accurate. In that case, the Court presumed that "the Agency's conclusion that the tests at issue . . . are accurate in the overwhelming majority of the cases" was correct.

9. In the criminal law context, the Court recognized the connection between the Fourth Amendment right of privacy and the Fifth Amendment prohibition against compulsory self-incrimination as early as *Boyd v. United States,* 116 U.S. 616, 630 (1885):

The principles laid down [in the British common law prescriptions against unreasonable searches and seizures] affect the very essence of constitutional liberty and security. . . . they apply to all invasions on the part of the government and its employees of the sanctity of a man's home and the privacies of life. . . . Any forcible and compulsory extortion of a man's own testimony or of his private papers to be used as evidence to convict him of crime or to forfeit his goods, is within [those principles]. In this regard, the Fourth and Fifth Amendments run almost into each other.

10. The Court has been sensitive to the effect of government regulations on employment status in other contexts. A contractual right to continued employment may, under certain circumstances, be "property" within the meaning of the Fifth and Fourteenth Amendments' due process clauses. This has been held to be the case with tenured teachers. See *Perry v. Sindermann,* 408 U.S. 593 (1972); *Connell v. Higginbotham,* 403 U.S. 207 (1971); *Slochower v. Board of Education of New York City,* 350 U.S. 551 (1956); and *Wieman v. Updegraff,* 344 U.S. 183 (1952).

11. *Secretary of Transportation v. Railway Labor Executives Association,* 13 O.S.H. Cas. (BNA) 2065.

12. Ibid., 2071–2076.

13. See Hattis, Rothenberg, and Ashford, *Some Considerations for the Design of OSHA Policy,* cited in Chapter 1, note 30.

14. The Court of Appeals for the District of Columbia Circuit has upheld OSHA's authority to require a mandatory MRP program as part of the lead standard. *United Steelworkers of America v. Marshall,* 647 F. 2d 1189, 1228–1238 (D.C. Cir. 1980), *cert. denied,* 453 U.S. 913 (1980). The court specifically noted that the MRP program would facilitate worker cooperation with biological monitoring. See also note 10 in Chapter 9.

15. 29 U.S.C. § 651(b)(1) (1985).

16. In general, the parties may come to any agreement through collective bargaining that does not otherwise violate the law. See "The National Labor Relations Act" in Chapter 11 for a discussion of union access to health and exposure data through collective bargaining.

17. Even if the procedure is not performed by a medical professional, ordinary rules of negligence should mandate such a result. An employer might argue, however, that he or she would not have undertaken to perform human monitoring in the absence of agency regulation, and thus claim insulation from liability for any damages that flow from that monitoring. Unless the employer is specifically ordered to perform an unreasonably dangerous procedure, this argument should prove unpersuasive.

18. An excellent statement of the theoretical basis of the doctrine is found in *Cobbs v. Grant,* 8 Cal. 3d 229, 242, 502 P. 2d 1, 9 (1972), in which the court identified four touchstones upon which informed consent can be said to rest:

The first is that patients are generally persons unlearned in the medical sciences and therefore, except in rare cases, courts may safely assume the knowledge of patient and physician are not in parity. The second is that a person of adult years and in sound mind has the right, in the exercise of control over his own body, to determine whether or not to submit to lawful medical treatment. The third is that the patient's consent to treatment, to be effective, must be an informed consent. And the fourth is that the patient, being unlearned in medical sciences, has an abject dependence upon and trust in his physician for the information which he relies during the decisional process, thus raising an obligation in the physician that transcends arms-length transactions.

19. See, for example, *Wilcox v. Salt Lake City Corp.,* 26 Utah 2d 78, 484 P. 2d 1200 (1971); *Lotspeich v. Chance Vought Aircraft,* 369 S.W. 2d 705 (Tex. Civ. App. 1963); and *New York Cent. R.R. v. Wilner,* 124 Ohio St. 118, 177 N.E. 205 (1931).

20. See *Cobbs v. Grant,* 8 Cal. 3d 229.

21. However, because the OSHAct expresses no congressional desire to infringe on the physician–patient relationship, and because OSHA itself has been careful to limit its intrusions into this relationship, OSHA monitoring regulations do not appear to preempt state laws regarding informed consent without a specific statement to this effect.

22. "Code of Ethical Conduct for Physicians Providing Occupational Medical Services," *Journal of Occupational Medicine* (1976) 18(8):703.

23. At the New York Conference on Ethical Issues in Occupational Medicine, Donald Whorton and Morris Davis offered an alternative formulation to section 7 of the American Occupational Medical Association Code [ibid.]: "The occupational physician shall fully inform the employee in writing of consequences of job changes or continuation that may affect his or her health status and shall not make nor participate in restrictive decisions regarding the employee's ability to work without the participation and concurrence of the employee" [D. Whorton and M. Davis, "Ethical Conduct and the Occupational Physician," *Bulletin of the New York Academy of Medicine* (1978) 54(8):733, 740].

Chapter 11. The Use of Monitoring Results

1. In the absence of regulation from the Occupational Safety and Health Administration, employees would arguably still have a right of access under common law or state statute in many jurisdictions. See G. Annas, "Legal Aspects of Medical Confidentiality in the Occupational Setting," *Journal of Occupational Medicine* (1976) 18(8):537.

2. 29 C.F.R. § 1910.20 (1988), as amended. See also 45 *Fed. Reg.* 35,221, et seq. (May 23, 1980) and 53 *Fed. Reg.* 38,140 (September 29, 1988). The regulation has survived constitutional challenge in the Fifth Circuit Court of Appeals, *Louisiana Chemical Ass'n v. Bingham,* 731 F. 2d 280 (5th Cir. 1984). Various challenges to the original rule are, as this book goes to press, still pending in the District of Columbia Circuit Court of Appeals and will be analyzed in light of the revised rule [see *Industrial Union Dept. AFL-CIO v. Marshall,* No. 80-150, and *National Construction Assoc. v. OSHA,* No. 80-1820].

3. See 53 *Fed. Reg.* 38,140 (September 29, 1988).

4. 29 C.F.R. § 1910.20(c)(5)–(6) (1988).

5. Ibid., § 1910.20(e)(1)(i), emphasis added.

6. See "Preamble to OSHA Final Standard on Access to Exposure and Medical Records," *Occupational Safety and Health Reporter* (BNA) (1988) 18(19):985, 1001; 53 *Fed. Reg.* 38,140 (September 29, 1988), citing 46 *Fed. Reg.* 40,490 (August 7, 1981).

7. 29 C.F.R. § 1910.20(c)(1)and(e)(ii) (1988).

8. Ibid., § 1910.20(b)(3), emphasis added.

9. The rule specifically acknowledges that employers may maintain their records on "an in-house or contractual (e.g., fee-for-service) basis" [29 C.F.R. § 1910.20 (b)(3) (1988)]. The preparatory agency comments to the revised rule note that "employers cannot be penalized if they make reasonable efforts to comply with the access rule when using contract services if such efforts fail for reasons beyond their control" ["Preamble to Final Standard," 990].

10. 29 C.F.R. § 1910.20(e)(2)(ii) (1988).

11. Ibid., § 1910.20(e)(2)(ii)(C).

12. Ibid., § 1910.20(e)(2)(ii)(D).

13. See 45 *Fed. Reg.* 35,273 (May 23, 1980).

14. 29 C.F.R. § 1910.20(e)(2)(i)(B) (1988). In the explanatory comments to the revised rule, OSHA noted that access to the exposure records of other workers is to be granted "only in the absence of personal exposure or workplace records adequate to determine the nature of an employee's exposure, and only to the extent necessary to determine the subject employee's exposure adequately" ["Preamble to Final Standard," 1001].

15. 29 C.F.R. § 1910.20(e)(2)(i)(C)–(D) (1988). In the explanatory comments to the original rule, OSHA noted that this would include "area, grab, or wipe samples which would not specifically characterize the exact exposure of any one employee" and "material safety data sheets and other records which simply reveal the identity of a toxic substance or harmful physical agent" [45 *Fed. Reg.* 35,273 (May 23, 1980)].

16. 29 C.F.R. § 1910.20(c)(13) (1988).

17. See "Occupational Safety and Health Administration Proposal to Modify the Access to Medical Records Rule," *Occupational Safety and Health Reporter* (BNA) (1982) 12(7):164; 47 *Fed. Reg.* 30,420 (July 13, 1982).

18. "OSHA Proposal to Modify Access," 170.

19. The definition includes "any item" [29 C.F.R. § 1910.20(c)(10) (1988)]. As noted in the preparatory comments to the original rule, "the definition . . . is meant to be all-encompassing" [45 *Fed. Reg.* 35,265 (May 23, 1980)]. Further, even without such a broad definition, physicians and other health care professionals who perform the monitoring would likely be inclined by professional nature (or induced by fear of malpractice liability) to keep accurate records.

20. 29 U.S.C. § 664 (1985) provides as follows:

All information reported to or otherwise obtained by the Secretary or his representative in connection with any inspection or proceeding under this chapter which contains or which might reveal a trade secret referred to in section 1905 of title 18 shall be considered confidential for the purpose of that section, except that such information may be disclosed to other officers or employees concerned with carrying out this chapter or when relevant in any proceeding under this chapter. In any such proceeding the Secretary, the Commission, or the court shall issue such orders as may be appropriate to protect the confidentiality of trade secrets.

21. In its comments to the original rule, OSHA noted "an apparent Congressional intent in balancing competing interests" in this area [45 *Fed. Reg.* 35,249–35,250 (May 23, 1980)].

22. See "OSHA Proposal to Modify Access," 174.

23. See 29 C.F.R. § 1910.1200 (1988). Although it does not pertain to monitoring information, this regulation will be of interest to workers seeking information regarding workplace exposures. It requires employers to disclose to employees the existence of certain chemical hazards in the workplace, and to make available to workers Material Safety Data Sheets pertaining to these chemicals.

24. *United Steelworkers of America v. Auchter,* 763 F. 2d 728 (3d Cir. 1985).

25. The agency's comments on the revised rule make specific mention of the definition in the hazard communication standard, which was revised in response to the *Steelworkers v. Auchter* case [see "Preamble to Final Standard," 1005].

26. 29 C.F.R. § 1910.20(f)(1) (1988).

27. The original rule required the employer to provide access to all "chemical or physical agent identities, including chemical names" [see 29 C.F.R. § 1910.20(f) (1987)].

28. In vitro tests for metaphase arrest, an abnormality in nonreproductive cell division, produced by a number of chemicals in the hydantoin (2, 4-imidazoladine-

dione) family, for example, produced widely different results [see A. MacKinney, "A Comparison of Potency of Hydantoins in Metaphase Arrest and Inhibition of Microtubular Polymerization," *Molecular Pharmacology* (1980) 17(2):275].

29. Chemicals are commonly indexed by their individual Chemical Abstracts Service number.

30. This is particularly the case where the route of entry (e.g., inhalation vs. dermal exposure), particle size, synergism with other chemicals, or metalobic conversion is a critical factor in correlating exposure with health effects.

31. 29 C.F.R. § 1920.20(f)(2) (1988).

32. Ibid., § 1910.20(f)(4).

33. Ibid., § 1910.20(f)(4)(ii).

34. Ibid., § 1910.20(f)(8).

35. Ibid., § 1910.20(f)(11)(i).

36. Ibid., § 1910.20(f)(11)(ii).

37. 45 *Fed. Reg.* 35,275 (May 23, 1980).

38. 29 C.F.R. § 1920.20 (f)(5)(ii) (1988).

39. Ibid., § 1910.20(f)(5)(iii).

40. 15 U.S.C. § 2613(b) (1982).

41. Ibid., § 2613(a)(3).

42. See 20 U.S.C. §§ 151–169 (1985). The right to refuse hazardous work is found in two places: section 7 of the NLRA, and section 502 of the Labor Management Relations Act. For a general explanation of the right, and a comparison with the companion right available under the OSHAct, see N. Ashford and J. Katz, "Unsafe Working Conditions: Employee Rights under the Labor Management Relations Act and the Occupational Safety and Health Act," *Notre Dame Law Review* (1977) 52(5):802. Since the time of that article, however, the National Labor Relations Board has narrowed its interpretation of "concerted action" under section 7.

43. Initially, there were three companion cases: *Minnesota Mining & Mfg. Co.,* 261 N.L.R.B. 27 (1982); *Borden Chemical,* 261 N.L.R.B. 64 (1982); and *Colgate-Palmolive Co.,* 261 N.L.R.B. 90 (1982). *Minnesota Mining* was the lead case. Citing *Minnesota Mining,* the Board then decided *Plough, Inc.,* 262 N.L.R.B. 1095 (1982).

44. See, for example, *Gulf Power Co.,* 156 N.L.R.B. 622 (1966), enforced, 384 F. 2d 822 (5th Cir. 1967).

45. *Minnesota Mining,* 261 N.L.R.B. at 29.

46. *Oil, Chemical and Atomic Workers Union v. National Labor Relations Board,* 711 F. 2d 348 (D.C. Cir. 1983).

47. *Minnesota Mining,* 261 N.L.R.B. at 32. Only three members out of five signed the majority opinion. One concurring member would have granted broader access, while the other would have provided more protection for the employer.

48. For an excellent treatment of the *Minnesota Mining* cases, and the union access issues that those cases did not resolve, see M. Mentzer, "Union's Right to Information about Occupational Health Hazards under the National Labor Relations Act," *Industrial Relations Law Journal* (1983) 5(2):247.

49. See, for example, D. Schechter, "Medical Records Access: Who Shall See What, and When?" *Occupational Health and Safety,* (1982) S1(7):23; G. Collings, "Medical Confidentiality in the Work Environment," *Journal of Occupational Medicine* (1978) 20(7):461; A. McLean, "Management of Occupational Health Records," *Journal of Occupational Medicine* (1976) 18(8):530; and L. Warshaw, "Confidentiality Versus the Need to Know," *Journal of Occupational Medicine* (1976) 18(8):534.

50. Depending on the state, this right may be part of the common law, may be created by statute, or both [see Annas, "Legal Aspects of Medical Confidentiality"]. At

present, there is no federal common law right of privacy beyond that embodied in the Constitution. Many states have recognized the common law tort of invasion of privacy [see, for example, *Biederman's of Springfield, Inc. v. Wright*, 322 S.W. 2d 892 (Mo. 1959); *Hull v. Curtis Publishing Co.*, 182 Pa. Super. 86, 125 A. 2d 644 (1956)].

51. See "Monitoring in Response to Agency Directive" in Chapter 10. See also *Whalen v. Roe*, 429 U.S. 589, 598–604 (1977) (state system of monitoring sales of prescription drugs did not pose a threat to patients' reputation or independence sufficient to invade any right to privacy).

52. See, for example, *Whalen v. Roe*, 429 U.S. 589.

53. Much of the information found in medical records—such as details of the patient's sexual activities, marital relations, and emotional difficulties—may often have little relevancy to the workplace.

54. Any state law of confidentiality would probably be preempted by the federal statute creating agency access [see, for example, *General Motors Corp. v. Director of National Institute for Occupational Safety and Health*, 636 F. 2d 163, 165 (6th Cir. 1980)].

55. 429 U.S. 589 (1977).

56. Ibid., 598–604.

57. Ibid., 602, emphasis added.

58. Ibid., 605, emphasis added.

59. 29 C.F.R. § 1913.10 (1988).

60. Ibid., § 1913.10(d), (h)(4), and (j).

61. Ibid., § 1913.10(b)(1), emphasis added.

62. Ibid., § 1913.10(b)(3), emphasis added.

63. Ibid., § 1910.20(e)(3)(i).

64. See H. Walderman, "Investigative Authority of the National Institute for Occupational Safety and Health," in *Legal and Ethical Dilemmas in Occupational Health*, J. Lee and W. Rom, eds. (Ann Arbor, Mich.: Ann Arbor Science Publishers, 1982), 131.

65. *General Motors Corp.*, 636 F. 2d at 166.

66. Ibid.

67. See J. T. O'Reilly, *Unions' Right to Company Information*, (Philadelphia: University of Pennsylvania Industrial Relations and Public Policy Series, No. 21, 1980).

68. *Minnesota Mining*, 261 N.L.R.B. 27; *Plough, Inc.*, 262 N.L.R.B. 1095.

69. *Plough, Inc.*, 262 N.L.R.B. 1095. In *Minnesota Mining*, the union asked only for access to medical records from which all personal identifying data had been removed [261 N.L.R.B. at 30]. In *Plough, Inc.*, the union requested access to "the results of all physicals taken by employees" for a particular time period [262 N.L.R.B. at 1095]. Noting that it did not agree with the administrative law judge's conclusion that this information would lose its value if all identifying data were removed, the NLRB conditioned disclosure on the removal of such data [262 N.L.R.B. at 1096].

70. *Oil, Chemical and Atomic Workers*, 711 F. 2d at 363.

71. 29 C.F.R. § 1910(e)(2) (1988).

72. "Preamble to Final Standard," 1002.

73. 29 C.F.R. § 1910.20(e)(2)(i)(B) (1988).

74. Ibid., § 1910.20(e)(2)(ii)(B).

75. See, for example, *Cort v. Bristol-Meyers Co.*, 385 Mass. 300, 431 N.E. 2d 908 (1982). The "legitimacy" of an employer's interest, of course, will be shaped in part by federal and state statutes forbidding certain kinds of discrimination, and by the public policies inherent in other state and federal statutes, such as the OSHAct [see text accompanying notes 82–147 in this chapter].

76. If the company doctor takes in personal information unrelated to employer

needs, he or she is arguably acting on behalf of the employee, not the employer. To this extent, there *is* a physician–patient relationship between the employee and the company doctor.

77. The employee may have a cause of action against the doctor for invasion of privacy [see Annas, "Legal Aspects of Medical Confidentiality"].

78. 45 *Fed. Reg.* 35,243 (May 23, 1980). The quote is attributed to Mattillion of the United Auto Workers.

79. Ibid.

80. The Supreme Court's recent decision upholding the compulsory alcohol and drug testing of railroad employees in certain situations [*Secretary of Transportation v. Railway Labor Executives Association,* 13 O.S.H. Cas. (BNA) 2065, 2073] notes that although the required information-gathering procedure

> permits the Government to learn certain medical facts that an employee might prefer not to disclose, there is no indication that the Government does not treat this information as confidential, or that it uses the information for any other purpose. Under the circumstances, we do not view this procedure as a significant invasion of privacy. Cf. *Whalen v. Roe,* 429 U.S. 589, 602 (1977).

81. See N. Ashford and S. Owen, *Draft Report: Expanded HMOs for Providing Comprehensive Health and Safety Services to Small- and Medium-Sized Firms* (Massachusetts Institute of Technology, Center for Policy Alternatives, 1977).

82. See 53 *Am. Jur. 2d, Master and Servant* §§ 49, 123 (1970).

83. Ibid., §§ 50, 123.

84. A number of courts have held that an employer may be liable in tort if the discharge of an employee violates a clear mandate of public policy [see, for example, *Parnar v. Americana Hotels, Inc.,* 65 Hawaii 370, 652 P. 2d 625 (1982) (tort of retaliatory discharge recognized when plaintiff was discharged as inducement to leave jurisdiction in order to prevent her from testifying against employer); *Palmateer v. International Harvester Co.,* 85 Ill. 2d 124, 421 N.E. 2d 876 (1981) (tort of retaliatory discharge recognized when employee was discharged for informing police of fellow employee's suspected criminal behavior); and *Lally v. Copygraphics,* 85 N.J. 668, 428 A. 2d 1317 (1981) (cause of action upheld for wrongful discharge of employee who had filed workers' compensation claim)].

85. See, for example, *Cussimanio v. Kansas City S.R.R.,* 5 Kan. App. 2d 379, 617 P. 2d 107 (1980).

86. See *Dairy Equip. Co. v. Department of Indus., Labor and Human Relations,* 95 Wis. 2d 319, 290 N.W. 2d 330 (1980). Pension plans, obviously, may affect the terms of the discharge.

87. Section 5(a)(i) of the OSHAct imposes a general duty on an employer to "furnish to each of his employees employment and a place of employment which are free of recognized hazards that are causing or likely to cause death or serious physical harm to his employees" [29 U.S.C. § 654(a)(1) (1985)]. In addition, many states have statutes creating a similar duty, and there is a generally recognized common law duty as well [see, for example, *Shimp v. New Jersey Bell Tel. Co.,* 145 N.J. Super. 156, 368 A. 2d 408 (1976)].

88. One key to judicial treatment of this issue at common law may be the extent to which the employee can be otherwise compensated for his or her loss of employment. A federal district court in Georgia took this approach some years ago in *Jones v. Central of Georgia Ry. Co.,* 220 F. Supp. 909 (N.D. Ga. 1963). Although that case did not involve exposure to toxic substances, it did involve a worker who was discharged as the result of a job-related injury. After receiving a permanent disability award through the workers' compensation system, the worker brought suit to regain his former job. The

court reasoned that he had been compensated for lost future earnings through the award of disability and was thus not entitled to receive those earnings a second time through subsequent employment. Accordingly, it dismissed his suit. The applicability of the *Jones v. Central* rationale to the use of human monitoring data is unclear. If a worker has been incapacitated by toxic substance exposure and a right of compensation clearly exists, this doctrine may apply. But in cases in which the worker is discharged merely because he or she displays an increased *susceptibility* to disease from toxic substance exposure, either because of past exposure levels or because of a perceived genetic or biological predisposition, there is likely to be no compensation for lost future earnings.

89. If the courts apply the rationale of the "retaliatory discharge" cases (see note 84 in this chapter), it is not clear that reinstatement or job reassignment would be available remedies. The employer would still bear the cost of removal, however, in the form of damages to the discharged employee.

90. 20 U.S.C. § 654(a)(1) (1985).

91. Ibid.

92. Under the OSHAct, the primary burden of ensuring workplace health and safety rests with the employer. As noted in a Senate committee report to Congress on the general duty clause, *"employers* have primary control of the work environment and should insure that it is safe and healthful" [Senate Report No. 1282, 91st Cong., 2nd Sess. 9, reprinted in *U.S. Code Congressional and Administrative News* (1970) 5177, 5186, emphasis added].

93. 29 U.S.C. § 660(c)(1) (1985).

94. Although an employee has no right to prosecute a violation of the general duty clause because OSHA is the "exclusive prosecutor" of OSHAct violations [*Oil, Chemical and Atomic Workers Union v. Occupational Safety and Health Review Comm'n,* 671 F. 2d 643, 649 (D.C. Cir. 1982), *cert. denied,* 456 U.S. 969 (1982)], this is mainly a *procedural* limitation on the employee's exercise of his or her right to a workplace free of serious hazards, not an eradication of the right itself.

95. Section 11(c) provides a procedure for redress against the employer [29 U.S.C. § 660(c)(2)(3) (1985)]. The aggrieved worker must file a complaint with OSHA within 30 days, and OSHA must then conduct an investigation. If OSHA "determines that the provisions of [section 11(c)] have been violated," it must then institute legal action to obtain "all appropriate relief" [29 U.S.C. § 660(c)(2)(3)]. Although the extent to which the worker may be able to compel OSHA to take action under this section is not yet clear, at least one court has held that OSHA is liable in tort for negligently representing a worker's interest under section 11(c) [*Chadsay v. United States,* 11 O.S.H. Cas. (BNA) 1198 (D. Ore. 1983)].

96. *Whirlpool Corp. v. Marshall,* 445 U.S. 1, 21 (1980).

97. 29 C.F.R. § 1977.12(b)(2) (1988). See also Ashford and Katz, "Unsafe Working Conditions."

98. *Whirlpool Corp. v. Marshall,* 445 U.S. at 21.

99. *Marshall v. Whirlpool Corp.,* 9 O.S.H. Cas. (BNA) 1038 (N.D. Ohio 1980).

100. *Oil, Chemical and Atomic Workers Union v. American Cyanamid Company,* 741 F. 2d 444 (1984).

101. See notes 2–10 in Chapter 9, note 30 in Chapter 1, and note 45 in Chapter 2.

102. As used here, the term *discrimination* means nothing more than treating a particular worker, or class of workers, differently from the majority of workers. This discussion assumes that the discrimination in question is based on *human monitoring data* and not some other reason. It assumes that the excluded workers would be qualified to perform the work in question if the monitoring data were ignored.

103. For more extensive treatments of this issue, see Rothstein, *Medical Screening of Workers,* and McGarity and Schroder, "Risk-Oriented Employment Screening."

104. 20 U.S.C. §§ 701–795(q) (1985 and 1988 Supplements). For a detailed discussion of the federal act, see C. Sullivan, M. Zimmer, and R. Richards, *Employment Discrimination,* Vol. 3 (Boston: Little, Brown, 1988), Chapters 25–29. As of 1983, 41 states and the District of Columbia reportedly had laws prohibiting employer discrimination against handicapped individuals. For a listing of the state statutes at that time, see M. Rothstein, *Medical Screening of Workers,* 1436–1437.

105. See, for example, *E. E. Black, Ltd. v. Marshall,* 497 F. Supp. 1088, 1100 (D. Hawaii 1980).

106. 20 U.S.C. §§ 701–795(q) (1985 and 1988 Supplements); section 503–§ 793(a).

107. See, for example, *D'Amato v. Wisconsin Gas Co.,* 760 F. 2d 1474 (7th Cir. 1985); *Davis v. United Air Lines,* 662 F. 2d 120 (2d Cir. 1981), *cert. denied,* 456 U.S. 965 (1982); and *Rogers v. Frito-Lay, Inc.,* 611 F. 2d 1074 (5th Cir. 1980), *cert. denied,* 449 U.S. 889 (1980).

108. 29 U.S.C. § 794 (1985); see, for example, *Pushkin v. Regents of University of Colorado,* 658 F. 2d 1372, 1380 (10th Cir. 1981).

109. Rothstein estimated in 1983 that "three million firms—about half the businesses in the country—may be covered by the Act" [Rothstein, *Medical Screening of Workers,* 1439].

110. According to Rothstein, state handicap discrimination laws "usually only exempt small employers" [Rothstein, *Medical Screening of Workers,* 1437].

111. Most of the state laws are modeled after the federal law. Some, however, are more restrictive.

112. See, for example, *Dairy Equip. Co. v. Department of Indus., Labor and Human Relations,* 95 Wis. 2d 319, 290 N.W. 2d 330 (1980); and *Chicago, Milwaukee, and St. Paul R.R. v. Washington State Human Rights Comm'n.,* 87 Wash. 2d 802, 557 P. 2d 307 (1976).

113. See, for example, *Advocates for the Handicapped v. Sears, Roebuck & Co.,* 67 Ill. App. 3d 512, 385 N.E. 2d 39 (1978), *cert. denied,* 444 U.S. 981 (1979); *Burgess v. Joseph Schlitz Brewing Co.,* 298 N.C. 520, 259 S.E. 2d 248 (1979).

114. 29 U.S.C. § 706(7)(B) (1985). The Department of Labor has promulgated a set of implementing regulations that contain further interpretive definitions at 41 C.F.R. § 60-741.2 (1986). To prove discrimination under the act, the handicapped individual must prove that he or she was "qualified" for the job [see *Senate Committee on Labor and Public Welfare, Rehabilitation Act Amendments of 1974, Senate Report No. 1297,* 93rd Cong., 2nd Sess. 5, 24, reprinted in *U.S. Code Congressional and Administrative News* (1974) 6373, 6390]. The Supreme Court has held that the handicapped person must be so qualified even though he or she is handicapped; it is not sufficient that he or she would be qualified if there were no handicap [*Southeastern Community College v. Davis,* 442 U.S. 397 (1979)].

115. Rothstein, in fact, cautions that "because a handicapped individual must have an impairment that substantially limits one or more major life activities, the Rehabilitation Act may not prohibit the most arbitrary, illogical, and baseless form of discrimination—that based on an individual's slight medical or genetic imperfection" [Rothstein, *Medical Screening of Workers,* 1451].

116. The definition of *handicap* was revised in 1974 [see note 114 in this chapter].

117. *Senate Committee on Labor and Public Welfare, Rehabilitation Act Amendments of 1974, Senate Report No. 1297,* 93rd Cong., 2nd Sess. 39, reprinted in *U.S. Code Congressional and Administrative News* (1974) 6373, 6389–6390.

118. 497 F. Supp. 1088, 1100 (D. Hawaii 1980). For further proceedings, see *E. E.*

Black, Ltd. v. Donovan, 26 Fair Empl. Prac. Cas. (BNA) 1183 (D. Hawaii 1981).

119. 497 F. Supp. at 1100.

120. Ibid., emphasis added.

121. Ibid., 1100–1102. A similar approach to the general issue was taken by the Sixth Circuit Court of Appeals in *Jasany v. United States Postal Service,* 755 F. 2d 1244 (6th Cir. 1985).

122. See, for example, *Senate Report No. 318,* 93rd Cong., 1st Sess. 18–19, reprinted in *U.S. Code Congressional and Administrative News* (1973) 2076, 2092.

123. See note 114 in this chapter. Although this appears to place the burden on the worker to prove that he or she could properly perform the job if given the opportunity— rather than requiring the employer to prove that the worker could not do so—it also appears to remove from consideration the various economic arguments that may be available to employers asserting a "business necessity" defense under Title VII or the Age Discrimination in Employment Act [see "Civil Rights and Age Discrimination" in this chapter]. Indeed, the court in *E. E. Black, Ltd. v. Marshall* declined to consider employer cost in determining whether or not the applicant was "qualified." Nonetheless, many of the factors relevant to a consideration of the "business necessity" defense may still be relevant here.

124. See, for example, *Strathie v. Department of Transportation,* 547 F. Supp. 1367 (E.D. Pa. 1982).

125. McGarity and Schroeder note, "Almost all state handicap laws contain some reference to employer defense" [McGarity and Schroeder, "Risk-Oriented Employment Screening," 1035].

126. See ibid. for a short discussion of the types of defenses available. Although the wording of each statute's defense should be examined with care, three general classes of defense may be identified: (1) those that require the employer to establish a "bona fide occupational qualification" [see note 139 in this chapter], (2) those that require the employer to establish "business necessity," and (3) those that require the employer to prove that the handicapped individual cannot perform the job (similar to the federal act, but a shifting of the burden).

For a discussion of the applicability of the "business necessity" test to discrimination based on human monitoring, see "Civil Rights and Age Discrimination" in this chapter.

127. 42 U.S.C. § 2000e (1981).

128. See, for example, *Mass. Gen. Laws Ann.* c. 151b.

129. 29 U.S.C. §§ 621–678 (1985) and, for example, *Mass. Gen. Laws Ann.* c. 149, § 24A.

130. That is, the policies will not be discriminatory *on their face.* For example, they will not by their express terms exclude blacks, even though they may exclude persons who have the sickle cell trait. An employer would be engaging in *per se* discrimination if he or she required genetic screening for male but not for female employees. Such discrimination, however, would be based on sex, rather than on human monitoring data.

131. For example, an employer might have a neutrally worded policy requiring genetic screening for all workers, but might screen only men. Here again, the discrimination would be on the basis of sex.

132. The court recognized disparate impact in *Griggs v. Duke Power Co.,* 401 U.S. 424 (1971).

133. See "The Cost of Growing Old: Business Necessity and the Age Discrimination in Employment Act," *Yale Law Journal* (1979) 88(3):565.

134. *Albermarle Paper Co. v. Moody,* 422 U.S. 405 (1975).

135. "Significantly" refers to more than mere *statistical* significance. Guidelines

established by the Equal Employment Opportunity Commission suggest that a difference of more than 20% (i.e., where the selection rate for the racial, sexual, or ethnic class in question is less than 80% of the rate for the group with the *highest* selection rate) should be sufficient [29 C.F.R. § 1607.4 (1988)].

136. See, for example, *OTA Report*, 91; Calabrese, *Pollutants and High-Risk Groups*, 153. The sickle cell trait is reported to be more prevalent in equatorial Africa, parts of India and Middle East, and the countries along the Mediterranean.

137. The permissibility of "fetus protection policies," which exclude fertile women from the workplace to avoid exposure to reproductive hazards, is beyond the scope of this book, because it does not involve discrimination on the basis of monitoring data [see "Equal Employment Opportunity Commission Guidelines on Reproductive and Fetal Hazards," *Occupational Safety and Health Reporter* (BNA) (1988) 18(21):1052].

138. The business necessity defense is available only in cases of disparate *impact*. If a practice is discriminatory on its face or involves disparate treatment, the employer may avoid liability only by demonstrating that the basis of the discrimination constitutes a "bona fide occupational qualification" (BFOQ). This defense is available under the Civil Rights Act for discrimination based on sex, national origin, or religion (but not race or color) [42 U.S.C. § 2000e–2(e) (1981)] and under the Age Discrimination in Employment Act [29 U.S.C. § 623(f)(1) (1982)]. The BFOQ defense requires the employer to establish that the discriminatory practice is "reasonably necessary to the normal operation of . . . business" [42 U.S.C. § 2000e–2(e) (1981)]. The Supreme Court has characterized the BFOQ defense as an "extremely narrow" one [*Dothard v. Rawlinson*, 433 U.S. 321, 334 (1977)].

139. See *Wards Cove Packing v. Atonia*, 109 S.Ct. 2115 (1989) (as to Title VII).

140. *Griggs v. Duke Power Co.*, 401 U.S. at 431.

141. *Robinson v. Lorillard Corp.*, 444 F. 2d 791, 798 (4th Cir.), *cert. denied*, 404 U.S. 1006 (1971).

142. *Wards Cove Packing v. Atonia*, 109 S.Ct. 2115; *Albermarle Paper Co. v. Moody*, 422 U.S. at 425.

143. These anticipated "costs" might include an employer's future liability to pay workers' compensation or, in some cases, a tort judgment; adverse publicity from having a high incidence of occupational illness at the workplace; decreased productivity associated with occupational illness; and the expense of training replacement employees.

144. *Wards Cove Packing v. Atonia*, 109 S.Ct. 2115.

145. McGarity and Schroeder, "Risk-Oriented Employment Screening," 1049.

146. In *E. E. Black, Ltd. v. Marshall*, the court indicated that employees who were offered reasonable alternative positions would not be considered "substantially" limited—and thus would not be considered "handicapped"—under the federal handicap law [497 F. Supp. at 1099].

147. There are a few federal statutes that apply to certain specialized industries, but the great bulk of workers are under the various state workers' compensation systems.

148. For a survey of the various state laws, see *Analysis of Workers' Compensation Laws* (Washington, D.C.: United States Chamber of Commerce, 1988). This is an annual compilation.

149. In its purest sense, "strict liability" means that Party A is liable to pay compensation to Party B if A caused B's injury, regardless of questions of fault.

150. U.S. Department of Labor, *An Interim Report to Congress on Occupational Disease* (Washington, D.C.: Department of Labor, 1980), 4.

151. In some states, however, the tort system has been modified by state statutes that have placed a cap on certain kind of damage awards (most commonly, awards of pain and suffering for certain types of injury).

152. See, for example, *Blankenship v. Cincinnati Milacron Chemicals, Inc.*, 69 Ohio St. 2d 608, 433 N.E. 2d 577 (1982), and *Johns-Manville Products Corp. v. Contra Costa Superior Court,* 165 Cal. Rptr. 858, 612 P. 2d 948 (1980).

153. See, for example, *Beshada v. Johns-Manville Products Corp.,* 90 N.J. 191 (1982), and *Karjala v. Johns-Manville Products Corp.,* 523 F. 2d 155 (8th Cir. 1975).

154. U.S. Department of Labor, *An Interim Report to Congress on Occupational Disease,* 3.

155. R. Doll and R. Peto, "The Causes of Cancer: Quantitative Estimates of Avoidable Risk of Cancer in the United States," *Journal of the National Cancer Institute* (1981) 66(1):6. For criticism of Doll's and Peto's estimates, see D. Schmähl, R. Preussman, and M. R. Berger, "Causes of Cancers—An Alternative View to Doll and Peto (1981)," *Klinische Wochenschrift* (1989) 67:1169–1173; S. S. Epstein, "Losing the War Against Cancer: Who's to Blame and What to Do about It," *International Journal of Health Services* (1990) 20(1):53–71; M. A. Schneiderman, D. L. Davis, and D. K. Wagener, "Lung Cancer That Is Not Attributable to Smoking [letter]," *Journal of the American Medical Association* (1989) 262:904; and O. Axelson and L. Forrestiere, "Estimated Increases in Lung Cancer in Non-smokers in Italy," Workshop on Increasing Cancers in Industrial Countries, Collegium Ramazzini, Carpi, Italy, October 20–22, 1989.

156. C. Caldart, "Are Workers Adequately Compensated for Injury Resulting from Exposure to Toxic Substances? An Overview of Worker Compensation and Suits in Tort," in *Chemical Safety Regulation and Compliance,* F. Homburger and J. Marquis, eds. (Basel: Karger, 1985), 92.

157. Of course, if the attributable risk were higher than 50%, all of the exposed workers with the disease theoretically would recover.

158. The plaintiffs reportedly were prepared to offer such evidence in the suit brought by the families of eight leukemia victims against W. R. Grace & Co. and Beatrice Companies, Inc., over contaminated drinking water in Woburn, Mass. [see M. Pacelle, "Contaminated Verdict," *American Lawyer* (1986) 8(10):1].

159. See L. Gara, "Medical Surveillance Damages: Using Common Sense and the Common Law to Mitigate the Dangers Posed by Environmental Hazards," *Harvard Environmental Law Review* (1988) 12(1):265.

160. The emerging rule seems to be that one cannot recover for increased risk unless one can establish that the risk of contracting the medical condition in question is greater than 50% [see for example, *Sterling v. Velsicol Chemical Corp.,* 855 F. 2d 1188, 1205 (6th Cir. 1988); *Hagerty v. L & L Marine Services, Inc.,* 788 F. 2d 315, modified *en banc,* 797 F. 2d 256 (5th Cir. 1986); and *Herber v. Johns-Manville Corp.,* 785 F. 2d 79 (3d Cir. 1986). Some courts have allowed recovery where the risk was less than 50% [see *Brafford v. Susquehanna Corp.,* 586 F. Supp. 14 (D. Colo. 1984), and *Herskovits v. Group Health Cooperative of Puget Sound,* 664 P. 2d 474 (Wash. 1983) (decreased chance of survival for a cancer patient)]. See J. King, "Causation, Valuation, and Chance in Personal Injury Torts Involving Preexisting Conditions and Future Consequences," *Yale Law Journal* (1981) 90(6):1353, for a theoretical justification of this approach. It does involve something of a conceptual leap, because a court must be able to recognize that being placed at a moderately higher risk—say 20%—of contracting a fatal disease, is a harm in and of itself. Recovery for emotional damages for having been put at risk is a separate potential source of compensation; see *Sterling v. Velsicol Chemical Corp.,* 855 F. 2d at 1207, where the court did allow recovery on this basis, up to a fixed maximum of $9,000 per year per person.

161. J. Descotes, *Immunotoxicity of Drugs and Chemicals* (New York: Elsevier, 1986).

162. See R. Rothman and A. Maskin, "Defending Immunotoxicity Cases," *Toxics Law Reporter* (BNA) (1989) 3(39):1219, and the cases cited therein. (This is very much written from the corporate defendant's point of view.)

Chapter 12. Policy and Ethical Considerations

1. J. Ladd, "The Task of Ethics," in *Encyclopedia of Bioethics,* W. T. Reich, ed. (New York: Free Press, 1987), 400–407.

2. J. Ladd, "Legalism and Medical Ethics," in *Contemporary Issues in Biomedical Ethics,* J. Davis, B. Hoffmaster, and S. Shorten, eds. (Clifton, N.J.: Humana Press, 1978), 1–35.

3. Ibid., 34.

4. This view of the law has its origin in Blackstone. See W. Blackstone, "Of the Nature of Laws in General," in *The Sovereignty of Law: Selections from Blackstone's Commentaries on the Laws of England,* G. Jones, ed. (Toronto: University of Toronto Press, 1973), 27–45.

5. Ladd questions the appropriateness of the law and legal categories to resolve moral problems of medical ethics [Ladd, "Legalism and Medical Ethics," note 2 in this chapter].

6. For a useful discussion of corporate responsibility, see J. Ladd, "Corporate Mythology and Individual Responsibility," *International Journal of Applied Philosophy* (1984) 2(1):1–17.

7. "Film Recovery Executives Sentenced to 25 Years for 1983 Employee Death," *Occupational Safety and Health Reporter* (BNA) (1985) 15(5):76.

8. K. C. Davis, *Discretionary Justice* (Urbana: University of Illinois Press, 1971).

9. Prior to 1970, it was not general practice to disseminate risk information to workers [see P. A. Schulte and K. Ringen, "Notification of Workers at High Risk: An Emerging Public Health Problem," *American Journal of Public Health* (1984) 74(5):485–490].

10. R. Ilka, "Necessity and Adequacy of the American Occupational Medical Association Code of Ethics," *Seminars in Occupational Medicine* (1986) 1(1):59–65.

11. We are indebted to Claire Nader for this insight. See also D. Bollier and J. Claybrook, *Freedom from Harm* (Washington, D.C.: Public Citizen and Democracy Project, 1986).

12. See for example, S. Samuels, "Medical Surveillance: Biological, Social and Ethical Parameters," *Journal of Occupational Medicine* (1986) 28(8):572–577; G. Atherley, N. Johnston, and M. Tennassee, "Biological Surveillance: Rights Conflict with Rights," *Journal of Occupational Medicine* (1986) 28(10):958–965; M. Lappe, "Ethical Concerns in Occupational Screening Programs," *Journal of Occupational Medicine* (1986) 28(10):930–934; R. Bayer, "Biological Monitoring in the Workplace: Ethical Issues," *Journal of Occupational Medicine* (1986) 28(10):935–939; and P. Derr, "Ethical Considerations in Fitness and Risk Evaluations," *Occupational Medicine: State of the Art Reviews* (1988) 3(2):193–208.

Index